PRAISE FOR

I Know What I Saw

"The shadowy realm of monsters and weird human-animal hybrids is not limited to the ancient, dusty past, but exists right alongside us today, revealing itself in terrifying ways. There is no better navigator through this bizarre and scary landscape than Linda S. Godfrey, one of the most outstanding researchers in the cryptid field. This book will both thrill and chill you." —Rosemary Ellen Guiley, author of *The Encyclopedia of Angels*

"The most frightening monsters you can imagine may be lurking in your own backyard. In this unsettling collection of testimonials and anecdotes, veteran monster-hunter Linda Godfrey shows how ancient myths and indigenous legends inform modern sightings of walking wolves, dire dogs, deer people, and other strange beasts in rural America. You will think twice before driving down a country road at night after reading this book." —Scott G. Bruce, editor of *The Penguin Book of the Undead* and professor of history at Fordham University

"Linda Godfrey continues to position herself as a much-needed journalistic voice in an often overlooked subject. *I Know What I Saw* presents not just a fascinating, terrifying, scintillating series of spooky stories, but begins to pull at the strings that tie together some of the greatest mysteries of all time. Do real monsters exist? The answer might shock you." —Seth Breedlove, filmmaker at Small Town Monsters

"From ancient burial mounds to mysterious woods, reports surface of strange creatures that *seem* to be flesh and blood, but that, paradoxically, have supernatural abilities. Come with Linda Godfrey as she seeks for answers to the mystery and skillfully guides us through the monstrous mayhem!" —Nick Redfern, author of *The Bigfoot Book*

I KNOW WHAT I SAW

Modern-Day Encounters with Monsters
of New Urban Legend and
Ancient Lore

Linda S. Godfrey

A TarcherPerigee Book

tarcherperigee

An imprint of Penguin Random House LLC
penguinrandomhouse.com

First trade paperback edition 2020
Copyright © 2019 by Linda S. Godfrey

TarcherPerigee with tp colophon is a registered trademark
of Penguin Random House LLC.

Most TarcherPerigee books are available at special quantity discounts for bulk
purchase for sales promotions, premiums, fund-raising, and educational needs.
Special books or book excerpts also can be created to fit specific needs.
For details, write: SpecialMarkets@penguinrandomhouse.com.

Illustrations by Linda S. Godfrey

Library of Congress Cataloging-in-Publication Data

Names: Godfrey, Linda S., author.
Title: I know what I saw : modern-day encounters with monsters of new urban
legend and ancient lore / Linda S. Godfrey.
Description: New York : TarcherPerigee, 2019. | "A TarcherPerigee book." |
Includes bibliographical references and index.
Identifiers: LCCN 2019005259| ISBN 9780143132806 (hardcover) |
ISBN 9780525504696 (ebook)
Subjects: LCSH: Monsters—Folklore.
Classification: LCC GR825 .G5643 2019 | DDC 001.944—dc23
LC record available at https://lccn.loc.gov/2019005259

ISBN (paperback): 9780143132813

Printed in the United States of America

This book is dedicated to Steven Stanek,

mystery cat hunter, investigator, and recorder extraordinaire,

who has toiled quietly for decades on his quest, and whose

generous participation made the mystery cats

chapter possible.

Contents

Chapter 8

Phantom Quadrupeds and Other Nonconformist Canines 167

Indiana's Pendleton Spook Pooch · California Phantom Hound · Hawaiian
Flying Dogman

Chapter 9

Dire Dogs 181

The Dire Dog of Rock County · Legend of the Head Chomper of Nahanni
Valley · White Dire Dog · Knuckle-walking Dire Dog · Lake Mills Dire
Dog · The Red-Eyed Monster of Rusk County, Wisconsin · Great Gray
Dire Dog of Kenosha County, Wisconsin · Big Pooches on the Prairie ·
Dire Dog of Milwaukee · Florida's Two-Timer Dire Dog · More Florida
Freakishness · Unknown in Utah · Uncanny in Kansas · Nebraska Nemesis
· Ohio's Sacra Via Dire Dog · Monstrous in Missouri · Eerie by Lake
Erie · New York Dire Dog of the Corn

Chapter 10

Black Mystery Cats and Inconvenient Mountain Lions 217

Cougars: The Impossible and the Legendary · Arizona *Chindi* and the
Coronado Cat · Evil Spirit Cats · Wily Wampus · Paths of the Water
Panther · Black Panthers: The Darker Side of Great Cats · When Is a
Panther Not a Panther? · Newfoundland Black Panther · British Black
Cats · Cougars of the Midwestern US Hills

Chapter 11

Great Ghost Cat Nexus: Wisconsin's Baraboo River Watershed 237

Big Cats of the Wisconsin Hills · Flying Fence Posts of Hillsboro · A
Vertical Cigar · The Hillsboro Air Disasters · The Strange Range · Home
on the Range · Black Panther Goes Fishing · The Mystery Skull · The
Hillsboro Hairless Thing · Mystery Cat Conclusions

Chapter 12

I Saw Bigfoot! 259

Which Came First? • Unseen but Not Unnoticed • Shake, Shake, Shake! • More Than a Feeling • Iowa Sprinter • The Big Branch • Hairy Men of the Ancients

I KNOW
WHAT I SAW

Introduction

Which Came First, the Legend or the Beast?

"In cryptozoology we are studying legends. Legends are
the smoke above the fire."
　　　　　　　—Loren Coleman, *Cryptozoologist*, 2018

IN DECEMBER 1991, I trudged for days around a frosty corner of
southeast Wisconsin to interview people who claimed to have
seen what they said looked like a fur-covered werewolf on a rural
byway known as Bray Road, just outside of the small city of Elkhorn. And yes, they did say "werewolf," and no, that did not send
me running for silver bullets. Looking into topics of local interest
was my job as a reporter for the county's weekly newspaper, *The
Week*, based in Delavan, Wisconsin, so I was trying to keep an
open mind. It wasn't easy. Area residents were saying they had
seen what looked like a large wolf walking or running on its hind
legs, eating chunks of road-killed animals held in its upturned
paws, and generally acting in ways that normal eastern gray
wolves were not known to act. Moreover, there hadn't been a
known population of wolves breeding in and inhabiting southeastern Wisconsin for many decades. None of it seemed likely.

As I listened to stories of encounter after encounter, however, told by what seemed to be sincere and sober citizens, my mind reached for possible explanations of impossible claims. Were eyewitnesses seeing an actual wolf gone bipedal for some odd reason?

Most of the alternatives I could conjure up also seemed unlikely. I had heard folktales of other manimals, such as Maryland's Goat Man, that had supposedly become mutant monsters due to genetic experiments. Folktales and legends are generally not considered proof of anything, however.

There was also speculation that the creature could be something ghostly, more akin to the spectral black hounds of the British Isles than to a Hollywood-style human with fangs and fur. I even had to consider the chance that there was no real creature, no true sightings, just a hoax perpetrated by unknown jokers, perhaps.

The author's rendition of a goat man

After all, the long, cold winters of the Dairy State have been blamed for all sorts of odd behavior among its residents. Certain Wisconsinites have gained notoriety for activities ranging from the sublime to the shocking: from late-blooming, self-taught artists who spend long evenings by the fire creating visionary sculpture from rusty metal and concrete, to cannibalistic serial killers Ed Gein of Plainfield and Milwaukee's Jeffrey Dahmer. Admittedly, Gein and Dahmer were motivated by much more than ice and scant daylight, since psychological derangement figured prominently in each case. But the peculiar nature of their crimes was seriously weird—what I call bad weird, as opposed to good weird—in the extreme.

After listening to the Bray Road witnesses in person, however, I finally decided that no matter what the origin of the mystery creature sightings, the stories had already spread far enough locally to have reached campfire-tale status. That meant the phenomenon I'd dubbed "The Beast of Bray Road" could be considered folklore in the making. I realized I'd been given a rare opportunity to observe and document the birth of a new legend, and I felt obliged to record whatever I found for future reference.

Back in 1992, the likeliest scenario to my mind was that the upright creatures were just what they looked like: flesh-and-blood wolves or wolf-dog hybrids that were able to walk upright and often did. The ability to walk on hind legs, or bipedalism, is not a supernatural act for animals, but it is unusual. When seen in the wild, bipedal locomotion usually indicates an injured forelimb. Given healthy limbs, and YouTube videos of dancing dogs aside, quadrupeds rarely live their lives in a vertical posture, since their skeletal frames are not designed to support their whole weight on their hind legs.

And yet, many who witnessed the upright canine creatures thought there was also something otherworldly about them . . . some kind of knowing, uncanny intelligence in their glowing, yellow eyes. As famed Bigfoot researcher and author Ivan Sanderson said in his book *Abominable Snowmen: Legend Come to Life*, "A lot of myths are straight history; a lot of history is pure myth."[1]

It seemed obvious to me in those early days that I'd have to look at many more reports to have any hope of understanding anything at all about the creatures and why they were being sighted. Luckily, the reports continued to roll in from all over the

United States, Canada, and other places, even though I hadn't been actively soliciting them, and after ten years or so I began to publish them online and in my books.

Alas, interesting as these reports were, I have found it is much easier to record encounters than to understand them. Twenty-six years of "chasing" monsters later, it still comes down to this: Are these sightings simply a combination of mistaken species of known animals, truly undiscovered animals, hoaxes, and coincidence, or are they somehow—perhaps through the power of myth and legends—intertwined with the human mind? Some researchers suspect these creatures spring from another reality, and that they use the human mind or spirit to project themselves into our world as perceivable beings. Many Native American beliefs hold the more specific view that Sasquatch, dogmen, and other such creatures use freshwater springs as portals between the spirit world and our own. According to the online Hočąk Encyclopedia, the lakes surrounding Wisconsin's state capital, Madison, all serve the spirit world as trans-realm conduits. It states, to cite just one example, "The old Winnebago Indian name for Lake Wingra was *Ki-Chunk-och-hep-er-rah*, meaning the 'place where the turtle comes up.'"[2] And also presumably goes back down.

When all speculation is said and done, however, there is still that question that fans, enthusiasts, and researchers of every stripe want answered: Are the creatures something we would consider "real," or are they entirely "other world"? My suspicion these days is that they may be both, and that our reality operates on a scale from dense matter to realms the human eye cannot see.

I'll do my best to keep seeking answers here, although nothing absolute is promised. There were and are countless other investigators and researchers diligently seeking the same truths about other cryptids (hidden or unknown animals) like Bigfoot and the Loch Ness Monster. Again, thanks largely to the Internet and TV shows about mystery beasts, more and more creature hunters continually join the ranks. There is now a small army of cryptid enthusiasts combing the far corners of the globe for unknown beasts and searching for the truth in legend and lore.

So why hasn't this small army yet proven these creatures exist? I don't believe it's entirely the fault of the investigators. Keep in mind that certain mysterious entities such as, say, werewolves, refuse to be limited to any one definition, and the stories told about them morph more swiftly than can the most talented human shapeshifter. And just when it seems we have one old legend pinned down to help prove an origin, another version or a bothersome contradiction will pop up and we have to start over or look elsewhere.

As the editors of the very helpful book *Medieval Folklore: A Guide to Myths, Legends, Tales, Beliefs, and Customs* put it, "In the nineteenth century, when the term *folklore* was coined, many people assumed that folklore, like a fossil, preserves a frozen image of the ancient past . . . To the contrary, through close observation, folklorists have noticed that folklore tends to be extraordinarily dynamic, extremely prone to change with changing times and environments."[3] That means we are shooting almost blindly at *two* moving targets—the legends and the present creatures they describe.

Knowing that these myths and legends change throughout time and location presents an extra, but not insurmountable, challenge. Despite adaptations, the creatures remain largely recognizable through the centuries, probably because their stories are so often repeated. We hear tales of Centaur sightings in twentieth-century Illinois, right across the river from St. Louis, and our imaginations conjure that same image so vivid in Greek mythology of a four-legged, equine body fronted with the torso, head, and arms of a man.

Still, thanks to the wide dissemination of today's many styles of art and illustration, the "Centaur" sighted today may not look *exactly* like the man-horse described in days of old. It may display a beefier torso and sport a contemporary hairstyle. It may also have forsaken its forest home to lurk—as reported in one sighting we will discuss later—near the St. Louis arch. Or it may choose to play hide-and-seek with Bigfoot rather than battle the Lapiths at Hippodamia's wedding. Either way, a Centaur is still thought of as half horse, half man. And if his majestic appearance ever begins to fade in our minds, we need only consult a book on Greek mythology or watch one of the films in the *Harry Potter* series to remind us of what a Centaur should look like.

Summing it up, the Centaur, the dog woman, the Bigfoot, the giant Man Bats, even the werewolfish Beast of Bray Road . . . all still pretty much resemble their immortal story selves in today's representations. That is how eyewitnesses know them when they see them, even as the legends grow ever darker as spooky things like killer clowns jostle their way into the spotlight. Perhaps something beyond mere literature of the distant past or Internet-fueled legends of today really does help preserve these basic forms and manifest the scream-your-face-off monsters we're all so anxious to see.

CHAPTER 1

Lake Snakes to Slenderman: Modern Legends

THE STUDY OF FOLKLORE is a scholarly discipline equal to any other and commands its own field of inquiry. The good news is there will be no pop quiz here. I'm strictly an amateur folklorist myself. But like any subject pinned down and formalized by academia, folkore has its own accepted lingo. Luckily, the short list will do for our purposes. But the terms—*folklore, legend,* and *myth*—are not as interchangeable as casual users might think. And merely pasting the correct label on the story type of a creature encounter won't prove the true nature of that cryptid. The folklore/legend labels are simply tools to help us categorize things that lounge beyond our comprehension—things such as, perhaps, legends of meat hooks guarded by dog women, to be examined in our next chapter. But before we run off with a pack of hounds to bay at Pennsylvania's October moon, let's go over the basic categories.

LEGENDS: SNAKE OF THE LAKE

Legends are stories from the past, ranging from far ancient times to mere decades or less. The stories are told as if based upon the experiences of some actual (if unknown) person or group of persons, and are sometimes still alleged to be occurring. They may contain an element of the supernatural, such as the Loch Ness–type situation that popped up in 1892 in Lake Geneva, Wisconsin, and lasted for at least a full decade.

The resort town near the Wisconsin-Illinois border became famous for modern-day sightings of a huge lake serpent spotted by area residents and tourists in the city's spring-fed Geneva Lake, one of the state's deepest bodies of water. (The city and lake are distinguished by the word order of their respective titles.) According to reports, the sinuous, scale-covered creature chased groups of boaters and was witnessed by a well-respected minister from nearby Delavan, the Reverend M. N. Clark. Some witnesses estimated the serpent's length as equal to that of a familiar lake vessel, the *Steamship Aurora*, which measured sixty-five feet! Residents nicknamed the serpent Jenny (or Genny).

Area newspapers recorded some incidents viewed by multiple witnesses. An article in *The Milwaukee Sentinel* reported one sighting by no fewer than six people in September 1902. The mystery creature disappeared soon after that date, fading with the tourist season, her origin and escape route still unknown. Perhaps as boat traffic became heavier, the lake could no longer protect creatures that needed to stick their long necks out of the water for air. But legends explaining where she might have gone already existed in the area.

Jenny wasn't the first outsize gigantic creature believed to swim in Geneva Lake. She was preceded by ancient legends of other lake monsters taken as a matter of course by the town's former residents, the Potawatomi, the last native tribal people to live on the shores of the seven-and-a-half-mile-long lake. Area chronicler Paul B. Jenkins and other local historians recorded local Native belief in several different water monsters, including a great, horned water serpent much like Jenny; a giant fish; and the strange water panther, or water spirit. (More on the latter creature later.)

Incidentally, the Potawatomi leader at that time was known as Chief Big Foot. This name had nothing to do with the large, hairy, humanlike creature now popularly called Bigfoot, a term that didn't come into use in that sense until the 1960s or so. The chieftain's name was said to have come from the large footprints he left by walking in snowshoes, or in mud that spread out and enlarged his tracks—whichever version you choose to believe. But he is the reason why near the Wisconsin-Illinois border, you'll find a small community named Big Foot, a Big Foot High School in the city of Walworth, a Big Foot Archery Club, and other places and things intended to honor the displaced chieftain. His footprints became a legend in their own way.

The lake monster stories told by the Potawatomi and other area First Nation folk were also published in a series of pamphlets by Charles E. Brown[1] and Dorothy Moulding Brown[2] in the Wisconsin State Historical Society from the late 1920s to the early 1940s. This was twenty to forty years *after* the decade-long lake monster flap in Geneva Lake (and many other Wisconsin lakes, as well), which showed that sightings of the aquatic creature weren't inspired by the Browns' later published stories.

To complicate the origins of these legends, the stories of battles between the water panther, lake serpent, and thunderbird are widespread in the lore of various Midwestern Native people, and may have been known to Big Foot's Potawatomi band before they moved to southeastern Wisconsin from the western shores of Lake Michigan around 1700 to 1800. For all we know, Big Foot's people may have localized the older story to fit their own observations of Geneva Lake. But that does not make the legend any less important, just more universal. And it is always thrilling to find a universal truth living in your own backyard.

We may trace Jenny the Lake Monster, then, from very old indigenous legend, to fairly contemporary sightings in the early 1900s, to written versions recorded by folklorists a decade or more after the sightings ended. With such strong oral and written background, the Jenny sightings really do seem like legends come to life.

So who saw her first, Big Foot's band, the turn-of-the-century tourists, or more ancient native inhabitants of Geneva's shores? If only we knew how long the sightings had been occurring, we might be able to associate the correct ancient lake monster legend with the modern Jenny. But given the time frame of the sightings, Jenny could also technically glide into the subject of our next category. . . .

URBAN LEGENDS:
THE KANDAHAR GIANT TO CRYBABY BRIDGE

Urban legends are stories of current or recent happenings, and often follow themes of horror and the supernatural. Urban legends distinguish themselves in a couple of important ways. They often skip from community to community, with only the names and minor details changed to suit each particular locale. The other main hallmark of urban legends is that they are contemporary events that continue to change and, with the aid of the Internet, may evolve quite rapidly.

This instant transmission of sightings and encounters has necessitated a whole category of sites dedicated to busting legend bubbles. Snopes.com, for instance, can run a search for most any current legend or computer scam and then explain in the calm manner of most automated websites whether there is any cause for worry. My personal Snopes favorite dates from 2016 and is titled, "U.S. Forces Killed a Giant in Kandahar." This story was rated "false."[3] The site explained, "In the summer of 2016, several personalities and websites dedicated to discussing supernatural myths and conspiracy theories began claiming that an American Special Forces soldier serving in Kandahar, Afghanistan, was killed in 2002 by an 1,100-pound, blade-wielding, 12-foot-tall giant from Old Testament times before the giant himself was taken down by the military. . . . A Department of Defense spokesman told us they have no record of such an incident."

That statement assuredly did not stop everyone from believing a twelve-foot-high biblical Nephilim (a term for offspring of angelic beings and humans) was gunned down and its corpse hustled off by government officials. Like most urban legends, retellings of the story have grown to gigantic proportions. But the Kandahar Giant's fame probably hasn't quite reached that of one of the most widespread Internet memes and local legends: a grisly story known as the "Crybaby Bridge."

This tug-on-the-heartstrings horror usually involves a child or children having been murdered and their remains tossed under a local bridge by the mysterious killer. Their spirits are then left to wail every night at midnight for as long as the bridge stands. In Michigan, for example, there's a typical Crybaby Bridge near Grand Rapids where some locals claim the devil visits every night to scream in triumph when the clock strikes midnight. I've been there, and the small metal bridge was creepy even though I had to leave before scream time.

So numerous and popular are such urban legends, whole books are dedicated to the ever-growing body of stories. One collection, *Urban Legends: The As-Complete-As-One-Could-Be Guide to Modern Myths* by N. E. Genge,[4] organizes its chapters by themes that range from intimate relations that end horribly to gastronomic terrors of food gone not just bad but deeply wrong. (Think fried rat in a bucket of fast-food chicken.)

The legend themes I most often find useful in the investigation of strange creature sightings, however, are those of teenagers attacked by monsters while parking in secluded places. Tales of creatures chasing speeding cars or popping up from roadside hiding places are also likely to feature some type of manimal as leering villain. And again, most entries in this category are set in fairly recent times, handily distinguishing them from the next category.

FOLKTALES AND FOLKLORE:
LUMBER CAMP CREATURES TO FOLK BELIEFS

Folktales and folklore are somewhat similar to historical legend in that their roots lie in the past. They may include heroic characters that elude or defeat whatever creature or danger threatens the populace of their day, but although they often teach a lesson, the stories are easily recognized as fiction. A good example of funny or instructional things we know never existed might be the slew of crazy creatures said to inhabit the forests of North America when the timber industry was king. The creatures were often associated with the giant lumberjack folk hero Paul Bunyan, and Babe, his equally gigantic blue ox.

No one would mistake these outlandish campfire favorites for actual animals. There was, for instance, the creature called the Tripodoro, a beast with legs that telescoped into itself so that the animal could shorten one side, the better to stand on a forested hill. Another was the Teakettler, a smallish canine that walked backward, had ears like a cat's, and whistled like a teakettle as it trudged hind end first through the pine woods. Researchers believe these stories—which also belong in the folk subcategory "tall tales"—first took root in logging camps of the late 1800s. They caught the public's fancy in the early 1900s as folklorists began to publish them, and they are still taught to schoolchildren as American folk literature.

Folklore comes in many other categories beside stories of outlandish or supernatural creatures, of course. Superstitions, medicinal home remedies, hauntings, and spook lights are just a few. One compilation of German American folk beliefs includes many startling gems of farm and household advice, such as the admonition to avoid picking up toads to prevent your cows from giving bloody milk, or how to cure whooping cough by hanging a live, fuzzy caterpillar in a small sack around the afflicted child's neck.[5]

Again, because these household hints belong to a specific national or ethnic group, and have been passed on within that group in recent generations, we label them as folklore. Stories about universal truths and long-ago doings, on the other hand, are quite different and so fall into the next category.

MYTHS: VIKING SAGAS OF RAGNAROK

Myths are stories or collections of related stories that usually hail from the *distant* past, and are likely to involve the actions of gods or supernatural heroes and villains rather than ordinary humans. The mythic literature of any culture often embodies moral teachings and creation stories, using allegories and metaphor to get the points across. Mythic literature may be passed on orally or written and is usually considered sacred by those whose culture it illumines. Because of that, I'm also offering a disclaimer: In this book, a myth simply means a story that fits the description given above, without any intent to decide, confirm, or refute matters of personal belief, truth, or religious faith. One person's myth is another person's bible, and we have respect here for both views. In other words, referring to something as a myth does not mean it lacks any truth.

I like the more succinct definition of *myth* offered by John Bierhorst in his introduction to *The Red Swan: Myths and Tales of the American Indians*: "A myth is an unverifiable and typically fantastic story that is nonetheless felt to be true and that deals, moreover, with a theme of some importance to the believer."[6]

The Viking sagas of the gods and heroes inhabiting the afterlife's great hall of Valhalla are one robust example of ancient literature generally considered mythic. The sagas are also creature-rich: megamonsters such as the massive wolf Fenrir populated the ancient Scandinavian spirit world as they waited to be set free in the planet's epic battle called Ragnarok, meaning "the fate of the gods."[7]

H. R. Ellis Davidson's *Myths and Symbols in Pagan Europe* describes this apocalyptic event: "*The escape of the bound monsters, when the wolf breaks loose from his chain, the serpent emerges from the depths where Thor laced it, and Loki escapes from his fetters* [emphasis mine] laid upon him by the gods," adding that this battle "is given a prominent place in *Völuspá* [title of the best known of the ancient Scandinavian poems, or *Eddas*, possibly dating back to the tenth century]."[8]

After the Scandinavian countries became largely Christianized around 1000 BCE, some scholars likened *Völuspá*'s concept of beasts loosed for final warfare to apocalyptic Bible prophecies. Ragnarok does bear some startlingly similar comparisons to the Christian Bible's book of Revelation, chapter 16, which predicts devils or miracle-working spirits will be set free in the end time to gather the armies of the Beast against the Christian believers.

There are differing opinions on whether the verses of the *Völuspá* refer to past events, the future, or even present times. Some modern day Scandinavians predicted Ragnarok would occur on February 22, 2014, according to an article in the UK's *Daily Mail* titled "Norse Myth Predicts World Will End This Saturday."[9]

Others have pointed out that the so-called Viking experts cited in that prediction may have intended it as a marketing ploy. One scholarly blogger, "A Clerk of Oxford," called out those claiming Viking Armageddon was close at hand:

"I'm all in favour of popularising England's Viking history, and getting people to talk about the Vikings is always good. But this year, to promote their annual festival, they've decided to invent the concept of 'Ragnarok 2014,' in which they pretend that Norse mythology predicted the end of the world would arrive on 22 February (the last weekend of the festival)."[10]

Obviously, Ragnarok did not occur on that date or things would be looking a lot different around planet Earth. But some have suggested that a still-upcoming end of the world may be the reason why sightings of Bigfoot, dog men, humanoid flying creatures, and the like seem to be increasing both in numbers of sightings and in media portrayals of end time events such as Ragnarok and Armageddon.

The word *myth* is also frequently used today to mean a popularly believed falsehood. I'll try to avoid that usage. But if you thought Fenrir and Ragnarok were scary, wait until our next category where we will touch on urban folklore's new kid on the block.

CREEPYPASTA: BEYOND TERROR

Creepypasta is a term with an origin very unlike the traditional categories above. It refers to a product of the electronic age whose curious title says it all. Fans of Creepypasta may expect weird stories of frightening, imaginary people, creatures, and situations. The entities described in this category are mostly online offshoots of horror fiction, however, rather than anything a person might actually encounter in a forest or dark alley. Creepypasta combines urban legends, folktales, and traditional horror themes in a dark mix of make-your-own-legend stories contributed by online readers.

A surprising variety of sites now devote themselves to this literary form that first began to draw big fan interest around 2010. The term was birthed from the Internet slang word *copypasta*, which had in turn hatched from the antiquated "copy and paste" command that first made it easy to share information and creative efforts online. Creepypasta contributors share their tales in order to be part of the shocking but literate culture generated by these collaborative, never-ending stories. A quick glimpse at these shadowy cyber landscapes may be gleaned by plugging *Creepypasta* into any search engine and spending a little time title-surfing.

One of the genre's most popular host websites, Creepypasta Wiki, breaks its massive story log into categories with titles like "Animals," "Beings," "Dismemberment," "Hospitals," and "Military." I was most drawn to the "Beings" category, which contains a section on hidden or unknown creatures that is further divided into stories about legendary entities such as The Rake, Wendigo, Goat Man, Michigan Dogman, and Skinwalkers, whose online entries add depth of subject matter with additional taglines like, "The Melonhead Illustration," "The Beast of the Dam," and "The Six-Legged Centaur."

SLENDERMAN, SHADOW MAN, AND HAT MAN

It should be noted that some of these stories are better left to mature audiences. Most readers of extreme science fiction and fantasy understand that horror fiction is fiction, but there are unsettling exceptions. In May 2014, a popular Creepypasta meme titled "Slender Man" was seized upon by two twelve-year-old girls from Waukesha, Wisconsin, who somehow concluded that Slenderman would invite them to live in his mansion in a forest—if they killed someone to prove their devotion. There are a number of stories that link him to fictional missing children in fictional towns. And so, these preteens connected all the wrong dots and then allegedly stabbed a twelve-year-old friend nineteen times. They left the girl for dead, but she survived her massive wounds to tell what had happened. The two Slenderman fans were charged with attempted homicide. Their example is an extremely unusual and tragic case, but it shows that myth and legend may affect our contemporary lives in unexpected, even shocking, ways.

Whatever cachet it is that creates a fascination with things like faceless monsters, Slenderman owns it. I went to the experts to find out why. When you want to know what's behind a subject going viral, the perfect consultants are those most keenly interested in advertising: professional marketers. As Chicago's Quality Logo Products (QLP) blog said of the slender gent, "He seems to be everywhere nowadays, having grown from his humble beginnings on a forum to several dedicated web series, multiple blogs, songs, games and even an upcoming movie. He has 'blown up,' as the kids might say."[11]

Slenderman epitomizes a new, faster day in the spreading of urban legends. And yet, as the Bible says, there is nothing new under the sun. Even a skinny, expressionless meme like "Slendy," as some bloggers now call him, had to begin somewhere. I believe parts of Slenderman have lurked in the literature, folklore, and traditions of many cultures, and that traces of these other, earlier legends may still be identified in his eerie persona.

The most familiar traits are the inhumanly thin silhouette, the literally blank face, and the shadowlike, colorless figure dressed in formal or business attire with some type of hat. Entities with the latter uniform are known in today's ghost-lore parlance as Hat

Man and Shadow Man. The phantom forms are often observed standing just outside a normal conversational distance, such as the end of a dark hallway, but may also show up in bedrooms. Researcher Heidi Hollis has spent years collecting examples and has published several books about them. She believes, based on the many reports she has received, that they are evil and malicious beings that can be vanquished by rebuking them in the name of Jesus, but that they are also real. Unlike Slenderman, some of the hat men display visible, ghoulish faces.

STICK PEOPLE

Inhumanly thin, or "stick," people are another type of widely spread folk entity whose emaciated frames are echoed in Slenderman. In America, we can find them in the lore of Native Americans, the Pennsylvania Dutch, and even modern sightings. We'll start with the latter.

In December 2014, a former US Marine spotted something very thin with skin the color of gray asphalt just as his car crested a hill near Carmel Road outside of Hillsboro, Ohio. The creature was walking or running across the road and came within ten feet of the witness's vehicle. The witness estimated its height at seven feet and said that it had muscular legs with knees that appeared to be backward. This is a common observation from people seeing a quadruped walking upright, because most quadrupeds walk on their toes or toe pads, putting the hock joint above the ground to create the illusion of a "backward" knee joint.

The witness could not see any arms on this creature, and although he couldn't make out the head very well, either, he said it also appeared to lack a jawbone. The sketch he made reveals an impossibly thin creature with legs more reminiscent of an insectoid "walking stick" than any known mammal. The story was published in Hillsboro's *Highland County Press*,[12] from information received by Mutual UFO Network (MUFON) member Ron McGlone.

The *Highland County Press* story contained another statement that came directly from the former Marine's wife. She had been in the car at the time of the sighting but evidently did not see the creature. She said, "My husband saw it. He is a skeptic—almost sixty years old—and a proud Marine. He wouldn't have admitted to seeing it if he hadn't been in shock."[13] She added that she asked him to make a sketch when they returned to the house. He produced a drawing of a faceless torso with sticklike legs, one jutting forward at an almost ninety-degree angle to the other.

After publication, a site called Doubtful News that specializes in skeptical views of various types of sightings declared that what the Marine saw must have been a deer standing on its hind legs.[14] It does seem logical. Deer can stand upright to feed on birdseed stands; I've seen it happen at my own feeder. They do have those skinny legs, too. But they don't usually walk across highways on two legs. It's also hard to miss a deer's big ears and white tail. The eyewitness was only ten feet away with good light from his headlights, and his wife asserted that he was deeply shocked by what he saw.

All in all, this sighting seems like a very idiosyncratic, one-off sort of event. But in August 2018, another man contacted McGlone to report he had seen a stick-thin creature in Ohio on July 31, read an article by Nick Sabo in the *Mount Vernon News*.[15] It was also about seven feet tall, hairless, and seemed focused on crossing the road, which it did in a few bounds. This witness also first mistook the creature for a deer, although he didn't mention "backward" legs. The sighting occurred near Mount Vernon on Ohio State Route 13. The witnesses in each sighting drew sketches of near-literal stick figures to accompany their reports. Neither news article ventured an opinion as to why these tall, nearly skeletal creatures have been observed racing across roads in southern and central Ohio, but they surely do fit the legendary archetype of the Stick Man.

As an aside, the term "Stick Man" is also the English name many tribes of the northern west coast, such as the Salish and Pullyap, use for various legendary creatures including dangerous, man-eating Bigfoots to hairy dwarves. But sometimes actual humans can be scarier than unknown humanoids.

KILLER CLOWNS

The transition of clowns from funny, endearing characters of the mid-nineteenth century to today's menacing figures of terror seemed to happen swiftly in the entertainment world. *Smithsonian* magazine featured a July 2017 article on the recent history of this macabre makeover, citing some of the first examples—such as a child's grinning doll struggling to yank the boy under his bed in the 1982 film *Poltergeist*, or the grinning alien clowns in the bizarre 1988 cult classic *Killer Klowns from Outer Space*.[16]

Most people don't realize, however, that clowns did not originate as entertainment for the kiddies. They have always served to shake the worlds of grown-ups, mocking and mirroring their own cultures from Native American, stripe-clad Hopi tricksters to the court jesters of Europe's royal palaces. But now we have evil clowns parodying evil clowns. A whole generation has grown up watching Matt Groening's cartoon series *The Simpsons*, in which a clown named Krusty tosses off cynical one-liners like this quip from a 2011 episode titled "The Food Wife," when Krusty chuckles to his child audience: "Krustyland has a new ride, the Eyeballs of Death. It only passed the safety by a 3 to 2 vote. And that third vote didn't come cheap."[17] Yikes.

BLACK-EYED CHILDREN

Far creepier than *The Simpsons* cartoon characters are the strange figures of young people said to have appeared in the real world to a growing number of people. Black-eyed children or kids, also known as BEKs, seem to be solid, fully dimensional young people except for one unique feature: their eyes are completely black, like liquid pools. They also behave as if they don't quite understand the niceties of social interaction, and usually ask very brusquely to be allowed inside people's homes or vehicles. Said to have originated in the 1990s in two articles by an Abilene, Texas, reporter named Brian Bethel, they have achieved full urban legend status according to Wikipedia,[18] have been the subject of their own 2015 movie, *Black Eyed Children: Let Me In*, and have been covered on the TV show *Monsters and Mysteries in America*.

FAKE NEWS VERSUS TRUE ENCOUNTERS

In a world besieged by false or sensationalized information known as "fake news," telling fact from fiction becomes harder and harder. Televised accounts of people claiming to have seen UFOs, werewolves, and nine-foot-tall ape-men have exploded over the past few years. Why the sudden interest?

Perhaps it's because the creatures of the present often display a dual nature. They may vanish into thin air, fly, or glow, yet they still often *appear* to be solid and living within the bounds of our reality as they leave footprints, tear up shrubbery, and devour deer and domestic animals with gusto. Modern reports of fatal attacks by cryptids on humans are rare and, as far as I know, officially unsubstantiated, while monsters from the past such as France's Beast of Gévaudan didn't hesitate to kill humans whenever possible. I think this sense of uncertainty about the true nature of contemporary monsters adds to their mystery and makes us even more curious about them.

And yet, in the absence of truly monstrous behavior, the oversize, fur-covered "human ape" known as Bigfoot begins to feel more like some long-lost relationship that has always been here. Perhaps it has. In full disclosure, I've had my own Bigfoot sightings (which I'll divulge later), long after the Beast of Bray Road first showed its hairy head. These incidents have convinced me that the huge, hairy hominids are more than mere legend.

But again, what are they?

Most people believe legends and myths are akin to fairy tales, and there is scant hard evidence to prove otherwise. That doesn't stop us from scouring the countryside in hope of finding real proof.

The urge to chase monsters seems to be in our genes, helping us swallow our fear in exchange for a crumb of truth. Perhaps the master of modern terror said it best. According to Alfred Hitchcock, "Fear isn't so difficult to understand. After all, weren't we all frightened as children? Nothing has changed since Little Red Riding Hood faced the big bad wolf. What frightens us today is exactly the same sort of thing that frightened us yesterday. It's just a different wolf. . . ."[19]

Or how about a different canine? We will start our search with the legend of a dog woman and her unsettling connection to a mysterious meat hook in a stone chamber in southeast Pennsylvania.

CHAPTER TWO

A Meat Hook
and a Dog Woman

WERNERSVILLE DOG WOMAN

In October 1972, high school students within driving distance of Wernersville, Pennsylvania, were excited about something far more exotic than the usual Halloween and homecoming festivities. Everyone southwest of Reading was whispering that a vicious "dog woman"—a feral half-canine and half-human creature—lurked in the shadows of South Mountain, a wooded rise that borders the outskirts of Reading. People said the weird beast frequented the grounds of an abandoned resort complex that had been known as the Grand-View Sanatorium until 1927, when the sanatorium closed. The buildings were razed by a controlled fire in 1967, but remnants such as a stone chapel and roadside walls remain.

The creature, according to local legend, often appeared at one stone wall that contained a chamber furnished with one unsettling item embedded in the rock . . . a massive iron meat hook.

The legendary meat locker door,
COURTESY OF TERRY WEINHOLD

*The stone wall from which the unknown canine jumped to the road in front
of Terry Weinhold and friends,* COURTESY OF TERRY WEINHOLD

The meat hook carried its own bloody legend and the stone chamber where it hung was known as "the meat locker," according to an article in the *Reading Eagle* published in November 2010. Reporter Darrin Youker called it "the stuff of horror films."[1]

The story of the meat locker was grisly, no argument there. An unknown murderer had killed five people, so the legend went, and then butchered their remains and packed them into the chamber that had once been used for cold food storage. Muffled screams of the victims were supposed to emanate from the chamber on dark nights. Was any of this true? Not according to the reporter who investigated it for the *Reading Eagle*. "The story is pure bunk," said Youker.[2]

Adding the story of the ferocious dog woman to the meat hook tale probably didn't increase its general believability among the public, but it definitely boosted the legend's supernatural scare factor. The students reacted in various, predictable ways; many scoffed, some were frightened out of their wits, while a few were intrigued with the idea of exploring something so mysterious right in their own community.

Three brave high school seniors—Terry Weinhold and friends I'll call "A" and "B" (names withheld on request)—fell into the latter group. I learned about them when Terry contacted me online, and I was able to conduct email and phone interviews with him and with A. B's whereabouts were unknown.

But it seems that back in 1971, the three had decided to do more than just wonder about the legend. Terry recalled one unpleasantly memorable evening in October 1972, when they set out at dusk to find the dog woman. It wasn't their first attempt. After A had first heard of the creature from two other students on their school bus, he, Terry, and B had driven to the area several times after school to look for the dog woman, with no success. They decided their chances might be better after dark, when strange creatures seemed likelier to roam. The trio hopped in A's green Chevy pickup, B riding shotgun and Terry stuck in the middle, excited at the prospect of seeing the beast with their own eyes.

The wall was easy to find. It stood (and still stands at this writing) about eight to ten feet tall on one side of Grandview Road, which once fronted the resort's wide acreage. A slowed the truck to a crawl as they approached the spot. When they rolled past the open chamber, they heard a horrific sound Terry described as simultaneously a deep roar and a fierce growl. Terry then heard B, who was peering out the passenger side window, gasp. B excitedly told Terry and A that there was a large, fur-covered creature standing on its hind legs screaming at them from the top of the stonework. Before they could react, the creature hopped off the wall and dropped heavily to the pavement while continuing to emit earsplitting screeches. B screamed for A to hit the gas, and the truck lurched off down the narrow road. The creature, however, followed close to the rear bumper and kept pace for several hundred feet, still shredding the air with its vocalizations.

Terry added that A later said he could hear the creature's heavy footfalls padding on the asphalt as it chased them. Terry confessed he actually never saw the creature, partly because of his place in the middle of the truck seat, and partly because he was too afraid to look. "I was only seventeen," he told me. "I was scared out of my wits . . . It seemed like it was going to jump in the back of the pickup truck."

Despite the level of fright the boys were feeling, once the creature stopped chasing them, A decided he wanted to take one more pass for a better look at the creature. B and Terry adamantly opposed this idea, but A was driving, so he turned the truck around and approached the meat locker door once again. B was almost hysterical, said Terry, and was holding a large flashlight plugged into the cigarette lighter in the dash. Despite his fear, he aimed it out the window, perhaps as much in hope of scaring the creature as in seeing it.

They could tell it was still there by the growling sound, said Terry, and A said he could see glowing eyes. Terry and B yelled once again for him to step on the gas, and he did. At that point, the flashlight fell from B's hands but remained plugged into the dash. "The flashlight was banging against the side of the truck as we drove away," remembered Terry.

The creature did no harm to A's truck, but Terry knew another student who had been out to the chamber several years earlier and had claimed a large canine had dragged its claws across the trunk of his '57 Chevy. Terry also told a secondhand story from a friend and neighbor who said he had dared to enter the stone room, only to see a furry limb with sharp claws burst out of a hole in the wall and jab at his chest. These two stories cannot be corroborated, of course, and admittedly sound like any number of other urban legends about animals or entities popping out of desolate places to frighten young people.

But there were many other stories of local interactions with the dog woman, Terry said. Many of the stories were much older than 1972, since he remembered hearing older people talk about the creature when he was a child. "I've told this story to no more than three to four people," said Terry. "Everything I told you was the truth, exactly as it happened."

I'm willing to bet that, right now, especially given this last item about claws slashing a '57 Chevy and popping out of a wall to paw at an intruder, readers are struggling to sort out the story's details. Was this event fact, fiction, folktale, or urban legend? How can we know what to believe about such unusual accounts?

And which came first, the monster or the myth?

PEOPLE KEBABS OR JOKERS?

Our desire to reach a definite conclusion about the truth of this story is natural. The human urge to evaluate a dangerous situation—especially when the danger is something new and unidentified—is an instinctive and critical skill. For instance, it was likely only idle curiosity that drove the three teens to the rock wall in the first place. But curiosity quickly turned to terror as the snarling animal leapt off the rock ledge at them.

At this point, they had to react to one of two possibilities: Was this thing an actual flesh-and-blood predator capable of turning humans into people kebabs on that giant meat hook, or was it some joker acting out a Halloween legend? The unanimous and instant conclusion was that the creature was no kid in a gorilla suit, and the teens' mutual zest for self-preservation compelled them to flee.

Was their reported encounter proof of the story that a half-woman, half-canine creature had haunted the place for at least several decades? Probably not. Taking their story at face value doesn't rule out something explainable such as, say, a large, weirdly acting but otherwise normal, flesh-and-blood wolf or a dog with some unknown attachment to the wall—perhaps the meat hook still carried a cadaverous scent ingrained from its days as a meat locker accessory. The first option still smacks of something super-natural, a conclusion that will send most folks running for alternate theories. But the second option also seems unlikely, since wolves and large dog breeds rarely live more than ten to twenty years in the wild, and this creature was believed to have been prowling these grounds for many decades. Any natural animal should have met its fate long before Terry and his friends paid it a visit. There would have to be a breeding population.

It's easy to suggest something simpler than either option: The Grandview "beast" may have been a stray, mixed-breed farm dog merely wanting to chase intruders from its territory. It was dark outside at the time of the encounter, and visions of dog women had been dancing in the young men's heads. Perhaps most important is the fact that neither of the eyewitnesses described anything identifying it as a female. But Terry remains convinced to this day that the creature was more than some roving farm pet.

As with most sightings of unknown creatures, there isn't much hard evidence for any of these views. The creature's fearsome roar convinced the teens the beast was real, but the sound they described is only hearsay to those who weren't there. The claw marks on the Chevy could be considered at least circumstantial evidence, if only we had a few photos of the marks. But even great photos aren't necessarily seen as more than inconclusive evidence. I have taken photos of car trunks on two occasions in Wisconsin, which the auto owners said were inflicted by unknown canines chasing their cars on hind feet, but the photos didn't prove what had made the scratches.

And yet there were three witnesses—two who laid eyes on the canine animal and three who could testify to the teens' visit to the rock wall and to the roaring growl and the thump as the creature landed behind them. There are also photos of the rock wall and chamber door to support the story's location. That's more substance than can be found for many legends.

The story sent me looking for other tales of wolf women and dog ladies to see whether there might be similar legends to lend credibility to the tale. I did find a lively litter of reports of female, upright canines, and several are worth a quick study as relevant comparisons.

DOG LADIES: WHAT'S IN A NAME?

The tale of the Dog Woman of Wernersville, Pennsylvania, has at least one great thing going for it: its name. *Dog woman* evokes a whiff of old sideshow characters, faraway races of dog people (sometimes known as the cynocephali and famously reported by Marco Polo), or a mad scientist's genetic experiments. It especially reminds me of the story of the Dog Lady of Monroe, Michigan, which also has a fabulous moniker but is a very different, still thriving legend.

The Monroe Dog Lady has a backstory—and perhaps an end story, too, based on known facts. And despite the name, she was all too human. I have discussed this partly true tale in *Weird Michigan: Your Travel Guide to Michigan's Local Legends and Best Kept Secrets*, and I'll share a shorter version here.

THE LEGEND OF DOG LADY ISLAND

The first settlers called it Fox Island, but locals have known an overgrown little isle south of the Lake Erie port town of Monroe as Dog Lady Island since the 1960s. That's when area teenagers began to use the forlorn, weedy site as a perfect place to meet up and par-tay as only teens can do. This may sound as much like a classic monster-versus-teens horror movie as did the Pennsylvania meat hook story, but the Dog Lady, as everyone called her, was hardly a threat. Even the pack of dogs (some say they were Doberman pinschers) that followed her stayed mostly hidden from the carousing young people who visited the island on weekends.

The lady was known to spy on partygoers as she hid in nearby shrubbery, and those who occasionally glimpsed her said that despite her ragged appearance, she would definitely be classified as wholly *Homo sapiens*. It was her uncombed hair and overall lack of grooming that lent her a feral appearance. Her alleged habit of crawling around on her hands and knees, tearing at the flesh of dead animals along with her Dobermans, added the final touch of wildness to her image.

She lived alone on the island in a tiny shack that was once a caretaker's cottage, people said. Some teens swore she growled at them, licking her chops . . . until she lost her tongue. There are alternative versions of the story of how that happened. One story, and I emphasize *story*, claimed that a hound chewed it right out of her mouth as they tussled over a raccoon carcass. Another version said that a motorcycle gang cut her tongue out to prevent her from telling anyone about their commission of atrocities.

The facts, feral traits aside, were that there really was a lone, elderly woman living on the isle, and that she had once had some type of relationship with a prominent family, the Kauslers, that moved there in the 1800s. Their son, George, was born on the island in 1906, according to the Monroe Historical Society's records, but the family later moved into the city of Monroe. Sometime after that, the Kauslers hired a couple to live in a small cottage and watch over the mansion.

By the mid-60s, the husband had passed away and his wife remained alone on the island. And local historians say the lady—whoever she was—probably wasn't as weird as legend has it.

According to an archivist I spoke to years ago at the Monroe Historical Society, there is no evidence that the lady actually turned feral. It's also doubtful any teens or the lady were actually caught, tortured, and killed by a motorcycle gang as alleged in various versions of the lore. But a number of teens claimed to have seen her leap to the roofs of their cars and scratch at the windows with her claws, spittle flying from her curled lips.

That is a classic "attacked teenagers" legend trope, very similar to the actions attributed to the Pennsylvania dog woman. I think we can safely assume that this rather sad story of an elderly, dog-loving woman who may have suffered some age-related dementia was touched probably not by an angel but by an urban legend.

The island is still there, but the woman is gone, although some visitors claim they still feel her watchful presence on Dunbar Road near the old island causeway. And it wouldn't be a legend if eerie howling wasn't heard coming from the island when the moon is full.

Again for comparison's sake, we will look at another alleged female of the part-human, part-animal kind. If dog women can be immortalized in legend, then why not wolf women?

THE MOBILE WOLF WOMAN

A flap of sightings of a stunning female creature from Mobile, Alabama, hit that city's newspapers in April 1971, only about five or six months before Terry and his friends set out to look for a female, werewolf-like creature in Pennsylvania.

The phone calls to Mobile police started coming right around April Fools' Day, and by April 8 the *Mobile Press Register* revealed at least fifty concerned citizens had phoned in to say they'd seen something with the face and long hair of a beautiful woman but the body of a wolf or large dog. One caller added, a bit redundantly, that "it didn't look natural."[3] The bulk of the sightings occurred around Davis Avenue and the community of Plateau, an industrialized suburb founded and built by freed African slaves after emancipation. Once known as Africatown, it is listed on the National Register of Historic Places. Its original inhabitants sought to live according to their own culture there, and the initial population included a chieftainship and an official medicine man.

The 1971 Wolf Woman seemed to have appeared out of nowhere. She was more a curiosity than a terror, however. Although people were understandably apprehensive about running into the creature, she wasn't viciously attacking people. No one reported injury—not even so much as a stray claw mark—although one man claimed the creature chased him home from one of the area's many marshes. After a few days of continual reports that kept residents looking over their shoulders, the sightings abated and the town went back to normal. The Wolf Woman retreated as quietly as she had come, and has not been reported there since, to my knowledge.

I have another, somewhat fanciful suggestion, however. Perhaps the Mobile Wolf Woman decided to travel north to cooler climes along the Mississippi River, took a hard right at the Ohio, and arrived in Pennsylvania around October of 1971, just as the rumors of her began to spread around Wernersville. Considering both the unique concept of a female wolf monster and the relatively short time span between sightings in Alabama and Pennsylvania, it seems possible these two modern folklore-in-the-making stories are related. Remembering our earlier discussion of urban legends and the fact that they're often transmitted from location to location, it makes sense. Granted, Mobile is a long way from Wernersville, but strange news travels fast, and unknown creatures travel even faster.

THE TEXAS LOBO GIRL

There is one more story, this one from a publication of the Texas Folklore Society.[4] As this tale is quite well known and dates back to the 1830s, it might just possibly qualify as the root of all American dog woman, dog lady, wolf woman, wolf lady legends. I'm including it here because of a particular quote from the Texas Folklore Society author that made me think of the story in a new light. We'll get to that soon. But the saga actually began in another state, along Georgia's Chickamauga Creek.

Everything started, legend says, when two fur trappers had a row over a woman named Mollie who was officially engaged to one of the trappers, John Dent. When Dent's trapping partner, Will Marlo, met Mollie, he decided she should marry him instead of Dent. They also quarreled over their trapping agreement. Violence ensued, and Dent ended up killing Marlo. Dent had to skip town, but sneaked back to grab Mollie and marry her at last. The pair eloped to a small colony of English people on the Devils River in Texas, in the region of today's Carrizo Springs. Mollie became pregnant, and John Dent died in a lightning storm as he rode to get help for her delivery. Mollie passed away during childbirth, but the child was mysteriously taken from her. Those who discovered her body saw only *lobo*—Spanish for "wolf"—tracks and no trace of a baby.

After a decade had passed, people around San Felipe began saying they'd seen what looked like a human female with very long hair running with wolves—sometimes on all fours. Some recalled Mollie Dent and her missing baby and began to wonder whether this *lobo* girl could be that baby, somehow raised by the wolves. Area Native Americans reported finding human footprints in the sand along the riverbanks. Inevitably the young female was caught and discovered to be a normal human, although she was "excessively hairy."[5] She also cowered, spat at other humans, screamed, and made other strange, animalistic sounds. Her caretakers noticed unusual muscle development of her hands and arms (probably from running on all fours). They took her to a nearby ranch, where she spent much time howling to her *lobo* companions for rescue. The wolves soon attacked the ranch and somehow the girl escaped and fled with her beloved pack.

About seven years later, she was reportedly seen again on the banks of the Rio Grande as she sat nursing two wolf pups. She leapt to her feet and ran off with the little ones, and that seemed to be the end of her story. But next came the part that made me sit up and take notice—the quote I alluded to earlier.

The author wrote, "In the border country, a wolf has occasionally been found with a *marked human resemblance*, and for many years now '*human-faced' wolves*, so called, have been considered the final culmination of a Georgia murder and elopement. If a man can bear the 'mark of the beast,' why may not beast bear the mark of the man? Speaking only for myself, I will say that despite the fact that over a century has passed since the beginning of the incidents just related, yet during the past forty years I have in the western country met *more than one wolf face strongly marked with human characteristics*."[6] (All emphases mine.)

The implication is that Mollie's daughter was able to mate with a wolf and reproduce hybrid young, even though there is no indication from the author quoted above that the wolf pups she carried had any human features. And since humans and canines are not genetically compatible and modern genetics technology didn't yet exist, I doubt the little wolf-human hybrids existed. The pups, of course, might have been actual little wolves or even human babies covered with dirt so as to appear furry from a distance. Whatever they were, their story had taken on its own life, and could have helped seed legends of similar canid-humanoid creatures such as Mobile's Wolf Woman and Michigan's Dog Lady.

As far as folklore origins are concerned, the story of Mollie Dent's feral daughter doesn't have to be *true*; it simply has to have been known and repeated enough to travel due east of west Texas and arrive in Mobile and Wernersville by the 1970s. The Dent story was published in 1937, which gives it over three decades to have made the journey by printed page and word of mouth.

HAIR TODAY, DOGGONE TOMORROW

Does this mean the creature that jumped off the meat hook chamber and chased Terry, A, and B was merely a phantom apparition of an old folktale? Not at all! We still don't know what it was. Its description and behavior are very consistent with what other people have been seeing along American highways and byways since at least the 1930s, and it could be a member of that unknown, upright canid family. It could also have been a feral mutt or a defensive farm dog that loved to chase trucks.

I have another proposed explanation for the Wernersville and

Mobile "canine women," although it requires acknowledgment that yet another mystery creature does exist in a flesh-and-blood, solid, procreational sort of way. The idea struck me one day when I came across a particular description of not a canine, not a human, but a female Bigfoot! It was described by Alan Hall, a Haisla Nation storyteller of the British Columbian coast, in Robert Pyle's excellent 1995 book, *Where Bigfoot Walks: Crossing the Dark Divide*.[7] The incident Hall related had been told to him by his grandfather, who had shot at what he thought was a group of black bears. To his horror, he saw that he had accidentally killed a female Sasquatch that stood among what turned out to be a group of Bigfoots rather than bears. He said that she had humanlike breasts and little to no body hair. Hall's grandfather barely escaped with his life as the remaining Sasquatch band pursued him to his canoe. But I started to imagine what this female may have looked like.

Hall hadn't said she was bald, so she may have had long hair, and if her torso was hairless, perhaps her face was, too. And if there was one female with a fur-free body, perhaps there were others with varying amounts of body and facial hair. And what if there were some with long hair on the head, a furless torso, but fur on the lower legs and arms?

I know people who have observed a couple of female Bigfoots in Salt Fork State Park, Ohio, and said the creatures looked unexpectedly human and even pretty. Many Native Americans have traditionally seen Bigfoots as either fully human or a subspecies of humans that could actually mate and produce hybrid, less hairy offspring. Might a partly smooth-skinned, female offspring be taken for a dog woman, especially if seen outside her normal element? Bigfoots are known to run on all fours in areas of human habitation, presumably to keep a lower profile, which would enhance the impression they were some weird, large canine. I think it's a possible way to look at both the Wernersville and Mobile incidents and as good an explanation for dog women as any—except for one more thought I have.

This one requires a bit more backstory. We will have to start with the tale of a flesh-and-blood creature from the region west of Reading. Much of the information comes from an unpublished article, "The Thing," that was shared with me by its author, Reading area historian and author Charles J. Adams, and discussed here with his permission.

THE THINGS OF SHEEP HILL AND BIG VALLEY

Across the Schuylkill River and over a few hills from the Wernersville area in the mid-twentieth century lurked a creature so strange and unprecedented that it was known to local Pennsylvanians simply as "the Thing." While its main stomping ground was Sheep Hill in North Coventry Township, Chester County, it terrorized the folks of neighboring counties—including Berks County, home to the later dog woman legends.

The many witnesses could not get an exact bead on its description but seemed to agree it was a large predator with dark fur that could "scream like a banshee, howl like a wolf, and growl like a grizzly," with the ability to leap twenty feet in a single bound. According to the *Coatesville Record* of Coatesville, Pennsylvania, eyewitness Thomas Rhodes said, "The creature was larger than a fox with a sleek black coat, a long body, short and pointed ears and a long, thin, tail . . . Lester Thompson, of Couglasville, described the sequence of the calls: 'It starts sort of low-pitched, gives a couple of short bursts first, then it lets her rip.'"[8]

Guesses as to its species ranged from black bear to big cat or black "panther"; a Jersey Devil; an English-style, huge phantom dog known as "Black Shuck"; and—most encouraging for our dog woman studies—a werewolf.

And yet, as Adams says in his written account, "It was not a fiend that threatened superstitious folks in an unenlightened time. It was a monster that terrorized a civilized area in November, 1945." Just what we were looking for!

Even the Associated Press began to pick up some of the stories accumulating in area newspapers, quoting farmer John Hipple, who claimed, "It was like a big cat. I shot at it and it leaped twenty feet into the air, screamed, and disappeared."

I presume that he used the word *disappeared* to mean that the animal leapt out of his sight, but with this kind of report, we can only wish that he had been questioned a little more closely about that aspect of the incident. Witnesses of unknown animals will sometimes use the word *disappear* in a more literal sense as well. The fact that it was compared to a phantom hound, the Jersey Devil, and a werewolf tells me that there was at least some speculation as to the creature's true nature.

The Thing evidently looked and acted more deadly than it really was. The only depredations reported were chickens and turkeys gone missing or killed. In fact, the greatest danger to area citizens was other humans, as people set out to find, capture, or shoot the creature. A car crash caused by one driver's panic injured two people, and two others were accidentally shot in separate incidents. Adams said, "Armed posses, some comprised of on-duty law enforcement officers and accompanied by hunting dogs, spread across the countryside for weeks."

Even the Pennsylvania State Police got into the action, warning residents to avoid the countryside, day or night, and assisting citizens in the placing of sixteen bear traps baited with cattle entrails on Sheep Hill. The Thing was evidently too smart or too well fed on farm poultry to touch the traps, however. The sightings soon stopped, and people assumed the Thing had moved on to some other hunting ground with fewer rifles and bear traps.

I found this story interesting for several reasons, chief among them the great diversity of descriptions made by the eyewitnesses, and their tendency to suggest legendary or supernatural creatures such as the Black Shuck, Jersey Devil, and werewolf as their best guesses. I also note that two of these, the phantom hound and werewolf, are canine-type entities, and that, as in the case of the Wernersville Dog Woman, there were no actual attacks on humans, and only minor loss of farm animals.

Adams documented another Pennsylvania "thing" in his book *Pennsylvania Dutch Country Ghosts, Legends and Lore.*[9] This one stomped around rural Lancaster County, which is noted for its large Amish population, in 1973. According to Adams, the journal of the Society for the Investigation of the Unexplained (SITU) reported that two Amish brothers were plowing a field in the Big Valley area with a team of horses when a heifer-sized animal covered in gray fur and running on its hind legs came at them full tilt. That caused the horses to rear up and the brothers to tumble to the ground. Luckily for them the white-maned creature ran off, and the brothers were okay. But they couldn't forget its formidable fangs that looked like those of a tiger, nor its long, sharp claws and curved, goat-like horns. And they weren't the only ones to encounter this terrifying animal. A nearby farmer claimed he was attacked by the same creature only a day later. Luckily he was armed with a scythe and was able to take a good swing at the beast as it neared him. Not so luckily, he realized the scythe was no match for the powerful creature. It simply batted the tool out of the farmer's hand and then chewed and ate the wooden handle. The panic-stricken man was able to make his getaway, and the beast did not follow.

There was one more encounter the day after that when a neighboring woman spied the same upright, horned creature creeping around her farmyard after dark. Evidently the creature had already helped itself to her poultry shed, because it flung one of her geese—stone dead—at her and then bounded off into the night, a rude farewell indeed.

WHAT OF THE DOG WOMAN?

Could any of the above encounters or legends in this chapter have been related to the Wernersville Dog Woman, which had been seen in roughly the same part of the state within one to twenty years of one another?

I think a better case can be made that the creatures were linked by legends rather than by physical association. Even if my hybrid female Bigfoot idea could account for most sightings in Alabama and Pennsylvania, there was nothing to indicate the sex of the canine creature glimpsed by Terry and his friends. It's just possible that over the space of twenty years or so, stories of the Thing combined with the tales of the Mobile Dog Woman, and then both merged with the legend of the meat hook chamber to *become* the legend of the mysterious Wernersville Dog Woman, guarding the chamber from trespassers. Again, the physical distance between Wernersville and Mobile is no problem; a nice trail along the Appalachians leads from Alabama to southeastern Pennsylvania, offering a pathway for both urban legends and flesh-and-blood predators to spread from high school to high school. Memories of scary experiences can become legendary in very little time. . . . I've seen it happen in less time than that on Wisconsin's Bray Road, for instance, where a cluster of sightings of a werewolf-like creature became known nationally in only a few weeks. That legend is still very alive almost three decades later.

None of this speculation, however, lessens the real fear Terry felt that night when some type of all-too-real animal jumped off the top of the stone chamber, just as the legends said it should. Whether the fulfillment of a legend or spooky happenstance, the event was a true life-changer to him and his friends.

CHAPTER 3

Those Dear, Deer People

THE OGLALA DEER WOMAN

THE IDEA OF MONSTERS with feminine attributes is not an isolated concept, either in ancient mythology (think of Medusa, the snake-haired woman of the Greek pantheon) or in contemporary sightings. In 2009, Patrick Waters described seeing a woman-beast about three years earlier that might support my "hybrid female Bigfoot" idea. Patrick encountered a creature with a very human, female torso but an animal structure from the waist down. Patrick wrote (edited slightly for punctuation and format):

Have you heard of the deer people, like deer woman or the deer man? . . . I have a strange encounter to relate to you. I live in Rapid City, South Dakota, and am an enrolled member of the Oglala Sioux tribe and often travel to the reservation.

This happened three years ago when it was late at night. I was traveling with a former acquaintance. We were about fifteen miles from the town of Hermosa and it was pitch black and really dark that night. I was asleep in the passenger seat when my traveling partner woke me up, saying he just passed a nice looking woman standing in the tall grass near the edge of the road. He was wondering if we should pick her up.

I've heard stories from my late mother about picking hitchhikers up late at night near the reservation; she told me of shape shifters and other less savory supernatural entities, of goatmen, dogmen, and deer people.

I told him to drive—if there was a woman standing there at two in the morning, she could find her own way home. A couple minutes passed and he said, "There she is!" He was pointing to the side of the road; there was a female human figure standing there but I couldn't see her legs. I told him to keep driving and put some umph in the gas pedal.

We were nearing a part of Battle Creek when he said, "There she is again," except he had a slight twinge of fear in his voice. I looked and she was standing on the pavement. She was wearing a dress-type piece of clothing and had small hooves where her feet should have been. She had a human upper body, long dark hair, but her eyes reflected white in the headlights, pretty face, kinda like the Disney version of Pocahontas, maybe about 5'9" around 120 lbs.; we really didn't get a good look at her legs the first time, but the sighting a few miles later showed she definitely had deer legs and a tail, mule deer color and markings, and she had human hands for sure.

He hit the gas and I looked behind us. There were vaguely deer-shaped figures running not far behind our Tahoe, and we were doing like eighty miles per hour on a small two-lane country highway. It [the road] was very curvy and had a lot of blind turns. We got to Hermosa and hid out at the truck stop for a couple hours. It was very unnerving, . . . really strange, and I [now] don't go near the reservation at night or even near evening. It felt like I was seeing things for a while.

According to Patrick, he and his friend are not the only people who have seen what more accurately should be called Mule Deer Woman. He added, "A lot of people tell stories about encountering her between June and November during powwows and other ceremonial gatherings; she's like the boogeyman to us, like a succubi, [sic] in the Christian sense. [A succubus is a female entity of old European lore that appears to men at night for apparently carnal purposes.] She entices men away from crowds and they are never seen again or they have been trampled to death. There are reports of some survivors in other tribes and reservations."

Patrick also experienced a frightening encounter in 1987 or '88. He was only five years old, and it was just after dusk in the early fall. He was helping his older cousin load a truck for a planned hunt to take place in the morning, he said, when they heard a blood-chilling scream from a nearby pasture. Again, in his words:

He put me in his truck and we drove to the pasture and found a couple of our horses laying on the ground but still moving, but as we drove closer I seen eye shine, from about seven feet off the ground we estimated later. My cousin turned on his spotlight and there were these huge dogs with bright yellow eyes, dark in color, eating the open bellies of the horses. They [the dogs] started for the truck and, I'm not too proud to say it—I was little—I wet myself.

My cousin pulled his gun, a Colt 1911. He fired it empty and jumped in the truck and we left to get help. I don't recall how much later we came back to the property. My cousin dropped me off with my mom and left with five other trucks filled with people armed to the teeth for something. A short time later in the canyons behind our property, it sounded like the Fourth of July.

The next morning my cousin was telling my grandpa [the dogs] were big and didn't scare easily but they got six of them and burned the bodies. Fast forward to when I was thirteen and I asked him about that night, he said they were big dogs that reared up on their back legs and walked. It took a lot of fire power to bring them down but they weren't "HIM." (HIM is how we describe Bigfoot.)

As a footnote, Patrick added that his cousin died in a car accident when Patrick was nineteen, and his mother died from cancer when he was fifteen. He also added: "A few years later [at about the age of eight], I was hiking around our old property and found some bones and a huge dog skull in a medium [burial] mound in one of the canyons. And I moved away from South Dakota in 2016 and now live in Illinois."

Another, much more recent report of a close encounter with deer women occurred in Colorado on April 6, 2018, when a man and his girlfriend, who was driving, were looking for a place to eat near Colorado Springs one night during a misty, light snowstorm. They weren't having any luck finding a restaurant, he wrote me, but both felt compelled to keep looking despite a growing fear that something was wrong. They were debating turning back when they noticed six or more deer running on a hill to the right of their car. Nearby them was a fence with what looked like a limp, dead deer hanging from it. They also discovered a restaurant just ahead and pulled into the parking lot, only to be met with a truly strange spectacle, said the man.

"As we pulled in we saw them," he said. "The deer people. That is really the only way to describe them. There were about a dozen scattered about." (I presume he meant the same creatures they had just seen running nearby.) They appeared to be about six feet tall or a few inches under, he said, standing upright with thin waists and legs, but looked somewhat humanlike. The strange part, he added, was their upper bodies, which had very wide shoulders with wide necks and heads that seemed too big for their bodies and were covered with fur. Their faces, however, resembled those of deer. Their eyes were wide set and black, and they had large ears. A few had antlers.

He and his girlfriend both saw them. The man said they seemed fully physical to him, but his girlfriend, whom he describes as a "materialist" and a teacher with a degree in biology (he is a computer technologist), thought they looked "out of phase."

The writer did not say whether they stayed to eat or left immediately, but I presume they left. One of the creatures, however, seemed to have followed them home. The next night as he lay in bed he heard footsteps and heavy breathing and then saw a tall, dark shadow in his room. Not long after that, he was smoking on his apartment balcony and saw a large figure standing on a nearby riverbank, staring at him. It had the same oversize head and neck and the deerlike muzzle as they had seen while driving. He ran to get his girlfriend to witness it, but by the time he could bring her to the balcony, it had disappeared.

The deer people are interesting in that they blend the traditional human/monster mythology of all cultures with the well-known modern urban legends involving attractive (at first glance) people spotted along roadways as they entice travelers to stop. And the large, dark canines with the shining eyes evoke thoughts of black phantom hounds that date back many centuries in the British Isles and Europe, such as the Black Dog of Bungay that attacked churchgoers during worship in Bungay and Blythburgh in 1577. But just to show that not all older legends lend themselves to such associations or hybridizations, I'd like to mention a pure and benign example of the female human/animal on the western prairies.

WHITE BUFFALO CALF WOMAN

As stated above, there are female, human/animal spirit creatures in the Sioux and other tribal traditions that are not ill-intentioned toward people. Quite the opposite! One of the best known and most sacred to many tribal people of the US is White Buffalo Calf Woman, a spirit woman that appeared in the distant past to help her people. According to legend, widespread among North American Native peoples, she promised when she had finished her work she would visit earth again as a white buffalo calf and that her appearance would help to usher in a new era of mankind.

Legend became reality when the long-awaited birth of such an animal (not an albino but a true, white-colored calf) did occur on August 20, 1994, in Janesville, Wisconsin, on a farm near the Rock River on the city's southern edge. Many Sioux and other First Nation people traveled to see the calf named Miracle, who became a worldwide sensation. I interviewed a few of these sojourners at the farm for a Walworth County, Wisconsin, newspaper, *The Week* (the same paper from which I broke the Beast of Bray Road story).

Chief Joseph Standing Horse of the Lakota Sioux was one of those who had made the pilgrimage from South Dakota to see Miracle. He told me she had originally come in the shape of a woman to bring a message of future peace. The spirit woman gave the Lakota a sacred pipe bundle to keep for the day she would return, and then transformed herself into a white buffalo, changing back into a woman when she went back to the spirit world.

The Buffalo Calf Woman, then, was quite different from the Dog Woman and the Mule Deer Woman, not only in her intent and behavior but in her appearance: either wholly human or wholly buffalo, never as a half-animal, half-humanoid siren (a mythical Greek aquatic temptress). She was also a pure and sacred entity who is still revered, the opposite of the mule deer lady, which is to be avoided at all costs.

TO THE MOON, DEER MAN, TO THE MOON!

I must also be clear that deer people are not always devious in Native American traditions. Patrick mentioned hearing of their lore in other tribes, and according to Canadian ethnologist and linguist Basil Johnston, the Ojibwe of the northern forests of the US and Canada had their own legend of a deer man spirit who could appear as a man or a deer. This deer man was associated, interestingly, with a "sky craft"[1] that looked like a closed clamshell (very similar to today's archetypal flying saucer) and left a circular pattern in the grass where it landed on the earth after slowly hovering downward on its visits.

As Johnston told it, a young Ojibwe man named Eshkekbug witnessed this spectacle one day and watched as ten beautiful young women debarked from the sky craft to play and dance. A deer man appeared to Eshkekbug as he stood admiring the women's dancing, and generously helped him win one of the sky-people as his wife. The deer man also gave Eshkekbug the power to transform himself into the shapes of various animals and even, on one occasion, a tree.

I'm going to sound a digression alert in order to mention other peculiar details of this story that, while perhaps not directly related to the spirit/animal creatures, may interest readers. The clamshell-shaped sky craft, for instance, was said to be composed of "shining rainbow material," with "dully glowing sides." That sounds like an advanced technology not likely to have been imagined by the pre-space-age people of this story. Also, the vessel was supposed to be capable of space flight from Earth to the moon and back, and seemed to exist just for that purpose. However, since the story was translated and retold in modern times, it is possible that these details may have been added to the older core of the story.

Also, although there may seem to be a very direct correlation between the ancient sky craft described by Johnston and modern descriptions of UFOs, I must also caution that there is no estimated date of origin available for Johnson's stories. We may assume that the core storyline is probably many generations old, and that his purpose for writing stories down as he heard them directly from tribal storytellers was to preserve the ancient oral traditions. But he also states in prefaces to his books that certain details may change as the stories are adapted through time to honor and include the experiences of tellers and listeners. Despite all that, the sky craft still sounds to the modern ear like a UFO. And I thought of one less obvious but significant correlation between the shining craft of the tale and present spacecraft technology:

Johnston noted that the craft's propulsion system was operated by sound, via a very special song sung by the young women. The idea that vocal music could launch and propel any kind of airborne craft seems purely fantastical, but I decided to run a quick search for sonic propulsion systems anyway. I found that in 2011, the Ohio Aerospace Institute released a statement suggesting a possible spacecraft propulsion system that could be powered by light or sound waves. These waves are carried in the magnetic fields of plasma that can be supplied by the sun.[2] The most useful sound waves would be those of radio frequencies kHz to MHz. In Johnston's story, only females could sing the sky craft's "music." This also seems a fanciful notion, unless it is a reference to the higher sound frequencies usually generated by female voices, in which case it is revealing rather specific information about the craft's operation.

This kind of speculation is always risky, especially for laypeople such as myself. But it's rewarding to discover possible correlations hiding inside legends or religious myth. And as long as I've started, here are a few more: In Johnston's story, Eshkekbug's mother felt that she, too, had once known something about the sky craft but was frustrated that she wasn't able to access the exact memory. UFO buffs may immediately think of modern abductees who describe the same sense of knowing something important had been wiped from their memory. (Some would declare this part of the modern legendry of UFOs.) The mother later managed to recall the flight song she had heard as a child.

The sky craft also possesses the bizarre characteristics of time slips, missing time, and other temporal anomalies experienced by modern UFO eyewitnesses and abductees. For instance, Eshkekbug is a mortal who will grow old and die, but the sky women do not age, nor do they experience time as do ordinary earth dwellers. As Johnston tells it, "Alas, time for the sky people has little force and meaning."[3]

Eshkekbug and his wife had a son, Zhawano-gizig, which meant "blue sky." This boy was said to be "tall," and the fact that this was the *only* description of their child's appearance seems possibly significant. I couldn't help but think of the Bible's passage in Genesis that describes Sons of God descending to Earth to mate with Daughters of Men, with resulting children described as giants.

As long as I'm mentioning giants here, let's keep in mind that the term *giant* is relative. Since humans come in so many heights, there is no standard measurement to denote true giant status in every population, and it may refer to any individual noticeably taller than others of that time and locale. It's more like, we know one when we see one. For instance, there have been many newspaper articles that describe skeletons of ancient Native Americans found in burial mounds as "giants," when they measure seven or seven and a half feet tall. (some have been found whose height was estimated at eight or nine feet.) When the rest of the population averages five and a half feet, a person of such stature may well seem like a giant. But in this day and age we would probably just call this person a professional basketball player.

The Ojibwe story presents another parallel to the Genesis passage that is actually an interesting turnabout: here we still have celestial entities descending to Earth, but this time it's the *daugh-*

ter of a god that descends and mates with a *son* of men—even if it was his idea rather than hers.

Eventually in the story, Zhawano-gizig was able to ride to the moon with his mother to meet his grandparents. They sent him back to Earth to fetch his father, commanding him to collect and bring them one of every bird species on Earth when he returned (reminiscent of the Bible's Noah and his ark containing a pair of every animal species).

All in all, the Ojibwe Deer Man proves as kind and beneficial to humans as did the White Buffalo Calf Woman, and was entirely different in character and appearance than the fear-inspiring mule deer and dog women.

Finally, I still see one more association between the Deer Man's story and the spirit-animal theme of these first chapters that may be worth considering, as we compare human/animal legends and modern reports. There *have* been a number of cases from contemporary UFO research that involved both UFOs and strange, animal-humanoid creatures that look and act like they're not from around here. "Present-day UFOnauts," "entities," and "beings"[4] are some of the terms scientist and UFO researcher Jacques Vallee uses for them in his book *Passport to Magonia*, a work he describes as a "bridge" that spans the uncertain places "between a fancy and a myth."[5]

More precisely, Vallee lists those UFOnauts and entities as "beings of giant stature, men indistinguishable from us, winged creatures, and various types of monsters."[6] In most stories of UFOs piloted by otherworld beings, the pilots seem to be chosen from a different roster of candidates and are usually seen as dark, hairy, gnomelike creatures, sylphs (spirits of the air described by Paracelsus in the sixteenth century), or elf-like creatures. Some sightings involve mixtures of all these things. In Johnston's culture story of the Deer Man, we have the beautiful, sylphlike maidens or sky people whose sonic emanations pilot and power the sky craft, and we also have a possible giant in Zhawano-gizig, the "tall" son created by the union of the daughter of the sky people and the son of men.

The gang's all here, as the old song goes. Well, perhaps not all. There's one more.

"WHEN THAT FIRST 'DEER' STOOD UP": OHIO MANWOLVES

There are times when people think they are seeing deer, but they have another think coming. An Ohio man who once lived in East Liverpool, Ohio, wrote me about an incident that occurred in winter 1998, in the vicinity of that town. What he saw seemed so bizarre to him that he figured he must have simply hallucinated the whole thing, until he heard me discussing upright-walking canines on a radio show. I'll call him by his requested pseudonym, Dale. He wrote:

> After listening to you on *Coast to Coast* I have come to realize that I really saw this. Now, I will be honest with you. I have had a lot of paranormal experiences since I was a child, but it always involved the more spiritual aspect of the supernatural, never anything like Bigfoot or other such "monsters" beforehand.
>
> I was living in East Liverpool, Ohio, back in 1998. I lived at the top of Calcutta Smith Ferry Hill. Now the hill is fairly steep, and in the winter it can be treacherous climbing, and worse com-

ing down, so you always had to take it easy on the road. I worked night turn [shift], and often did not head home until after three a.m. most nights. I cannot recall exactly what night it was that this occurred, but I know it was at the tail end of November going into December.

I had been working, and was getting sicker and sicker as the night went on, to the point that I had to leave and go home. It had really snowed earlier that day, and the roads were just covered with ice. I believe it was about one thirty in the morning that I started up Calcutta Smith Ferry Road. The snow made it really rough to get up, and I was really taking it slow as I went up the hill. I can't recall if it was a full moon, but I remember it was really clear, and the moon was seriously shining. With all the snow and ice it really lit up the night, and I could see very well.

As I cleared the crest of the hill and started down the other side, I had to really take it slowly, as I started to slide sideways. The rear of my car started to pull to my left, which edged my car to slightly face to the right, into a farmer's field.

As I was sliding, I managed to get the car back under control without event, but I took notice that as my car slid, a family of four deer had come out of the woods from Beaver Creek. What struck me as odd was that when they came out, they started running pell-mell towards my car. I thought it was weird that they were moving so fast, but put my attention back on the road as I started sliding again. My car actually went into a 360-degree spin. I got myself collected and found myself facing towards the field. I was set to back up, when I saw the deer stop about three hundred feet away.

Up until now I had no clue anything was weird, but then two of the deer stood up and I could see that they weren't deer, but really weird wolves. I would say they stood about six feet high, and I remember their eyes were a strange green color. Deer eyes, I believe, glow red. So yes, I panicked and got back onto the road and took off like a shot, and they followed me (running on all fours) for roughly two hundred yards. After that I stopped watching them, I made it home a minute later and ran into the house. After I got in I told myself that I was so sick I had seen things. I don't believe that at all now, though.

Dale revealed a few more interesting things as we continued to discuss the details of his sighting. I mentioned that the eyes of deer generally do not reflect red or reddish orange but rather a bright white tinged with some other light color. Bears, owls, and often Bigfoot are reported to reflect a reddish color. Canine eyeshine is normally yellow to yellow green. That the "deer" were actually canines makes perfect sense considering Dale's observation of greenish-colored eyes. He added:

They varied in size. The largest two are the ones that stood up. The other two were thinner and could have easily passed as does from a distance. The larger ones were definitely broader and more 'wolfish' in their looks. I know the primary one was male, but I'm not sure about the others. Their hands, now that I think on it, were less human and more like extended or lengthened canine paws. I would say that they ran like dogs do because I really thought they were deer up until I looked right at them. Had they run differently, it might have made me take note faster. I believe that in the moonlight they were brown. But color is tricky in moonlight.

One thing I just recalled. I believe they ran out of the woods with their tails down, not up like they were chasing something. But when they came after the car, their tails were up, which made it easier to believe I was in a fever dream state. But the one that stood closest to my vehicle had his tail out, as it was bristled. I even remember seeing his breath backlit by the moonlight. Honestly I can't recall how they followed the car because I was more concerned with getting away than anything else.

East Liverpool is very close to the Pennsylvania border, about thirty miles south of Youngstown. Both Ohio and Pennsylvania are well-known for sightings of upright canines as well as Bigfoots. And this particular spot on Calcutta-Smith Ferry Road is within a few miles or less from the Little Beaver Creek and also very close to the Ohio River. There are three state parks or forested nature areas just northeast, north, and northwest of the encounter site, and any online map will reveal the great amount of wooded cover perfect for any type of predator all along that hilly river road.

Supporting Dale's story was another report from eastern Ohio, about thirty miles northwest of Youngstown. This encounter occurred in fall 2006, in West Farmington, as the eyewitness drove east on Clark Road. In this case, however, the witness never thought the creature might be a deer or anything else. He wrote:

"I crossed Girdle Road and continued east. When I drove around the long bend in the road to the north, I saw something just at the outer reach of my headlights on the left side of the road. It was standing on its hind legs near the ditch." The witness said that when the creature noticed him, it dropped down on all fours and loped across the road, giving him a very good look at it. He then saw clearly that it was a huge dog or wolf about six feet in length plus a big, brushy tail. Its build was canine-like, too, with a beefy upper body that tapered to a slim midsection.

As the creature melted off into the brush, it reminded the witness of the dire wolf in the movie *300*. And interestingly, he had already heard reports of some strange animal—something with an appetite for chickens, goats, and other farm animals—from the Amish who lived in the area near Middlefield. "They all reported something different, from a black bear to a black panther," said the witness. The Amish eventually agreed that it was a black, or melanistic, panther, another creature not acknowledged by authorities to exist in that state. And what this witness and Dale both described sounded nothing like a great cat in appearance or behavior.

Neither did the report from yet *another* witness who on March 1, 2006, eight years after Dale's sighting, saw what he called a man-wolf that was also near Middlefield. He worked in that town, the man wrote, and was on his way home heading east on State Route 88, then south on Hoffman Norton Road. He did not know of Dale's sighting. He first described the terrain of that countryside as mainly consisting of a densely wooded, hilly public wildlife area that lay near an ancient Native American burial ground with a few Amish homesteads scattered throughout.

Soon after he made his turn onto Hoffman Norton Road, he said, "My high beams shone [on] a large and I mean very large animal. It was on all fours but I would guess it was every bit of six feet long from its head to its butt, not counting its very bushy tail, and stood at least three feet high on all fours to its back and shoulders."

The witness watched the creature leap into the ditch, illuminated by his headlights to reveal a white face and silvery-white fur. He called it a "magnificent animal." The creature did not act in a threatening way, he said, but stared at him in a deeply inquisitive manner. The witness added that he felt safe in his car with the windows rolled up.

Many other eyewitnesses have also noted that these creatures gazed at them in a way that formed a connection, established an attitude, or at the very least, implied intelligence and curiosity not expected from normal animals. This type of experience usually leaves a deep impression on the eyewitness.

Dale, the witness just previously discussed, indicated similar feelings when he said of his encounter, "This has really stuck out in my mind over the years . . . I have never forgotten it and actually consider it every so often. I will never forget when that first 'deer' stood up. Now I wonder what would have happened if my car had gotten stuck on the roadside."

I think Dale would agree it's probably better that he never did find out what would have happened if his car had gotten stuck. It indeed seems strange that the small pack of canines headed straight for his car as it began to slide around, almost as if they anticipated it might go off the road and somehow knew he would then be vulnerable. I also wonder how many people see what they *think* are deer and never give them a second glance or thought, when they are actually seeing something quite different. I have a feeling that many "deer man" legends are started by similar misidentifications.

CHAPTER 4

Witchy Wolves of Omer Plains

TRUE BURN NOTICE

WITCHES AND WOLVES have long been associated with one another in the realms of folklore and dark traditions. Many areas of Europe spent roughly three hundred years, from the late fifteenth to the early eighteenth centuries, waging a prolonged and zealous campaign intended to rid themselves of the perceived menaces.

These were dangerous times in which to be associated with occult practices. Anyone who was accused of being a witch or had even the slightest of charges against them—say, a weirdly shaped wart or a neighbor's blame for a dead cow—was tried, tortured into confessing, and quite often killed. Burning people alive at the stake was the cruel, standard method of execution for crimes the church considered heresy. Witches fell into this category because of the belief that they had renounced their Christian baptism in favor of devil worship.

Estimates of the total number of Europeans executed for witchery over these three centuries range as high as ten thousand people, many of them elderly or suffering from mental illness. Alleged werewolves, or people thought to be able to change bodily into or project their spirits as wolves, also fell victim to these grisly trials due to the logic of that time that shape-shifting could only occur through use of witchcraft, so those accused of changing into wolves or even merely attempting to do so must necessarily be witches.

Although the witch trials had finished for the most part in Europe by about 1630, they persisted for a short time in the fledgling American colonies with the famed Salem witch trials of 1692. The American version didn't necessarily dwell on the idea of wolves as spirit companions to witches, but the *concept* of supernaturally generated, wolflike creatures is something that evidently not only crossed the Atlantic with European immigrants but has endured in diverse places into the twentieth and twenty-first centuries.

The tiny city of Omer, Michigan, pleasantly situated only five miles from Lake Huron and bisected by the scenic Rifle River, is one such locale.

OMINOUS PLAINS OF OMER

When I visited in early fall 2014 to speak at the invitation of the Omer Little Eagles Nest Library, I was charmed by the town's old-fashioned ice cream shop and the restored county courthouse that now serves as a historical museum. The settlers who began to cluster here in the 1860s called it Rifle River Mills, but a sawmill owner and postmaster later changed it to "Homer," in honor of a local trading post owner. He eventually dropped the *H* to avoid confusion with another Michigan community already going by that name.

While I'm reasonably certain that no citizen of Omer has ever been burned at the stake or tortured on a rack on suspicion of being a wolf or a witch, the idyllic little burg has been known for many years as the home of phantom lupine creatures called the Witch Wolves or Witchy Wolves of Omer Plains. Various eyewitnesses over several decades have described sightings of the fierce, mysterious entities some believe to be guardians created by past shamans to watch over their sacred ground. Others say the legend was inspired by sightings of the gray wolves that once inhabited the Midwest until they were hunted nearly to extinction (wolves were considered officially eradicated in Michigan's Lower Peninsula by 1935), and that modern encounters are just glimpses of a recovering *Canis lupus* population.

OMER LEGENDS, THE BEGINNING

The local tales began with some strange and unsettling Civil War–era events said to have unfolded in a small cemetery about three miles upstream from Omer along the Rifle River, according to one of two articles in the collection of the Arenac County Historical Society that were sent to me by a society member. The anonymously written, undated article titled "The Witch Wolves of Omer" tells the story of several members of the Marvin and Sally Keeney family, who built their homestead near the cemetery in the scrubby, forested area now called the Omer Plains. It was this family's tragedy, says the article, that spawned the Witchy Wolves legend.

Before we start, I'd like to note that a Keeney family did exist in Omer in that time frame, as did the other people whose names are included, according to local newspapers and other historical documents I was able to access. Whether their experiences as described in the article are true or imaginary, I have no way to tell. But the following story as recounted many decades after the alleged events is part of the local lore regarding the Witchy Wolves and therefore deserves to be included.

THE CURSE OF SCORBUTUS

The great tragedy that befell the Keeneys was the death of their son, Corwin, who lost his life in 1865 in the notoriously brutal Confederacy prisoner-of-war camp known as Andersonville. Corwin had been assigned to Company H, the Fifth Michigan Cavalry, and was captured by rebel forces in Virginia at the 1864 Battle of Trevilian Station. I confirmed from online Civil War records that this part of the story was, indeed, true. The young soldier's remains were eventually returned to his family in Omer Plains in 1895—a full thirty years later—and the family placed the shoebox-sized package in a new, full-length coffin and interred it in the nearby cemetery. His grave number in Omer's Plains Cemetery is listed in historical records.

The following part of the story, which local reports said happened the following spring, is not so easy to affirm as known historic fact. It may or may not be true.

In May 1896, after the harsh Michigan winter had finally let up, some Omer citizens undertook their annual ritual of cleaning and tending the cemetery. The group set out for the graveyard armed with appropriate garden tools, intending to pay special attention to the grave where their Civil War hero lay. They were in for a shock; the new grave had been dug up and commandeered as a birthing den by a female wolf with pups. The cluster of citizens shrank back in defensive postures as the protective she-wolf sprang from her lair, snarling, and began to snatch at the humans. She wasn't alone in her defense of the pups. Several other full-grown wolves, likely her pack members, ran out from the woods at the sound of all the commotion, and the workers had to hold them off by brandishing their shovels and rakes as they beat a fast retreat back to town.

From that point on, said the article, the story of the events at the Plains Cemetery in Omer grew more and more sensational as each worker added his or her own creative flourish, some stating the beast was no ordinary she-wolf but a vampire, warlock, or "witchy wolf."

The thought of a magical wolf springing from a dead man's grave to wreak havoc and fury on the deceased person's survivors may seem far-fetched, but the townspeople of Omer did not make up the idea. One of them, a "Mrs. Gorrie" (another actual surname of early settlers in Omer, several of whom are buried in Omer's Evergreen Cemetery), told the others a rumor she'd heard about a similarly horrific "curse" her family in Tennessee had confided to her.

The Tennessee kinfolk said the curse was used by Confederate soldiers as a tactic of war learned from Native Americans. The soldiers, said the kinfolk, used rituals of magic to secretly place the curse on corpses of dead Union soldiers before returning the remains to relatives. This must have been what happened to Corwin Keeney, the Omer group decided. The curse could remain indefinitely in its coffin as it harbored the wolf spirit, waiting and guarding the contents. If the coffin was disturbed or opened, the supernatural creature was free to leap out and attack anyone in sight. The Confederates, so the story went, called the curse "scorbutus," a term for the debilitating disease caused by vitamin C deficiency that is most often known as scurvy today.

Records show that scorbutus was the exact cause of death listed on Corwin Keeney's papers (confirmed)! Scurvy raged rampant in prisoner of war camps of that time, and many soldiers died not from battle wounds but from severe malnutrition. The Omer villagers in 1866, however, may not have been aware of this medical condition nor of the term used for it. They had seen the angry wolf for themselves, however, and decided they had to rid themselves of it. They came up with a two-part plan.

First, they brought an area undertaker, Fred Menzer (name confirmed through the Arenac County Historical Society online records), to the cemetery to view the grave and its contents as several armed men stood watch over the woods. The citizens felt that Mr. Menzer's knowledge of human remains could help him confirm that the bones left in the coffin were indeed those of a Witchy Wolf and not an ordinary human. According to the story, Mr. Menzer agreed this was the case.

The villagers next brought the minister from the Omer Presbyterian Church, a Reverend Kay, to perform an exorcism of the cursed remains. The reverend led exorcism-oriented prayers for hours, until the undertaker ascertained that the wolf spirit was gone. Everyone heaved a sigh of relief, reburied the coffin, and went home.

But that wasn't necessarily the end of the story. "Remember," wrote the anonymous storyteller, "the she-wolf had pups!"

The writer added, "In later years, after the great world wars, young people from the surrounding county would go out to the old cemetery on nights of a full moon and do witch dancing and moon howling in attempts to get the Witchy Wolf to come back. But, the Witchy Wolf never did come back. It is now only a memory."

Well, make that a fairly recent memory for some folks, as legend time goes. I've found reports of alleged sightings of the Witchy Wolf (or wolves) from the 1970s, and one account dating back to September 3, 1925—the second anonymously written article I received.

THE LOVERS' LANE MASSACRE

The second article is titled "The Legend of the Witchie-Wolves," ominously subtitled, "Omer MI Search Continues for Missing Boys." The author gives an obvious pseudonym—Uncle Moss E. Loggs—and adds that he is retelling the original story from accounts "by Francis Ledrow and Davey Rau. May they rest in peace."

Styled as a newspaper account, the story begins, "Hundreds of volunteers scoured the boggs [sic] ridges and swamps of the Omer Plains today in hope of finding the two teenagers alive. Seventeen-year old Clive Robinson, Jr., and sixteen-year-old Stewart McLavey are feared to be dead. Eyewitnesses report that the two boys were taken down and torn apart by wild dog-like creatures."

The article described the eyewitnesses as the young men's girlfriends, Lottie Pestrue and Betty Will (I did find county records of area residents with last names of McLavey and Pestrue). The teens were on a double date and had stopped in a clearing off Tyler Plains Road to do some stargazing under a first-quarter moon. After a while, said the story, they began hearing sounds like a mewing kitten from the woods. Almost immediately, an elderly woman appeared and asked for their help in getting her kitten out of a tree. As the boys hopped out to help her, screams began to reverberate all around them. Even worse, as they took a closer look at the "woman," the teens all realized she had the face of a decidedly unfriendly wolf.

Other wolves came running into the clearing and began to attack the boys, while the girls took off in the car to get help. According to the article, Betty said, "Lottie was in a state of severe hysteria and began to vomit. That's when I realized that I too had lost all control and had soiled my bloomers."

Despite their hysterical condition, the young women soon reached the town and over a dozen men drove quickly back to the clearing, but there was no evidence of either teen. A large search party set out the next day—"almost 300 in total," said the (unnamed) county sheriff—but found only blood-covered ground, a few scraps of cloth, and a bit of bone at the clearing.

The only other possible proof left behind was a row of five-inch-long tracks that looked like wolf prints. The group showed them to a local tracker, S. Mayhew, also known as the Mountain Man, who examined the locale four days later. Sure enough, Mayhew found "a fresh set of Witchy-Wolf tracks leading down into the swamp." He set nine trained hounds after the tracks but only three came back, and Mayhew refused to hunt the "wicked she-wolves of Omer" after that.

The article followed with a short segment titled, "Update November 13, 1975, Deer Hunters and Belt Buckle in Omer Plains Area." It claimed that two deer hunters named W. Thick and H. Migut found a belt buckle partially buried in the clearing where the alleged attack had taken place. It was engraved "S. M. Hunter." Bill Thick was sure the initials stood for Stewart McLavey and gave it to Stewart's nephew, Mike McLavey.

The story concluded with the writer's observance, "Over the years there have been many reported sightings from those who have been thru [sic] the Omer Plains. Young ladies have used the name Witchie-Wolf [sic] to explain why they came home with their nylons torn. With any luck, perhaps a deer hunter will get the cross hairs on one of them and avenge the lives of Clive and Stewart . . . HA HA HA! And you thought Omer was only famous for our spring run trumpet mouth trout!!!"

My initial opinion of both articles, especially the second, is that they were written by a local wag who sprinkled the stories with actual names and places for believability, and then mixed in a generous dollop of legendry to produce a supernatural thriller. The story about the murdered teenagers is very closely related in form and subject to a form of urban legend discussed earlier in which young lovers parking in cars are interrupted by some monster that the teens only narrowly escape. In some versions, the monster shreds anyone foolhardy enough to leave the vehicle.

On the other hand, the fact that both stories included names of longtime Omer residents, some of whose occupations I verified, makes me unwilling to dismiss them out of hand. The stories also included dates, which meant it should be easy to check the area newspapers for what should have been front-page news on the dates of the she-wolf's grave invasion on May 1, 1896, the purported animal attacks on two male students on September 2, 1925, and the alleged discovery of the belt buckle with one teen's initials found by deer hunters on November 13, 1975. But Omer's newspapers weren't available on microfiche online, and some of the print files had been destroyed in a fire at the newspaper office years ago. I contacted members of the Arenac County Historical Society one more time to see if they had the resources to check those specific dates. One helpful volunteer agreed to search their records, to no avail.

1970S TEENS AND WOLVES

As I continued my research, knowledge of the legend seemed universal among Omer area residents. Another historical society member I spoke with during my visit said she remembered the Witchy Wolf stories from her high school days in the 1950s.

But there are newer claims of Witchy Wolf encounters.

Writer David Kulczyk grew up in northeastern Michigan and attended Pinconning High School, about twenty miles south of Omer Plains, in the 1970s. By that time the Witchy Wolf legend was common knowledge among teenagers within a wide radius of Omer, and driving to the old cemetery road with friends or dates was still a standard and frequent form of entertainment for young people looking for excitement. Kulczyk wrote an article for *Strange Magazine* #15[1] about his own experience amid the whistling pines of Omer, and permitted me to retell his story in *Weird Michigan*.

Kulczyk and his friends made the trip twice during his high school years, he said, but neither he nor his companions ever worked up the nerve to exit the vehicle and hunt for the monster.

Their understanding of the Witchy Wolf's background was also a little different than the view held by citizens of 1890s Omer. Kulczyk believed the legend came strictly from Native American lore.

"According to local Chippewa legend," explained Kulczyk, "Witchie Wolves [sic] are invisible spirit dogs that guard the graves of ancient warriors, attacking anyone foolish enough to venture out at night on foot."

The spirit dogs may have been invisible but they were not silent, he said. He and his friends heard the "hideous, high-pitched laughing bark" that seemed to ring out from every direction in the pitch-black forest. Kulczyk said that he did know a few people who had accepted challenges from their friends to leave their vehicles, and that the results ranged from later finding their automobiles scratched and dented to being knocked bodily to the ground by unseen, growling forces.

The website Michigan's Otherside featured another report, made by a woman named Lindsey Russell, who attended high school in the area in the 1990s. Russell affirmed that the legend had survived into contemporary times and that students were still alleging interactions with the creature well into that decade.

Her own brush with ghost wolves came when she was still in elementary school, while picking fallen apples from her family's orchard on the Rifle River. As she worked, she caught a glimpse of a pack of dogs crossing a road over a nearby hill. The dogs appeared huge . . . and looked like two-dimensional, black shadows. While frightened at the time, she eventually blamed her imagination. But about fifteen years later, she had to think twice about the reality of what she'd seen when her boyfriend spotted the same huge, black shadow dogs in that area. She added, "The legend is very much alive and well."[2]

INVESTIGATORS COME TO THE PLAINS

Two teams of Michigan paranormal investigators, the Eerie Temperance Entertainment (ETE) group and Michigan Paranormal Encounters (MPE) organization, were counting on that last statement when they arranged a joint expedition to Omer's Plains Cemetery in mid-March 2009. According to a story in the *Arenac County Independent* posted on March 23 of that year, the teams did not leave disappointed.

The team members heard footsteps and a recurrent pulsing sound in the woods around them, said ETE member Jon McConnell in the article. He added, "It was crazy. I've never heard anything like it."[3]

The teams also interviewed area residents who described odd phenomena that seemed unrelated to the phantom wolf legend. One woman said her daughter was driving through the plains area one night and rounded a bend in the road to see what looked like an elderly gentleman seated in a rocking chair, with no one else around. Another resident said his father knew people who claimed to have seen teams of white horses galloping through the plains on dark nights. The *Independent* received an email from a man who had witnessed glowing white orbs floating through the area.

The *Independent* article noted, "He says these balls of light were always suspected to be phosphorous reactions, but he also said that strangely enough, when people would try to walk away from the lights, the lights would follow them, but when people would walk towards the lights, the lights would retreat."[4]

The paranormal teams said some of their members also saw balls of light during their nighttime vigils in the plains. So did an

Independent reader who also had an "old man" sighting, and who sent a comment to the paper after the story appeared: "My cousin and a friend both described seeing an old man who looked dead, dressed in all white and had a sort of glow around him on two separate occasions. My cousin was the first to tell me about him, then a couple weeks later my friend told me he had seen him after he got his car stuck in a mud hole on a two-track in the plains. My friend had no idea that my cousin just weeks before had described seeing an old man fitting the same description as the one he told me about. I have also witnessed the lights that were described here as well, but that will have to wait for another time."[5]

Another area man, however, speculated that the many pine trees around Omer "howled" whenever the wind blew through them, and that the entire legend of the Witchy Wolves grew around tall tales invented to claim a supernatural origin for a wholly natural sound.

Could it really be so simple? If the legend of spirit wolf guardians originated from the sound of the wind playing through dense pines, it would certainly explain why people heard "screams" but saw no creatures.

But then, what about the soldier with scorbutus, the she-wolf denning in his grave, the young teens supposedly ripped to pieces, the many names of actual people discussed in the old articles possessed by the historical society? There are also the many area residents reporting other anomalous phenomena in the plains area such as balls of light or the old man sitting alone by the road.

We mustn't forget the old Chippewa tradition of wolf-guardians, either. Conjured witch wolves appear in the beliefs of other Native American tribes around the country. In her book *Wolf Nation*, Brenda Peterson quoted a Cherokee friend who worked for the Smithsonian Institute: "Navajos believe there are real wolves who are good and part of nature. But then there are also witches who disguise themselves as wolves. . . . You never know who you're dealing with. . . ."⁶

OTHER BEASTS BY THE BAY

And speaking of never knowing with whom one is dealing, it happens that there have been other unexplained creature sightings around Saginaw Bay. I received a letter about an incident that occurred in the mid-1980s, well within the time range of contemporary sightings. The location lies about fifty miles southeast of Omer as the seagull flies, near a rural home between Mayville and Vassar in Tuscola County. The man, whose name and contact information are on file, prefers to remain anonymous.

His neighborhood was mostly overgrown farm fields dotted with small woodlands, he said, and his house was situated several hundred feet from the road. His sighting occurred at dusk, so that when he noticed something moving near the road he wasn't sure what he was seeing. It struck him as odd, since it was too tall and dark to be a deer but didn't resemble a bear, either.

"It got under my skin as it got later," he said, "so I grabbed a flashlight and went out to where I thought it was, to look to see if I could find any sign or tracks. When I did this, I had the distinct feeling whatever it was hadn't gone far, like I was being watched; you know, that creepy feeling you get when the hair on the back of your neck stands up." He heard leaves crunching and twigs snapping as he scoured the ground with a flashlight, and then he discerned the sound of something large departing in a westward direction. He whirled and trained the flashlight on a large dark form, catching a quick reflection from its eyes as it continued to stomp away. His impression was that the creature was bipedal and at least seven feet tall, and that it was watching him as closely as he was trying his best to watch it.

He estimated it had been no more than twenty to thirty feet away from him in the brush.

He added that despite his life as a tracker, hunter, fisherman, and general outdoorsman, this was the first and only such unexplainable encounter he'd ever had. But to his surprise, two weeks later the *Tuscola County Advertiser* ran a report that several people had witnessed an animal that sounded similar to a Bigfoot crossing a road only five or six miles from his own encounter.

The man's sighting had every ring of truth to it, but combined with some additional comments he made in our ongoing correspondence, I had to wonder whether he encountered something other than a Bigfoot, especially since he did not get a clear look at the creature's identifying features. For instance, I asked about the color of the eyeshine, which is almost always described by Bigfoot witnesses as red or reddish orange. He replied, "The glimpse I got of the eyes was a weak/faint yellow, which I assume was the reflection back off the tapetum [membrane in an animal's eye structure that increases night vision ability and appears as 'shine' to a human observer]."

Bigfoot eyes are almost never described as light yellow, but the eyeshine color of dogmen or unknown, upright canids—and indeed, of any *known* canids—is usually some variant of yellow-green.

The man did not notice any odor from the creature, nor any sounds. But he added another detail that could be important:

"I think it [the creature] was eating/gathering acorns, as it was in a small grove of oaks that dropped a ton of acorns that year. Prepared correctly, white acorns are very good, I've eaten them myself."

So, what large animals eat acorns? Bears, of course, come quickly to mind. A black bear could sometimes stand seven feet tall, walk bipedally for a bit, and hide itself in the brush. A bear's eyeshine, however, is normally a dull, red-orange color.

But would Bigfoots eat acorns? Many Sasquatch eyewitnesses have noted the creature's large, solid teeth and big jaws that could crush nutshells as easily as we crunch popcorn. Even if our teeth possessed the same crunch power, humans can only eat acorns that have been processed to remove the tannin, an acidic, bitter substance found in some plant and tree products. Bigfoots have not, to my knowledge, been observed performing such complex culinary tasks, but their jaws and digestive systems are undoubtedly more robust than ours.

Finally, we must ask whether the acorn gourmand could have been a canine of some type. For comparison, a quick reference search of items in the diets of wild wolves shows that they will eat acorns—and even things like earthworms and berries—as a supplement to their usual meat menu. The fact that these were white oak acorns, which have less tannin than red oak acorns, makes this possibility even more likely.

I asked the eyewitness if he had at all entertained the notion that it could have been a seven-foot-tall, acorn-scarfing dogman watching him. He replied that until I mentioned it, he'd never heard of such a thing as a dogman and had to spend some time googling the topic. He did not rule it out.

THE OSCODA GUNNERY RANGE

There have also been other sightings of unidentifiable creatures around Saginaw Bay. I'll briefly mention two that are treated more completely in my previous book, *The Michigan Dogman: Werewolves and Other Unknown Canines Across the U.S.A.* The first occurred in 1977, as a policeman was hunting in an old gunnery range west of Oscoda. He was busily obscuring himself in a grove of jack pines when he heard persistent rustling sounds behind him. The man wrote that the sounds became so unnerving that he returned to the two-track road he'd come in on, while the sounds followed him and remained just out of the range of his vision. He hid again in an effort to see what the stalker might be, rifle at the ready.

What he saw was a shimmering, translucent entity that years later he would describe as similar to the alien hunter in the *Predator* film series. He shot at it with his rifle and also a .357 Magnum pistol and was sure the bullets connected with the form, but the thing was still standing. He described it as looking like "a hole in the woods." As he explained, "It kind of absorbed all color and light, yet at the same time was not a shadow. It was like those badges that show two different things if you look at them from different angles; one angle was forest, the other was this hole."[7]

I also heard from a woman from Essexville, just east of Bay City, who was driving home from school at dusk as a sixteen-year old in the late 1990s when she noticed a large animal just past the intersection of Jones and Arms Roads. It was running alongside her GMC Jimmy on all fours, its back level with the bottom of her window, which would have made it four and a half feet at shoulder level. It had shaggy, dark brown fur and was not shaped like a deer. As it ran, it banged into the side of the truck. At that, she stepped on the gas and left the creature behind.[8]

It's interesting to me that all three of these bay area witnesses seem unsure of the exact appearances or species of the animals involved. Even the couple mentioned by the Tuscola newspaper report noted above described it only as a "Bigfoot-*type* animal" (emphasis mine), which leaves some room for interpretation. If witnesses don't get a solid look at the head, jaw, ears, hands/paws, or especially the rear limbs, it can be difficult to tell one furry, upright creature from another.

I guess that what I'm saying here is that, based on other Saginaw Bay area sightings and the amount of corroborating historical events and identities, I think Omer's Witchy Wolf is more than just the invention of a town immersed in historic legend. The fact that there have been so many other sightings of weird, wolflike creatures in the northeastern part of Michigan's lower peninsula hints at something more widespread than I first suspected. We can look at other states for examples.

WITCHY WOLVES OR SKINWALKERS

A Colorado man wrote to tell me that his grandmother believed she'd had an experience with a supernaturally created, wolflike creature that is widely known among America's indigenous people as a Skinwalker. It has the appearance of a somewhat humanoid, large wolf that can walk upright or on all fours and whose eyes glow red (unlike most unknown canines), and is believed to result from magic or rituals conducted by trained, native sorcerers. The man asked to have his name withheld but said his family members are Ottawa and Ute. His mother grew up on an eastern Utah land reserve and the man spent his childhood summers in a small town adjacent to Utah's Skinwalker Ranch, a much-investigated tract of land that has become associated with eerie happenings and various wolflike beasts that can appear as phantoms or as flesh and blood.

He wrote, "My aunt used to tell me about an encounter she had with what she believed was a Skinwalker up near an area north of Roosevelt in the Uinta Mountains called Moon Lake. An upright canine creature with red eyes kept pace with her car along a gravel road. She lost it [the creature] when she hit the paved road and sped off. The local Native Americans believe, much like the area around Skinwalker Ranch, that Moon Lake is a hotbed of Skinwalker activity."

I can't help but think of the Michigan woman who also experienced an episode of car pacing on her way home from school. The creature she saw was on all fours and actually bumped her car. In contrast, the Moon Lake creature was upright, did not contact the vehicle and, unlike most canine reports, featured red eyes. I've often noted that when unknown canines exhibit red eyeshine, there is usually some association with anomalous lights, humanoid body shapes, "openings in the sky or land that are said to look like portals," or openings to some place that appears to belong in another reality. And we will get back to those large car-bumping beasts later on.

THE THING AT THE END OF THE BED

The story of the man's aunt was only incidental; he was actually writing to tell me about his own scary experience as a child. He was playing on his mother's bed around dawn one day in the winter of 1983 when he saw a flat, black shape that was upright like a human but had the head of a dog. He said:

> It had a long, pointed muzzle and long, straight, pointed ears. The shape of the head reminded me of a black Chihuahua we had at the time . . . her head was more or less shaped like a miniature version of a Doberman. The thing in the room, though, was much taller. I would say it stood about six feet, although that was just an impression since this was a long time ago, I was quite little, and I was sitting on a bed. The thing was not bulky but rather thin, and its posture was quite straight up and down. It carried its arms and hands bent and in front of its chest, like you might see a dog doing when it sits upright to beg for a treat.
>
> The thing moved along the foot of the bed in a sort of bobbing glide. It turned left at the bed's corner, making its way along the opposite side of the bed from where we were playing. When it got to the head of the bed and wall of the room, it disappeared. I must not have been too afraid of the thing because I remember jumping off and looking under the bed because I figured that's where it must have gone. Things don't vanish, after all. There was nothing there.

His mother did not see the thing, but she corroborated his memory. He said, "She says that I told her the thing looked at me as it moved along the bed. She also said I told her it was tall, like 'Daddy,' who stood about five feet, ten inches. She also remembers me saying the thing had short, slick black hair . . . but my memory of it doesn't have that level of detail. I simply remember a more or less featureless silhouette, and I think my three-and-a-half-year-old brain could have just been filling in details it didn't understand with something familiar [the features of his Chihuahua].

"Most prominently, my mom was struck at how, right in the middle of our playing, I suddenly said, 'What's that?' and then pointed and followed with my hand some unseen thing . . . she definitely believes that I saw something. The event made an impression for sure. It's probably one of my earliest and clearest memories."

The writer might be comforted to know he is not the only human to have seen some unknown, dark creature appear in his bedroom while wide-awake. I've written entire chapters in other books on "bedroom invaders" whose shapes range from tall, black replicas of the Egyptian god of the dead, Anubis, to shapes only vaguely canid, to all manner of other creatures and beings that invite themselves into human homes. Whether what he saw is related in any way to the hulking thing that chased his grandmother's car and kept pace with it is unknown, but again, I've seen many such reports of upright car chasers over the years.

I think what we may confirm so far is that while there seem to be many incidents of canine-like creatures that bear similarities to legendary beasts, when we inspect them closely we see they are related by a dark, weird thread of ambiguity. Red eyes that should be yellow, fierce predators that either lurk harmlessly in the trees or inflict scratches on vehicles like teenage vandals "keying" an auto's new paint job, deer that on closer inspection prove to be large wolves—what can we do in the furry face of such confusion? For one thing, we tell stories, which become legends we can then use to sort the monsters into understandable groups. As an example of this love of categories, we'll look next at a creature that appears as lupine as the Witchy Wolf but has stubbornly retained its own distinct story since antiquity.

CHAPTER 5

Haunts of the Werewolf

*Unknown upright canine,
as typically described by witnesses*

WHEN IT COMES TO LEGENDS, few creatures can beat the part-man, part-wolf entity best known in present-day Western society as the werewolf for its sheer longevity of mythic status and the degree of fascination humans feel for it. I have often said I don't believe in actual, Hollywood-style werewolves, but I believe that universal curiosity about possible lycans is the reason Elkhorn's Beast of Bray Road catapulted into the national spotlight so quickly and firmly. And by the way, readers may notice that many of the chapters in this book are a bit canine heavy and Wisconsin loaded. That is due to several reasons. First and foremost is the truth that—for better or worse—I've been associated with the unknown canines for so long that I receive more firsthand reports about them than I do of other things, and I find original accounts the most compelling.

I have more stories about Wisconsin than other places for much the same reason. I've lived here all my life and have many years of associations to draw upon. More than that, I find that this state is a weirdly inexhaustible microcosm of all the anomalies that are out there. I've bloomed where I was planted and found it rich soil. But weird things are everywhere, and I'm constantly asked *precisely* where.

WHERE TO FIND A WEREWOLF

People frequently want to know where they can go to see or search for werewolves, dogmen, or upright canines as I prefer to call them, and that is a tough question to answer. I believe, based on sightings, that they aren't as numerous as Bigfoot, nor are they normally associated with environmental clues like branch structures as are Bigfoot, so their hangouts are tougher to recognize. They rove large territories, I believe, which makes them unlikely to be in the same spot for any great length of time.

Just in case these creatures might be more than simple legends, I also like to remind people to use extreme caution, and to remember that many eyewitnesses are so shaken by their sighting experiences that they wish they had *not* seen one. Bearing these things in mind, one approach is to simply check out places the creatures are known to have been, if there is public access, and remember that most sightings seem purely random and are statistically more likely to occur when people are not looking for upright canines. But there may be another factor that could increase the odds of such an encounter, and that factor is habitat—especially graveyards, deserted buildings, campgrounds, and military bases or installations.

Cemeteries are ubiquitous in encounters with upright canines. I came across an old piece of correspondence the other day that described a run-in with a wolfman or werewolf in a cemetery on the shore of Upper Nashotah Lake in St. Francis (near Milwaukee) called Seminary Woods. The area is not a legendary stomping ground for upright canines, but it is supposed to be haunted by the figure of a black-garbed monk who lived there long ago. The man who wrote about his experience had gone to the old cemetery located in those woods at about 10:30 p.m. in June 2005 with several friends to photograph what he described as a Wiccan altar and a "vampire den," when something else grabbed their attention.

Only about fifty feet away, he said, stood a creature over six feet tall (judging by comparison to some trees adjacent to the figure) and covered in black fur, watching them. It had the head of a wolf. They instantly ran, hearing twigs crunch under its feet behind them as it gave chase. It also made low, guttural growling sounds as it ran, said the writer, and when they cleared the entrance to the woods, it emitted a howl he described as "half pain, half anger."

As afraid as he was after that encounter, the writer said he made numerous trips back to the woods but never saw the creature again. His friends wanted to just forget it; two moved out of the state and the other two stopped speaking to him (I hear that a lot about co-eyewitnesses).

Pondering the fact that this place was known for being haunted by a humanlike figure but turned out to be the site of an unknown canine encounter, I realized that there were many other times and places when people were looking for some particular spooky thing but found dogmen or other unknown canines instead. For instance, I think of the Michigan Dogman sighting made by college student Jon Lyons and two friends near a cabin on a gravel road outside Reed City, Michigan, in June 2005. The cabin—once a one-room school—was known for a local legend of ghost children crying or laughing in the night. The cabin's owner told me he had heard those sounds himself. The spectral children seemed to have left, however, and the trio instead found themselves stalked and pursued by a gray, seven-foot-tall canine on one occasion, and a slightly smaller, black-furred dogman on another.

That was the same place I staked out in 2006 in the wee hours of a hot, foggy night with a cameraman from the History Channel's *MonsterQuest* show and Lyons and his friends, and I actually saw the gray, furry spine of *some*thing. The unknown, upright figure partially revealed itself at the edge of a spotlight as it blotted out a seven-foot-tall reflective road sign while crossing the gravel road not more than thirty to forty feet from where we all stood. As often happens in these situations, the videographer had his camera turned the other direction. This was my only personal sighting of what could have been a dogman (though I've had far better luck with Bigfoot). But that original legend of crying children initially brought young people to the desolate location.

The hauntings-dogman connection also comes to mind when I think of the 2007 sightings by four other young people in Oak

Creek, Wisconsin, part of the Greater Milwaukee area, on East Fitzsimmons Road. This dead-end road leading to a bluff over Lake Michigan has a long tradition as a haunted lovers' lane. The four teens were hoping to see a ghost, but instead an upright canine jumped out of a cornfield at them and chased them back to the nearest streetlight. I was there to investigate the site within days, and found large canine tracks in a muddy part of the field, just off a tractor lane.

The wolf creature–hauntings connection is also borne out on Elkhorn, Wisconsin's Bray Road which has several old houses said to have been haunted before the Bray Road Beast's first known appearances in the 1980s and '90s. I've been a guest in one of the homes, and listened to tales of creaky stairs and glimpses of ghosts. Their main association to the upright, wolflike creatures, however, seems to be that they share a road where strange things seem to happen.

THE GRAVEYARD SHIFTY: NEW HAMPSHIRE

Many people walk gingerly through cemeteries. That's natural, considering what lies below. But we humans are not the only beings that tread dark places lightly. Spirits are also said to waft softly over headstones. And this next encounter involves something that was not human, not dead, and perhaps not even a canine. But it's another good illustration of unknown creatures and cemeteries, so here is the very detailed report I received of an incident in New Hampshire in mid-October 2014. The man, who wished to remain anonymous, wrote that he had come home one chilly Tuesday night that fall at about 12:30 a.m. and saw what he first thought was a deer (very reminiscent of some accounts we've seen earlier here). He realized it was not a deer as it walked on its hind legs.

He said, "It was tremendously thin and was taking poodle-like baby steps at a high rate of speed! I did not see any tail but I knew it was definitely not a Bigfoot. I could not believe it, but at no time did I feel threatened. I was not afraid, just surprised . . . I kept staring at it . . . I couldn't figure out what I was looking at. It did not seem to pay any attention to me at all."

He said he was not able to see its arms but it had a triangular head with small eyes and a short face, and struck him as both cat-like and wolf-like at once. Its fur was quite short. It seemed to have walked across a Commons area and was about sixty-five feet away, standing just inside the treeline of some woods. It appeared to have come from the direction of a nearby Colonial-era grave-yard. Behind the cemetery were some historic buildings and an embankment that led down to a river called the Mountain Stream. It continued to head south silently but at a fast pace and was soon lost from sight. He added that there were houses nearby, and speculated the creature may have taken shelter in a shed next to an old church.

He said, "Now I believe those stories people said about the hostile werewolf types, and I believe there are different types of these dogmen . . . I just happened to see the more timid of the types." He added that seeing people go into the cemetery had always made him cringe without knowing exactly why.

Cemeteries are just one type of site often connected with wolf-like creatures, especially upright canines that act like phantoms—

or bear a resemblance to Anubis, ancient Egypt's jackal-headed god of the dead—military zones. Following is one of the most recently submitted, although the events took place in the early 1970s.

GERMAN MILITARY WEREWOLVES

This story occurred in Germany in 1971. I've received other compelling reports of encounters at military bases or installations over the years, and several, like this one, have compared the creature to Anubis. One of the first and most startling of those accounts was published in *Hunting the American Werewolf* [1] and recounted the sighting made by three night guards at North Chicago's Great Lakes Naval Training Center on Lake Michigan in 1994. The grounds the witnesses patrolled included a military graveyard, too. In that incident, all three saw the creature standing at the edge of a small wood, at about three a.m., revealed by the large flashlights they carried as it stared at them with greenish-yellow eyes. The naval guard who wrote me about the encounter said it was black furred, with the body of a man and a jackal-like head that reminded her of Anubis. It stood six and a half to seven feet tall. One of the witnesses was Navajo, and he immediately began to repeat, "Skinwalker . . . Skinwalker," referring to the "conjured creature" discussed earlier that is usually associated with the American Southwest—and with the Navajo. Whether Skinwalker or Anubis, when it ran away into the darkness, it did so on its hind legs. So did the creature seen by the next eyewitness, Ian Robertson-Molden, a British officer who had yet another name for the creature—werewolf. He wrote:

In 1971 I had just finished military college and was posted to Fallingbostel in Northern West Germany as a Second Lieutenant, in the Royal Military Police, Special Investigation Branch, so I would have been regarded as a credible witness. During my first week at this location, I had to report to the Medical Reception Centre to visit a soldier. Several regiments, including my own, were in a specific area but the Medical Reception was around 500 yards away via a footpath surrounded by a wooded area each side. Halfway to the Med Centre was a small WRVS shop (a little like the American PX).

Having visited the soldier, I made my way back to my unit. The whole area was almost desolate, as the division was away on exercise, leaving myself and rear parties. As I approached the WRVS area, I noticed a dog in the undergrowth ahead of me. It looked like a German shepherd or Alsatian. This gave me a little concern as it was a high rabies area.

I stopped at first, then moved slowly towards the dog. There was no way of avoiding it as it was a mere ten feet from the path and there was no other way past. I stopped approximately forty feet from the animal to assess the danger. I was confused about its appearance, as the dog had the long snout of a German shepherd but incredibly long [tall] ears. It looked more like the dogs seen in Egyptian hieroglyphics [Anubis]. I think its snout and ears were much longer than I have ever seen on a dog. I think its weight is significant as it was very slender. Standing, it had more of a dog's width of a body but it certainly was designed to stand and walk as it was very steady on its feet.

Realizing there was no other route, I gingerly started to walk slowly down to the path, keeping it under observation. As I got to around twenty to thirty feet away from it, it stood up on its hind legs. It was around seven to eight feet in height. I had no chance to observe further as it started to walk towards me. Initially, I thought it was some sort of very thin bear, as its body was dog-like. But there are no indigenous bears in that area of Germany. As I mentioned, it resembled ancient depictions of Anubis but with a dog's body and not a human's.

Its colour was dark brown. From what I could see, a pretty persistent colour too. Had it been a dog, it would have had a lighter underside, which it didn't. It sat directly watching me and then stood in complete silence. It made no animal noises of any kind. I don't remember, I didn't recall at the time any peculiarity with its eyes. Just appeared to be dark like a bear's eyes. I certainly didn't get close enough to smell it, lol. I was off running, lol.

To be honest, I ran like hell back to the Medical Centre. In fact, I didn't stop running, as I was unsure whether it was following me. As I mentioned previously, there was no other easy way to get back to the garrisons and I eventually decided to take the long route back via the local town—a trip of around three miles. Several days later, still thinking I had seen some sort of dog unknown to me, I mentioned my experience to a female German clerk. She casually said, "Oh, you must have seen the werewolf—you were lucky to escape."

Werewolf was a word Ian had not considered. But his description of the camp's surroundings was certainly creepy enough to make a supernatural wolf-creature feel right at home. He continued:

"I knew little about Fallingbostel when this happened, as I had only been there a few days. Werewolves were quite believed there, apparently, as many sightings had been recorded. As an aside, the whole area was strange. The Fallingbostel cemetery had an armed guard at night—due to grave robbing, we assumed. It also had a heavily fenced grave there of someone called Camilla Karnstein, who, the inscription said, was either bitten to death by a Vampire or was a Vampire. My German wasn't that good at that time."

I asked Ian if he had any more information about the vampire story, and he discovered the name Camilla Karnstein was from a novel about a female vampire published in serial form around 1872, twenty-six years before the world was introduced to *Dracula* by Bram Stoker. The author, Joseph Sheridan Le Fanu, may have based his main character on true horrors such as Elisabeth Bathory, a Transylvanian countess known for grisly murders of hundreds of young girls in what is now Slovakia. Bathory lived from 1560 to 1614, and her shocking acts were well-known in Europe. She was said to have dabbled in cannibalism and also bathed in human blood in the belief it would keep her young. She was eventually imprisoned for her deeds, and Ecséd, Hungary, is believed to be the site of her body's final resting place.

Bad Fallingbostel (*Bad* translates to "bath" or "spa" in German) was once ringed by forests that did contain wolves, and the last known wolf in that region was believed killed in 1872 and is now memorialized with a large rock known as the Wolfsstein, or literally, Wolf Stone. That did not mean wolves would never come back to the area, however. Wolves have been seen in the former area of that forest as recently as 2012, forty years after Ian's sighting.

Also located near Bad Fallingbostel in the Lüneburg Heath area are some four-thousand-year-old stone dolmen structures made by ancient Europeans known as the Funnel Beaker people. The name may sound like something from a chemistry supply store, but it derives from the culture's most noted style of pottery: beaker-shaped jars with funnel-shaped necks. The Bad Fallingbostel dolmen are known as the Seven Stone Houses, although there are only five structures. They were probably used as burial chambers, according to most archaeological studies. I have not come across any particular legends about these dolmens, but ancient graveyards seem to do the trick all by themselves when it comes to attracting mystery creatures.

This report is not the only one I've received from a soldier who has witnessed a werewolf-like creature at a German military facility. In *Monsters Among Us*,[2] I told the full tale of a 1987 sighting at Hohenfels Training Area, a US military garrison base near Wolfsegg. Wolfsegg is about five hundred miles from Bad Fallingbostel. The eyewitness in that case was sleeping in his vehicle and awoke to see a six-to-seven-foot-tall creature with glowing red eyes peeping into his vehicle's window. It left large canine footprints in the nearby mud.

A third, entirely separate German military base encounter with an upright canid occurred at the Hahn Air Base near the village of Wenigerath in 1988, just a year after the Hohenfels incident. It's known as the Morbach Werewolf. The Profound History website[3] posted an account from a retired USAF staff sergeant on January 5, 2018, in which the sergeant noted that the local legend about the alleged creature was well-known but generally dismissed by American servicemen stationed there. One night, said the sergeant, a routine patrol group came across some strangely mutilated deer carcasses. The discovery was followed by startling, deep, loud howls from an unseen animal. An armed patrol called in saying they were in pursuit of a large, dark canine that was headed for the base command center. The sergeant, hunting with his own patrol unit, saw the huge figure clear a nine-foot fence and then stand upright against a tree as it turned to coolly check out its pursuers before rushing off into the trees.

In summary, we have just noted three different military bases in Cold War–era Germany separated by one hundred to five hundred miles, each with its own sightings of large, upright wolflike creatures from very credible sources. This leads me to wonder how many other bases involved similar sightings, and whether reports referenced only upright canines or anomalous phenomena, as well. I can say that there was at least one such instance of the latter, and the possible phenomenon involved UFOs—a known obsession of Adolf Hitler's. Take this odd tidbit for what it's worth: a weirdly synchronistic little find that came to light in early 2018 after I inherited a cache of family letters and photos.

MY GRANDMA AND THE UFO LETTER

The unlikely source was a German woman who was a close friend of my maternal grandmother, Elsie. The woman, Louisa, worked in the former 5th U-boat Flotilla in Kiel-Gaarden in the postwar British zone. I came across her information in a letter she wrote to Elsie in April 1950. The part of her letter that surprised me began in a joking way but ended with a very matter-of-fact statement. I had the feeling that Louisa wanted to convey something important but first had to make an effort to sound offhand and skeptical in case the letter should be read by someone else. I should add that my grandma Elsie was a farm wife with a fifth-grade education and no government ties whatsoever, and a devout second-generation German Lutheran with no interest in things like UFOs. I am not sure how she met or made friends with Louisa, but it may have been through my uncle stationed in occupied Germany as a mechanic. He had the letter in his possession when he passed away in early 2018, and I found it in his papers.

The six-page, handwritten letter seemed innocuous at first. After chatting about the weather, a bad stove, and problems with rats in the larder, Louisa wrote, "You sure will know the flying saucers which people in all parts of the world have seen. Say, did you see one? The Russians invented them in 1903??? I read so in the newspaper and am not surprised as they claim to have invented everything. But, did you ever hear of flying cups? I did and saw a picture of them in the Kiel newspaper, when these strange things were flying over Kiel. Like this they looked [see her small drawing in the photo of her letter on the next page] a dozen of them and a noise they made they lighted up the night. These cups appeared over our towns on April 1. On April 1, I can't believe our newspapers here, they print all kinds of foolish things. Do your newspapers do the same?"

(Note: now for the more interesting part . . .)

Louisa continued, "But by now we know that the flying saucers really exist, it is a kind of all-wing airplane with the wings revolving around the cabin and the motors are fitted in the tips of the wings." The drawing she made did look rather like an inverted teacup—or a bell. The Germans were believed to have created a bell-shaped flying craft. One was seen over Saint-Jean, Haute-Garonne, France, in 1944 by a sixteen-year old riding her bicycle. She drew a sketch that was reproduced in a booklet by Richard H. Hall, *From Airships to Arnold*, that is not far off from Louisa's little drawing.[4]

The 1950 letter from employee of a former German military base to author's grandmother, COURTESY OF THE AUTHOR

My intention here is not to foist off these anecdotes as any kind of "proof" that werewolves or UFOs manifested around the mentioned military areas, although it does seem odd that the reports occurred in so many places. I suspect there are many more that have remained secret. The facts are, though, that Hitler was more than mildly interested in possible military applications for the wolfman of ancient folklore. He was also heavily invested in the acquisition of new, unconventional aircraft patterned after the flying saucers that many believe have circled the planet for millennia but are now often publicly scorned as urban legends of the twentieth century. The extent to which Hitler succeeded in actualizing his plans for these and other programs is still debated, but his obsession with all forms of mythic and occult knowledge is legendary in its own right. And as US servicemen and servicewomen returned home from the war, and people like my grandmother communicated with citizens of recently enemy nations, the legends grew.

Before we leave the graveyard–military base connection entirely, there is another sighting near ancient burial grounds to examine. In this case the burials are those of Native Americans, and the dates reach over three hundred years into the past.

MICHIGAN DOGMAN AND
MASSACRE BURIAL GROUNDS

Eyewitness: "It was like it rode the treetops."

This report actually contains three encounters that occurred in 2016 in rural western Michigan, close to Lake Michigan's eastern shore and adjacent to what has become known as the main stomping ground of the Michigan Dogman, the Manistee National Forest. The first of the three encounters begs an unusual question I haven't previously considered: Could a dogman travel from treetop to treetop in a snowy wood? Hard as it may be to imagine any canine at home in forest canopies, it seemed to the eyewitness that this may have been the case.

Unusual circumstances seem to rule this set of encounters. Local historians say the forests around the site are filled with hidden Native American burials. The remains of hundreds of men, women, and children were hastily interred here in 1642 after a large invading force of a branch of Iroquois massacred the resident

Potawatomi tribe. The White Lake Historical Society's locally published history booklet states, "Indian graves have been unearthed and undoubtedly many hidden remains of the unfortunate Potawatomi Massacre still remain. . . . Many artifacts of the Indians' culture of the Montague area have been found in this past century [the 1800s]."[5]

CREATURE ONE

As for the eyewitness, I'll refer to him by a pseudonym, Brad. He wrote:

> I've seen this creature that resembles a werewolf on the family farm here in rural south west Michigan. I'll start by explaining the property layout; the farm sits on 30 acres of woods, crick [sic] and marshlands. All of my encounters have come this year [2016] from February to about a month or so ago [early June]. The first came on or about the eighth of February at approximately 3:52 a.m. A heavy winter storm was hitting the area with some nasty weather. I was up early to get a jump on the snow shoveling, so the driveway was accessible for the propane delivery guy later that morning.
>
> As I was about halfway down the driveway I heard a loud splash in the crick to the south about twenty-five yards away; thinking it was a deer or two I stopped shoveling and scanned the crick and wood line for any movement. As I scanned the crick I came to the wood line and saw this pair of yellow/amber eyes about seven and a half to eight feet tall standing right next to a huge oak tree. It took off with a super burst of speed to the west,

it then leapt into the air and all I heard for the next few seconds was the tree tops clanging against one another. It was like it rode the treetops.

I stood there for the next few minutes questioning my sanity. For the six to seven seconds I saw this creature it stood on two legs that looked like a dog's hind legs. [It had a] big wolf-like head, with a snout and ears that resembled that of a German shepherd, and those eyes of yellow/amber in color.

CREATURE TWO

"The second sighting came on or about March 24, at approximately 2:38 p.m. I had decided to walk up the crick and clear brush. I always carry a firearm with me on these occasions. I had gotten about 450 yards up the crick that flows through [the] entire acreage of the property, it was strange to me how completely quiet or as I say, 'dead,' the woods were. I always jump something up whether it's a deer or turkey or ducks that are always there. I didn't even hear any birds which was really strange."

This spooky phenomenon of utter silence enveloping the area of anomalous events is known as the Oz Factor and is quite common in creature encounters. It was named by British author and investigator Jenny Randles after the strange, alternate kingdom portrayed in L. Frank Baum's book *The Wonderful Wizard of Oz*. It refers to the same type of disorientation experienced by Baum's protagonist, Dorothy, after a tornado transported her from a black-and-white world to a realm of color.

It was a brilliant way for the movie to portray Dorothy's transition from the known to the unknown, and works equally well to describe the Oz Factor. Those who have experienced it often say that all birds and insects suddenly go quiet, as a pervasive change in the surrounding atmosphere affects their emotions. I've received reports from people who said they felt either profoundly sad or paralyzed with terror. Sometimes the air seems to change color, often to green or gold.

Brad continued:

I rounded a bend in the crick when up ahead about 55 yards was what looked to be the back of a black bear that was digging into the bank of the crick. As I was setting my firearm down on one of the little islands in the crick I snapped a branch and it stopped completely what it was doing. I froze and watched as this thing stood up on two legs and started to turn around towards me. It stood eight feet tall and had a huge wolf-like head, snout and ears of a dog, and all black fur. In the first encounter the creature's fur was gray in color with some white, this one was all black.

It kept glancing over to the east and back towards me. It had not yet seen me, it put its snout into the air and looked like it was sniffing the wind. I'm completely freaking out at this point and reach to pick up my firearm to get out of the area quickly, when there was a splash up the crick. I looked up and now this thing was on all four legs, it still stood five to five and a half feet tall.

At this point I don't want to run out of fear that it will give chase, so I stay frozen. It looked at me and snarled, and I thought it was sizing me up and then all of a sudden it looked to the east, back at me one more time, and took two giant leaps toward the east, and onto the bank of the crick, that's about a twenty-five-foot distance. It then jumped towards the treetops and disappeared to the east. I stood there in total disbelief.

I got home and my mind just kept racing. So I decided to confide in my father about what I had seen and he looked at me as if I were an alien. Said I was crazy and I should get my head checked out. I know what I saw!

CREATURE THREE

The third and final encounter came on May 29, 8:52 p.m. My dad and I were having a fire down by the crick and we were getting low on wood. He asked if I could go get more wood for the fire from behind the pole barn. I hesitated and said in a few minutes. I was afraid of those woods, which is something I thought I would never say.

After about ten minutes I start to make my way towards the back of the pole barn, it's just about dark and I keep hearing this rustling and a lower growl like dogs are playing, and when I reach the back of the pole barn, it stops. I light a cigarette and look out into the woods which are ten yards away, again the woods had gone completely silent, it was eerie. Then there was a sound like a zipper being zipped up. It was about thirty yards to the south. I waited for a minute and decided to look out to where I heard the sound. As I glanced to my right I saw something move.

It was just about completely dark, and there was a stench in the air that was absolutely putrid. It smelled of rotten guts and urine. I figured it was a rotten carcass of a dead animal. And then as I was shining my flashlight a deep guttural growl, like a raccoon would make, came from the area I had heard the rustling sound. So I shone my light over towards the sound and I saw eyes about five and a half feet off of the ground, the eyes were red in color and were very shiny. The thing I saw didn't have paws on the front, they were long arms and had hands with claws!

It really didn't freak me out as a lot of critters have red eyes when exposed to light. Then this thing stood up on two legs, this thing was really tall, eight to eight and a half feet, it growled again and literally turned around and walked away to the south. I thought I had crapped myself, I came back home and my dad asked, where was the wood? I said I didn't feel well and was going to bed.

I went out the next day to look around the area. I heard the noise. I found only a deer skin, the rest of the deer was gone, including the head. Also two neighbors of mine have heard very eerie howls coming from my family's woods, saying they only come at dusk. They have been in the area for fifty-plus years and said they have never heard a sound like the one that they heard.

And one more thing. I set apples out for the deer every week and noticed the other day that all the apples were gone, and a rock was in every place where there was an apple. I have a trail cam on the area as I write this. I also found some tracks that look like a huge wolf's. There used to be deer around here all the time. Had a herd of fifty or so. Now you're lucky to see one or two, it's like they disappeared. Been really strange around here for the past couple of years and I don't know what to think about it.

In all three of my encounters the thing I saw reminded me of a werewolf. I no longer go near the woods. I was told by a family member that a lot of the wood acreage is Indian burial grounds. I don't share this with very many people at all in fear of getting laughed at or called crazy. Thank you for contacting me back and hope I gave enough detail on my encounters.

I'd say that Brad did well in furnishing details, and he was quite certain that the creatures he saw were canines. Two aspects, the fact that one of the creatures seemed to be moving through tree tops and also the exchanging of rocks for apples, are suggestive of Bigfoot action and behavior, but who am I to say that a wolflike creature couldn't do the same—especially considering that its paws were more like hands with long claws.

I was impressed that the legend-like existence of local Native American burials Brad had mentioned turned out to have a factual basis, with the tragic historic massacre of the area's Potawatomi at its core. Some researchers believe that large-scale, traumatic events imprint themselves not only on the psyches of survivors but on something in the landscape itself, resulting in tales of haunted places and ghostly animals. I think of the battlefields of Gettysburg, for instance, and the numerous sightings of ghostly soldiers and other apparitions reported there after Civil War took thousands of lives at that scene.

Although I agree with Brad that the creatures involved sound like upright canines, they had some traits that I usually associate with places where shamanic ritual likely occurs—often near Native American lands as we discussed earlier regarding Ute Skinwalkers—and creatures believed to be shape-shifters. In these cases, the eyeshine is usually red instead of the canine's standard yellow or yellow green. The paws look more like hands, and the creature's height is often estimated at eight feet or more. The fur is usually, but not always, black, and the creature may have actual shoulders, which ordinary canines lack and which are needed in order to truly swing through trees. The putrid stench comes standard with all models.

Whatever Brad saw, these were all powerful creatures and I wouldn't personally wish to share a farm with them. I must note that none of them actually threatened him physically, however. They just took off as upright canines usually do. And if they really were somehow connected to the massacre burial grounds, I'd be surprised if they didn't still take an occasional whirl through the trees just to check up on things now and then.

RED HILL WEREWOLF OF HAGERSTOWN

There are many other precedents for such connections between historic events and the appearance of strange animals. One example that occurred in the early 1980s was sent to me a few years ago by a resident of Hagerstown, Maryland. He wrote:

"Growing up, my father always told me stories of the Werewolf of Red Hill. My dad and his friends since I was a small child have sworn they used to see what looked like a werewolf on this mountain they call Red Hill because the clay is red. They have a story that they went looking for it in the daylight, and they came across some caves and they got rope and flashlights and a gun and went to explore the caves. Inside they found all kinds of Indian drawings and in [some] areas you had to squeeze through narrow passages and climb up ledges."

This is where things grew spooky. As the men continued climbing the ledges, something unknown shot out of the rock crevices and grabbed the man's uncle's wrist. He managed to break free and the pair hastily left the caves. The writer added, "My dad and his friends aren't the type to lie about things like this. They have a good many incidents that occurred with this thing. This area is very historical and a lot of battles have taken place, so there's a lot of supernatural happenings around this town."

I checked around and could not find a specific reference to the Red Hill Werewolf, so it may be just a localized legend that would require some on-site, deep digging and interviews to document properly. I did, however, discover there is an old graveyard known as the Red Hill Cemetery near the site of a church on Red Hill Road. Again, we find here the cemetery-werewolf combination, although it must be admitted that country cemeteries are not rare, and older ones that are not maintained make fine hiding places for all types of wildlife.

The connection in the Maryland legends between historic battles, hidden Native American rock art, old cemeteries, and the Red Hill Werewolf makes me wonder again about the true nature of the wolflike creatures Brad saw in Michigan. In both cases the creatures appeared to be flesh, fur, and blood animals, but many Native American sources believe certain animals may have a dual nature.

The concept of spirit guardians keeping watch over burials is common in Native American beliefs, and goes beyond the idea of an avenging spirit animal, as was the case with the Witchy Wolf discussed earlier. Other beliefs include spirit entities that can travel between worlds to appear completely solid and physical, completely spectral, or something in between. These would be different from the shape-shifters said to use ritual magic to go from human to animal as described above. If true—and of course there is no way to prove the ability to hop between worlds with our present science—it would provide another explanation as to how the creature seemed to be traveling through the trees, and also the non-canine appearance of the long "arms" and hands.

The alternative to the shape-shifter and realm-hopper models is the possibility that a physical, breeding group of bipedal canines lives in the western edge of the Manistee National Forest. Other sightings bear out that possibility, and most witnesses are adamant that they saw fully physical beings. The conjecture continues. . . .

TENNESSEE TWO-FER

Here is another report of upright, unknown canids of the extra-large kind that also occurred only a few miles from what once was very active Native American hunting land for several different tribes, and is now known as Burgess Falls State Park. The four cascading waterfalls of this preserve would have made this a special and sacred area to the area's indigenous people, as are most fresh springs. The Sparta area was home to a tribe led by a noted chief named Calfkiller, and was also situated near a charcoal lead mine whose entry the area tribes kept secret and which was never found by the white settlers who searched mightily for it.

Even more significant for our purposes—shockingly so—were the many ancient burial mounds located northwest of Sparta in the general vicinity of the encounters we are about to cover here. According to newspaper accounts and other records of the early 1800s, European settlers opened mounds sprinkled all over this section of White County to discover that they contained giant skeletons between six and a half and eight feet tall, as well as "pygmies" of about thirty inches in stature. Sophisticated pottery, artwork, and other grave goods were removed along with the human skeletons. There were also bones of a huge feline found in a nearby cave with skeletal remains of other large animals.

Such large-scale desecration of the burials of very ancient people—especially of such unusual individuals—is often connected, as we've seen, with later appearances of unknown creatures. For many more details on this county's fascinating history, see the website at DanielHaston.com for a paper titled "Legends and Stories of White County, Tennessee."[6] Between the astonishing grave remains and the park reserve splashed with great waterfalls, it's hard to imagine a more likely setting for anomalous beasts, whether guardian spirits, leftover energy spirits, or interested parties from distant realms. Here is a young woman's eyewitness story, name withheld on request:

In 2002 and then again 2003, I saw something that can't be classified (to my knowledge) using zoology, in [northwest of] Sparta, Tennessee. I saw this thing twice, once with a neighbor of mine and once with my oldest brother. It was a strange experience that I will NEVER forget.

The first time I saw this creature was in August of 2002. I was spending the night at my friend's house about two miles down Fanchers Mill Road from my parents' farm on Tollisontown Road. [Only about five miles from the Burgess Falls State Park.] It just so happened to be a full moon that night, and I remember this because it was an unusually large harvest moon. My friend and I went outside to smoke a cigarette without getting caught by her parents. Being stupid young teenagers we saw what appeared to be a cow out in the field behind her house and decided to try our luck at "cow tipping." [For readers not from dairy states, cow tipping is a supposed pastime in which several people try to push a standing cow over on its side. It is considered a rural legend by many who have researched the possibility, since bovines can weigh between 1,400 and 4,000 pounds. The general consensus is that there's a slight chance it could happen, though, if the targeted cow was asleep while standing on a hillside. The dismal odds do not seem to keep hopeful young people from attempting the feat.[7]]

Originally we were about 300 yards away from this animal. We were walking towards it and when we got about 100 yards from it this thing stood up on two legs and turned toward us. It was a light tan color, not white, but certainly light enough to be clearly visible in only moonlight with kind of shaggy hair, not short like a cow's. On all fours it appeared to be the size of a cow, but when it stood up this thing had to be nearly eight feet tall. More than anything I remember the feeling I got when it turned and looked at us. I FELT like prey. Every nerve in my body told me to run, and I did . . . without looking back. My friend was faster than I was, but I remember hearing sort of a panting behind me. I never looked back until we were at the house and it was nowhere to be seen at that point. I don't know if it chased me or if I was hearing myself panting. We didn't stay to see any more, we turned and ran as fast as we could back to her house and stayed inside the rest of the night.

About eight months later, early summer in 2003, my brother and I were on our way to Wilmar Market driving down Simpson Road about a mile from Highway 70. It was dusk out, not quite totally dark, but most of the light had faded. A creature the exact same color, a light, almost sandy tan color with shaggy fur, ran out of the woods from our right, across the road about fifteen feet in front of my brother's car, and disappeared into a field on our left in about eight seconds. I have never seen anything move so fast in my entire life. For the brief moment it was in our headlights we got a good look at it. Its back was eye level with me, [as I was] sitting in a Honda Accord. Its back legs were jointed backwards and it moved like a dog. It had a pointed snout and pointed ears. It looked like a wolf, except about a four hundred pound wolf. Its shoulders were higher than its back legs. It had a long bushy tail. It ran by stretching its front legs all the way out and its back legs all the way out and brought them all together simultaneously.

On the day my friend and I saw it, it was huge, shaggy, and its head didn't sit on top of its shoulders, its neck almost appeared to be jutting forward. What I saw that day was more of a silhouette. However, the day my brother and I saw it, it was absolutely beyond a shadow of a doubt wolf-shaped . . . but the size of a horse.

It was so fast my brother did not even slam on the brakes. As soon as it was on the other side of the road, I remember him yelling, "What the HELL was that!?!" We looked behind us to see it disappear into a wooded area of this field. This thing was SO big. Its feet only hit the ground once crossing the road. I still to this day talk about it with my brother whenever we drive through that area. That was the last time I saw the creature, but about two more years after that, in either 2005 or 2006, my other brother and I went for a walk in a snow storm.

It was unusual because this is Tennessee and we got about eight inches of snow in just a couple hours. We were walking in some woods across from the family farm and we found a skull. The jaw bone of this skull was about six inches tall. With the skull sitting on top of [the jaw bone], the whole [head] was about a foot tall. It was carnivore teeth in the front with grinding sort of molars in the back. It had an elongated snout. We ended up losing this skull several years later, I'm still looking for it. The eerie part is that this skull LOOKED like some weird hybrid between a human skull and a dog skull, but about the size of a basketball.

I am fully convinced what we saw those times was not a creature I know . . . and there is something about it that screamed werewolf to my subconscious. My brother and I have since become obsessed with werewolf movies and folklore. I only wish we had brought the skull home, we kept it in a particular nook in the woods because it was so alien. The only skull I have ever seen similar to this was a bear skull, but it definitely was NOT a bear skull.

I don't remember it making any sounds the day that I saw it, but I have heard strange sounds when I was out on the farm. I find it really hard to describe this sound, it was something between a baby screaming, a rabbit dying, and this weird gravelly machine-like sound . . . strange right???

Now, on the scientific side of things. My parents' farm is in an area where there are HUGE coyote populations. There are at least two packs that run in our area. One of the packs seems to stay on our farm most of the time while the opposing pack seems to stay on our neighbor's farm. They regularly kill cows . . . I have myself found calf skeletons that were eaten entirely except for the bones and the head was still fully intact. In the same stretch of woods where my brother and I found the skull we also found about thirty dog skulls.

Also this part I always thought was weird . . . in the same woods we also found a wallet with a driver's license, social security card, and work I.D. in it. The license expired in 1985. It may be significant, or it may be that some hunter lost his wallet in the woods.

My brother (who found the skull with me) and I are convinced that there is something out there that hasn't been scientifically proven yet. I am so thrilled to talk to someone who doesn't automatically look at me like I'm crazy for this.

The eyewitness is correct about my perception of her; I certainly don't think that she is reality challenged because she had these two experiences. There have been other sightings in Tennessee of dogmen and Bigfoot. Both of these creatures, canine and ape/humanoid, have been observed by witnesses to take and/or eat smaller dogs, so the fact that she and her brother saw thirty dog skulls along with the larger, approximately "basketball-sized" skull doesn't surprise me. Usually the skulls of large carnivores can be identified by a zoologist, wildlife specialist, or even a taxidermist.

One other thing that may be worth noting is that these latter three reports have involved larger than usual specimens, with witness comparisons to the size of a horse or a cow. As I continue to receive reports of massive quadrupedal canines, we'll be coming back to them in another chapter.

I might add that her encounter and interactions comprise only one of many reports of large, anomalous creatures in Tennessee. About half an hour's drive south from Sparta, for instance, lies McMinnville, where a Bigfoot encounter as told in my book *Monsters Among Us* occurred. We've talked about possible origins and increasing numbers of these creatures, but in the next chapter we'll take another run at them with a slightly different slant.

CHAPTER 6

Made in the Shade:
Hybrids and Multiples

OHIO CLONE DOGS

SOME TOPICS WORK BEST when you just jump in like a kid cannonballing into the deep end of a swimming pool, and let things splash where they may. So we'll take a deep breath and plunge into a letter received in early 2017 from James W. Powell in Canton, Ohio, who encountered what looked to him like a team of unknown canines trained by skilled military march instructors. He wrote:

> Linda, have you ever considered the possibility that some, possibly a good percentage, of these "modern" dog-like creatures may be artificially manufactured? Possibly clones for some unknown purpose? Possibly the result of cloning experiments gone terribly wrong? Possibly by humans? Possibly by something else?
>
> I have had an experience that may be of interest to you. I am now seventy-one years old. This happened ten years ago [about 2007], when I was still in excellent health and running, as exer-

cise, on a regular basis. It occurred on a rubberized walking/ running track in a public park, within walking distance from where my wife and I used to live. The park is in a valley, actually the lowest point in Canton, Ohio, surrounded on three sides by wooded area. When on the track, a person is approximately three hundred yards from the nearest public street, which is an elevated street separated from the surrounding area.

For perspective, the oval track is a little over three miles' distance. A small creek runs through the center of the track—there are bridges over the creek at the south and north ends of the track. There is also a small lagoon at the north end. There is a railroad track located at the extreme eastern edge of the park, running north/south. The railroad track is at the base of a steep hill, on top of which is the public street that I mentioned above. There are no orchards anywhere in the general area that I am aware of . . . I mention these details because you have pointed out [such] details in your recent book as being applicable.

This event was experienced on a particularly bleak, late March afternoon in 2006, which I remember as gloomy, cloudy, cold, damp, and very depressing—typical for that time of year here. Even though it was relatively early in the afternoon, perhaps 2 p.m. or 3 p.m., there was no one else using the park track that afternoon, due to the foul weather. I was on the west side of the track, running southward, when I noticed something coming toward me in the distance, something low to the ground as opposed to standing upright in the likeness of a person.

The object seemed to be moving toward me at about the same pace that I was running toward it. It was not actually on the track but in the grass beside the track. As the gap closed between us, I began to see clearly that it was some type of animal.

As it drew nearer, I determined that it was a very large dog. At this point I became concerned because dogs and runners are not a good mix.

Now closer, perhaps one hundred fifty yards, I could see that it was not *a* dog but *two* dogs, each about the size of a typical German shepherd. I stopped and watched as these two animals approached. They were not acting like dogs are supposed to act. I know dogs very well. My wife and I were breeders and handlers of show dogs (English setters) in the 1970s, and I cannot remember a time when we did not own a dog. I know how dogs are supposed to look and I am quite familiar with dog mannerisms. Something was not natural as far as these two were concerned.

They were moving as if they were *imitating* a running motion. Usually dogs will sniff the grass or trees as they run, investigating everything within range. Also, dogs do not *canter* and they certainly do not canter simultaneously, in perfect lockstep. These creatures were cantering, faster than a trot but slower than a gallop, precisely in step with each other and they were looking straight ahead—never looking to either side, up or down, never deviating from this bizarre behavior.

Their general appearance can best be described as *artificial*. One was shades of gray, the other shades of brown. The hair was entirely too colorful, too thick, too shiny, almost synthetic looking. Additionally, the body parts seemed not in proper proportion to each other. The dogs seemed to be physically identical—like twins or *clones*. Their faces lacked expression; no tongues hanging out, no panting, mouths were neatly closed.

By this time, I was no longer concerned about being bitten; these things were totally oblivious to my presence. I turned and watched them canter past me at a distance of six feet or so and proceed northward along the side of the track until they were out of sight. I have not seen them again. I go to that park every day, weather permitting, and I always look for them. I haven't seen anything even remotely resembling those dogs in the following years since that dreary March afternoon.

Powell has given this strange encounter a great deal of thought, and plays his own devil's advocate very well. His conclusions are startling but well put, so I'll again just share his musings in his own words:

Am I suggesting that these were robotic dogs? No, I don't think they were robotic, although that option is not entirely outside that realm of possibilities. Don't misunderstand me; I certainly am not suggesting that these creatures were genuinely artificial. I never thought for a moment that these were not living, biological beings of some type. I have used terms like 'artificial' and 'synthetic' to illustrate the strangeness of this sighting. I am not suggesting that I have had encounters with android animals.

You may be thinking that I am suggesting there is something unique about this specific location. Perhaps something mysterious or paranormal about the local park track? I'm not suggesting any such thing. As far as I'm concerned, these incidents occurred at this park track simply by pure coincidence and in accordance with known laws of probability. I speak in terms of *probability* because I am now feeling confident that this kind of thing is a common occurrence and not fantasy or illusion, and certainly not a myth. Not only is it common today, but I also believe it has been occurring for many years, possibly thousands of years. It is a genuine experience, an observable phenomenon, and therefore subject to the laws of probability and hopefully, someday, to scientific scrutiny.

Over a period of perhaps twenty years, I have spent a substantial amount of time in the same locality. I think the probability of these incidents occurring in my presence, in this park, has most likely about the same chance as this mysterious activity happening anywhere else—in a mall, a restaurant, a suburban neighborhood, and just about any other public place.

What confuses me is the apparent inability of the creators of these entities to successfully duplicate even the most basic human characteristics such as walking as a human would normally walk, or in the case of animal replication, running as the animal would naturally run, and behaving as the animal would normally behave. To put this in the simplest of terms, they, whoever they are, cannot be exceedingly bright if they are essentially unable to produce a convincing human or canine reproduction.

TEAM TEEN-GRANDPA

Powell added a few notes, including the fact that he'd forgotten to mention the area's oldest, largest cemetery is located within a few blocks of the track, not a surprising circumstance given our previous look at graveyard associations. He also offered one real shocker: he'd had a similar experience with humans in the same park! This occurred half a year before the "cloned dogs" incident, in mid November 2005. His account is a bit lengthy, so I may abridge some parts, but I'll leave it as close to the original as possible.

I was enjoying my usual mid-afternoon run in the park. It was a typical November day—cloudy, cold and damp. I had been running southward on the east side of the track. I then crossed the creek using the bridge and turned north anticipating another two miles of running, followed by a ten-minute walk to my house.

Ahead of me, at a distance of perhaps three hundred yards, I saw the backs of a small group of people moving northward, as well. As I drew closer I was able to determine that they were a group of four teenagers. There were two larger boys, side by side, in the front, and two smaller boys side by side in the rear. The larger boys appeared to be fifteen or perhaps sixteen years of age and the smaller boys thirteen or fourteen. I was moving considerably faster than the group, therefore gaining rapidly. The two in front were slender and the two in the rear were chubby. One of the older boys was clearly the leader. He was continuously giving instructions or lecturing the others. No others were talking. All were listening attentively to the leader.

The older boys were walking slowly and clumsily in a somewhat straight-forward direction. The younger two were slow and awkward as well, moving in an erratic direction, meandering from side to side on the track, falling behind, catching up, appearing very disorganized. I had the impression that these four were suspiciously laboring to move in a normal and orderly fashion. Their behavior was similar to watching a person learning to dance, unsure of the steps and movements, clumsy and graceless. I can stretch the previous analogy a little further by suggesting that they seemed to be impersonating human motion—learning to walk like a normal human. They were not behaving in the same way as an intoxicated person would behave. This activity was something else altogether. It would be very easy to jump to the intoxication conclusion but I don't think that intoxication by drugs or alcohol was the case. It was very weird.

As I drew to within ten yards it became apparent to me that they were not going to open up their group and allow me to pass through. Instead, they were going to force me to go around them, which would have been nearly impossible considering [the] layout of the track at this particular location—elevation, water [on] both sides, etc.

When I was close enough, perhaps ten feet, I was able to hear fragments of the conversation, but nothing understandable. I was sensing that they were very much aware of my closeness and were not comfortable with my uninvited presence. Nor was I feeling comfortable. I wanted only to pass these people and be on my way. It was at this point that I detected a barely perceptive nod of the head by the tall leader. In response to this nod, the other older boy slowly turned to look directly at me, and when I saw his face I was stunned. Here was a teenager, fifteen maybe sixteen, with the face of a sixty-year-old man. I am familiar with Hutchinson-Gilford syndrome (juvenile-onset progeria), a rare condition with symptoms resembling normal human aging. This description is definitely not what I was seeing in this case. With Hutchinson-Guilford syndrome (as I understand it) the body declines along with the face. In this particular case the four bodies on the track were completely normal teenager bodies— normal with the exception of the facial discrepancies. Next, the tall one stopped walking and the group, following his lead, stopped as well as if a silent signal had passed among them. The tall one looked at me and I saw the same astonishing physical appearance. All four of these boys were exhibiting accelerated aging. It was very unsettling to say the least. I've not seen anything like that since then, and I don't expect that I will ever see it again.

At this point I was able to overtake them because they had stopped walking, intentionally waiting for me to go past. I could not go around them because there was a creek on the left and a steep slope on the right. I had to walk through the middle of the group. As I passed by each of the youngest boys I noticed that they would not look directly at me. They appeared to be looking through me, or beyond me at something in the distance behind me. The two older boys made direct eye contact with me, and continued the eye contact until I had passed through. As I passed through the group no one spoke, not to me, not to each other. There was no attempt to block my path, only tense silence.

After passing through the group I intentionally did not look back. Who would? After another minute or so, just enough time to walk maybe one hundred feet, I could not resist the urge to peek. When I turned around to look, no one was behind me. I'm not suggesting that they disappeared into thin air. What I can tell you truthfully and accurately is that there was no one behind me. They were gone. During that minute or so which had passed, they may have gotten off the track. There is a small bridge in that general area and when crossed there is a trail that leads to a nearby wooded hillside. They might have taken the bridge—I don't believe that to be the case, but they could have done so. Because it was November, there were no leaves on the trees in the wooded area, therefore it was easy for me to visually scan the hillside. I did scan the area thoroughly and methodically but saw absolutely no trace of these people.

Remember that after passing through the group and proceeding forward approximately one hundred feet, it was only a minute or so until I decided to look back. What distance can the average person travel in approximately one minute? I don't believe that one minute would have been sufficient time for them to exit the track, walk to and cross the bridge, enter the leafless wooded area, and be so far away that they could not be seen. I am convinced that it would have been impossible for them to walk (or run, for that matter) out of visual range under that time constraint. They simply were not there.

To be clear, when I use the term "wooded area," I am not talking about dense trees and undergrowth. This is a public park, after all. Once the bridge has been exited on that side, there are trees, more trees than in the open park area, but not nearly enough trees to block a view—not even in the summer when the trees have leaves. Additionally, park maintenance workers keep the undergrowth cleared away from any trees in that area for obvious safety and security reasons. If these guys were in that area, I would have seen them easily.

If they had exited the track in the opposite direction, it would have been necessary for them to struggle down a steep, muddy slope and then walk through waist-high water to the opposite steep and muddy bank, climb up and then enter the open park area. I also visually scanned this entire area as well and did not see a trace of them. Keep in mind that this was mid-November, and during that time of day when most people would have been at work. Therefore there were no other people there. Usually after Labor Day, the track is nearly deserted except for the occasional retired person. They weren't there.

So, who could these four teenagers have been, and what was their purpose? Certainly not four victims of Hutchinson-Guilford syndrome out for a leisurely stroll in a park, in Canton, Ohio. A study has shown that there is an incidence of 1 in 4 million births. Currently, there are 100 known cases in the world. Approximately 140 cases have been reported in medical history. What are the odds that four of these people would have been walking on the track in 2005?

Offspring of a human/alien breeding experiment? Possibly— assuming that aliens exist and they are here. It's for sure that these four persons were here, and then they weren't here—which implies that they came from somewhere and then they went back to wherever they came from—most likely by traveling through a portal of some kind.

The same possibility relates to animal species as well. We know that someone has been mutilating cattle for years—taking samples of flesh and organs. The possibilities are endless.

Wow. Powell's observations of these two incidents provide a lot of food for thought. Let's take the cantering canines first.

DOGGISH DUO

Many people have, through the years, suggested the possibility that unknown, upright canines (and perhaps also the very large, unexplained quadrupeds we will get to next), are the result of some super-secret government genetics program. I'm sure there are plenty of such programs, as the field of genetics moves into the bioengineering aspect of every known type of device and natural resource to open vast new opportunities for civil defense and offense, medical treatments, and more.

My first thought is that the two sleek hounds observed by this eyewitness were not bipedal as far as the gentleman could tell, so they don't help solve the conundrum of upright canines. We must then ask, what possible advantage could be found in the expensive and complex process of cloning dogs and training them to move at an unnatural pace and in complete synchronization? That synchronization is the most remarkable part of the observations, although I'm not sure it would be created by cloning alone. A cloned animal is still a separate entity with its own body rhythms, inclinations, and reactions.

The successful cloning of large mammals started officially in 1996 when scientists created the famed Dolly the sheep by replacing the nucleus of an undeveloped egg cell with another sheep's adult cell nucleus. Such cloning procedures have had several decades now in which to progress, in a world where new discoveries build exponentially upon one another. I think it's safe to say that any cutting-edge, experimental procedures are highly guarded by governments and private labs worldwide. And their true purposes may lie far beyond what the public can presently dream of.

In addition to this ability to clone exact genetic replicas, scientists can now create designer embryos of any species by manipulating their gene sequences and "on-off switches."

Given all the known—and suspected—scientific advances of this day and age, I think it's possible that the weirdness of those two dogs and four humans may have been the result of scientific tinkering. The question becomes how we can know that from simply observing them. The answer, of course, is that we cannot tell anything for sure, which is probably the only reason they were allowed to be seen by inquiring people. This brings us to another question, especially concerning the dogs.

THE MISSING HANDLER

Who would let two valuable, perfectly matched dogs out to roam a public park (Stadium Park in Canton) without a handler or trainer holding them on leash? This green space is not a dog park. I searched for any indication that dogs were even allowed in the park, let alone off leash, and found nothing, other than one dedicated dog area in a different Canton park. The dogs' behavior would have been strange enough under strict leash, but to imagine them walking in perfect lockstep on their own, totally ignoring their surroundings, goes beyond strange.

Now let's look at the squad of humans. Men with the bodies of youth but faces of old age. Head replacement surgery? That is not supposed to be far in the future, according to some recent news reports which have said the first human head transplant was set to be performed by an Italian neurosurgeon, Sergio Canavero, in China in December 2017. As of this writing, the grisly event hasn't yet occurred, to the best of public knowledge. Dr. Canavero has responded to doubtful critics in a *Newsweek* article, saying, "'There are so-called experts who have no experience because they have never done this before. They say 'no, this will never happen.' Canavero has just one goal—he says 'I work on it. We have the scientists, the experts, the teams in the U.S., South Korea and China working it and when we are ready to inform the public, we will do it.'"[1]

Another critic is Dr. Jaime Shores of Johns Hopkins, who noted in a *Popular Science* article, "There are countries with much less regulation and oversight than here in the U.S. where people have done some very controversial transplants that have resulted in the death of the patient."[2]

This sounds mind-blowing, perhaps literally so in some cases, but it is perfectly consistent with the mismatched bodies and faces Powell observed. If you were having your head transplanted to a new body due to any age-related disease, it stands to reason you would want a much younger body. But unless you had a ton of cosmetic surgery, your face would still look whatever age you were at the time of the operation, wrinkles and all. Hence, elderly heads on teenage bodies.

It is also logical that your old head and new body might need some time to get acquainted in order to work smoothly, and that would account for the meandering, disorganized attempt at marching. But since the Ohio sightings were made over a decade before the first attempted human head transplant was scheduled to take place, does that mean noggin-swapping could not have been responsible for the looks and actions of those four strange men? I don't think it's necessarily a deal breaker. All it would have taken, once animal experiments were successfully conducted, would be some private lab or shadow government facility with the requisite skill and a disregard for medical ethics and regulations. Taking that next step toward earthly immortality—and likely some earthly wealth—would just be too tempting to remain un-tried, I believe.

And if so, then perhaps somewhere in the world, some neuro-surgery lab has been swapping parts on animals and then testing them in the real world in out-of-the-way places such as a lovely stretch of soft walkway in Ohio where the delicate things wouldn't be hurt if they fell.

MARYLAND'S GOAT MAN

If my Big Uneducated Guess as to the nature of those Ohio mixed-age men is even mildly close, then perhaps some of the urban legends about science gone wrong are finally vindicated. The head transplant idea is actually closer to Frankenstein's monster than to the mad scientist legends of today, but there are plenty of the latter to keep fear of secret science experiments alive. One of those newer legends features the creature perhaps most often blamed on laboratory accidents: the goat man. Goat Man's usual description is a furry, upright creature with the head, horns, and hooves of a goat. Although various goat people legends—and sometimes sightings—are scattered from New England to New Mexico, I think the tale of the Goat Man of Maryland is the most classic of them all. I will briefly share it and a few others just to show how diverse legends about the same supposed creature can be.

Maryland may not be one of the nation's biggest states, but the area of Prince George's County rates high on the list of goat man–infested places if urban legends are your guide. It features three—count 'em—three related legends stemming from an unknown scientist's animal experimentation running amok at the USDA's Beltsville Agricultural Research Center, according to *Weird Maryland: Your Travel Guide to Maryland's Local Legends and Best Kept Secrets*. In all the legends, the scientist is driven to the woods, armed with an ax. One variant says his departure was due to his going mad over the experiments, another says it was remorse over ruining a cure for cancer, and finally, my personal favorite claims the scientist accidentally turned himself into a half-man, half-goat creature and fled to the nearby wilds where he resides today.

The rumors have also been fed by supposed associations with the nearby Glendale State Asylum, and by unexplained, periodic spates of pets gone missing. The Goat Man has been acknowledged by the area press and folklorists for decades, as demonstrated in a 2008 *Washington Post* article describing a University of Maryland library file dated 1971: "Goatman: Who he is, where he lives, and what he does."[3] That *Post* article also lists the creepy stalkings of another Maryland legend, Bunny Man. Bunny Man, a giant, somewhat humanoid rabbit, also carries an ax according to most versions of its story. This implies that both Bunny Man and Goat Man sport hands or at least opposable thumbs, which seem to be a given with most legendary creatures. There are actual contemporary reports of goat men, bunny men, and other genomic atrocities we can check out for more details. I'll start with the goats.

GOAT MAN OF ROSWELL, NEW MEXICO

Earlier, I claimed that goat man stories are scattered from New England to New Mexico, so it's time to make good on that assertion by quickly touching on two entries found online. From a short piece in *The Pipeline* blog comes the story of a goat man from—of all places—Roswell, New Mexico, best known for its alleged UFO crash and alien bodies.

A guest post in *The Pipeline* by someone signed in as Tyler told of a strange creature said to live in an area of pecan orchards just to the west of Roswell. "Crazy stuff goes on there," wrote Tyler. "Typically it is used as a place for teens to take LSD or have unprotected sex, it is also home to a man who was born with goat horns who lives in the trees to protect its pecans from trespassing thieves. This goat man has been seen for decades. Like La Llorona, the weeping woman who you can hear screaming late at night in [Roswell, New Mexico's] Cahoon Park, this goat man has a legacy."[4]

Tyler said a friend of his claimed to have seen the horned one lurking in the trees as he drove past the orchard one night. Tyler added that he had also visited the place at night and saw hoof-shaped prints in the ground. According to the legends, the goat man serves not only as a guardian to the pecans, which he eats, but to the orchard workers who keep his tasty treats coming.

GOAT MAN OF VALLEY OF FIRES

Sometimes even witnesses who get a good look at an unknown animal are confused over what its basic species might be. I have found this to be especially true of eyewitnesses who figure they must be looking at upright goats or deer, probably because both animals have hock joints farther up the leg than do humans, giving the appearance of a knee "bent backward." Many times, the witnesses will change their minds and decide that, based on other features such as upright ears or claws, they probably saw an upright dog or wolf. Ambiguity, as we've noted earlier, is always in play in even the clearest of these sightings.

Consider this second New Mexico tale that begs the question, when is a goat man possibly not a goat man? Originally posted on the Phantoms and Monsters website in 2011 on a page titled "Freaky Confrontations," it tells of two siblings aged sixteen and twenty-four who were driving near Carrizozo, New Mexico, near the area known as Valley of Fires.

Briefly, the elder sibling (gender unknown) was driving as they came around a bend on the uncrowded highway to see a mysterious, upright figure on the road to their left. It was four in the afternoon, so they were able to see it clearly, and it was proceeding at a normal pace as if oblivious to having been spotted. The writer described it as a "gray/salt&pepper, fur covered, very tall, very muscular 'man' with the characteristic dog legs (same bends). We screamed, I swerved, and we both thought instantly that we had seen a 'Goat Man,' although there were no horns. Some goats don't have horns so we didn't seem swayed by that detail."[5]

Oddly, this goat man wore some type of clothing over his fur, including a pair of denim, loose-fitting shorts. The writer added, "Goat Man simply makes no sense anymore. New Mexico is infamous for its Goat Man stories, though, so we assumed they are based on an idea planted by local history."[6]

I thought that last comment was both incisive and interesting, and is another reason I wanted to mention this sighting as an example of rare understanding of the impact that local legends might have on a person's perception of unknown phenomena.

CALIFORNIA SCREAMING: WATTS VALLEY WOLF APE

Speaking of monster mash-ups, I've mentioned that people often ask me whether Bigfoots and upright wolflike creatures could be variations of the same animal. They are both tall, upright, and furry, right? The trouble is that, according to the many eyewitnesses who get a good look at either creature, one is a primate and one is a canine. These are separate and quite different animal types that should be genetically incompatible. And yet, there is a place near Fresno, California, called Watts Valley, where people claim to have seen a tall, shaggy-furred creature that sports features of both.

The Watts Valley Wolf Ape, as it is known, shows up on a number of websites devoted to strange things. Most of the stories are repetitious, but one article from a 2008 post on *Weird Fresno* seems to predate many of the others. It describes the unknown creature as having "long, gray mangy hair and the face of an ape or baboon and has both human-like hands and feet."[7] The creature is also said to look sick, spewing foam and hacking up copious phlegm. All these characteristics, especially the humanlike hands, feet, and eyes with no visible ears, sounds more apelike than wolfish. Bigfoot is also said to produce much saliva and make garbled noises and deep huffs that could be interpreted as hacking or coughing.

There had been a fairly recent sighting, according to the *Weird Fresno* site, by two men who claimed the Wolf Ape chased them into a Watts Valley cemetery, from which they escaped by distracting the creature with a pack of chewing gum. The men later denied it happened when a Fresno radio show interviewed them.

Older tales of the Wolf Ape legend include another undated but lively story of the ravening creature, in which it invades a country school and forces the children to climb up a pile of desks to the ceiling while the teacher cowers in the bathroom. The beast, it was said, contented itself with scarfing down the children's lunches, and then it left. This tale has the gently humorous flavor of a Jack Link's jerky TV commercial, and I'm also not sure how the children could have assembled a stable, climbable tower so quickly. That should have been a big news story of its time, if true, but I'm still hunting for a trace of its true origin.

Another legend says a local minister shot and killed a wolf ape that measured ten feet in length. He nailed the carcass to the church wall and displayed it, perhaps as a lesson to any other half-ape, half-wolf creatures, referring to it as Satan's pet. He was said to have sold the putrefying carcass to a sideshow and moved to San Francisco, where he was gruesomely killed for some unstated reason, sparking the additional legend of a curse on killers of wolf apes. The creature must have had family to survive it, though, because one was seen at Bass Lake in Madera County in the 1990s, covered with fur as always and drinking on all fours by the lakeshore. (Bigfoots have also been seen doing that.) I wrote to the Fresno library to ask if they might have any information about the origins of these legendary incidents, but they did not.

THE UPRIGHT WOLF OF DALY CITY, CALIFORNIA

The author's rendition of a wolf man

It seems that encounters with upright, wolflike creatures may be increasing around Fresno. I used to hear very little from any part of California, but that's becoming less true as time shambles on. I received an email from a Daly City man telling me about a possible dog man. The surrounding habitat would certainly support a good-sized predator. It's less than two hundred miles from Daly City to Fresno, a doable roaming range for any roving beast's territory. But it seems that the California critters don't mind an occasional trip to town, either. This encounter was experienced by the grandson of the Daly City writer, who noted that Daly City is usually considered a suburb of San Francisco, and that the family lived in a semi-rural area with some wooded areas and a nearby canyon. And yet, this incident occurred in a retail area on Mission Street in Daly City. The grandson was waiting in a car as his grandmother picked up some food at a noodle shop in mid-September, 2016. It was mid-afternoon on a sunny day, and the grandson sat facing an area bounded by trees and brush near a small hill when he became aware of a wolf-like creature walking on its hind legs.

"He described to me a creature standing on its two hind legs, with big, bright yellow eyes, upright ears, and a long snout," said the man. "He did not mention teeth. I believe he was seeing it from his 9 o'clock position and it walked to the 10 o'clock position, which means he saw it from profile to rear quarter as it walked away from him. He described to me a classic wolf type dogman, with long black fur, short in some places, slender, with huge chest and arms, a dog's waist, hands with claws, and a large wolf head with pointed ears."

The grandson sat only twenty feet away from the creature as it approached from behind the store; it seemed not to notice the young man watching it from inside the Toyota Scion. It continued into the tree line, using its forelimbs and front paws to part the brush. The grandson felt the creature was very familiar with the parking area as it seemed to know its way around. His grandmother returned in about five minutes and was upset that he had locked the doors. He told his grandfather about it later.

The grandfather felt that the grandson's experience "freaked him out, but not severely," perhaps because of his familiarity with monster video games and shows. It seems the creature was also shockingly blasé to the presence of humans. One possibility is that it was a hybrid coyote-wolf, or coy-wolf, combining a coyote's bold penetration of populated areas with a wolf's power and size. The question here, as always, is why would such a creature walk on its hind legs? It's hard to see any advantage to walking upright in a place like a commercial parking lot where humans might notice a bipedal canine. As for motive, I suspect the creature might have been visiting the garbage cans and was too full of noodles to bother with a human safely locked in a car.

CHAPTER 7

Hidden Little People

I'M ALWAYS A LITTLE SURPRISED at the term *elf sighting*. Historically, elves, fairies, and magical little people are not hanging out around forest trails waiting to be spotted and then written up in reports for the Internet or books on strange creatures. Also, reports of elf-like or fairy-ish beings are rare compared to the thousands of sightings of meatier beasts like Bigfoot or dogmen. And like all anecdotal evidence, the usefulness of elf reports depends greatly on the person making the report, and upon the quality and amount of information offered. Still, I do receive an elf report now and then, however, and I enjoy them as a welcome change of pace from great, hairy omnivores. There are always associations to be teased out, and there is certainly no lack of legendry about mini-folk.

THE ELF OF VICTORIA, CANADA

This unusual report from a pleasant Canadian man was dated April 1, 2017. Note that month and day, if you please.

We may as well get a certain question out of the way. First, let me say I take care to vet each report I receive as best I can, and that this next story would not be in the book if I didn't feel it was sincere and truthful to the eyewitness's experience. But just to explain my process, I'm always sensitive to certain red flags that may signal a writer playing Prank the Investigator. A report or news article dated April Fool's Day in any year is an instant red flag, of course. But sometimes pranks backfire. Traverse City music radio host Steve Cook, for instance, presented his Michigan Dogman ballad about upright-walking canines on April 1, 1987, as a joke.[1] As it turned out, many listeners hotly responded that the creature in Cook's ballad was real, and that they had seen upright, wild canines themselves. Cook began filing the sightings, which continue to this day and seem just like those of any other state. But his original intention is a sample of why the chance of trickery is always on my mind.

I sometimes even feel the need to ask some eyewitnesses point-blank whether they are being truthful with me. Posing the question never gets less awkward. The Canadian eyewitness mentioned above, whom I'll call "B.," seemed genuinely surprised that I would question his story, but he also understood the necessity. He wrote, "I was not joking about the sighting, and I am still shaken after all these years." He added that he hadn't even noticed the date, as he isn't superstitious. He said, "I wouldn't prank anyone like that, it's not my character to do that sort of thing . . . I'm very pleased that you are interested in using my story, and I hope that it can help others understand this odd parallel existence."

Also helpful was the fact that he had first queried me a couple of months earlier, and that he had written messages on other dates, too, so that the April 1 report was only part of a series. People do write perfectly legitimate letters about all sorts of topics on that date every year. I think this was one of them. All that having been said, on to the elf sighting! B. began his encounter story by reminding me of his original email:

"It was about an Elf encounter, of what I suspect was an Elf. Sorry for not getting back to you, but here goes. The date for this encounter was late July of 2014. Most likely the last week of that month. Early in the morning just before sunrise. Around 5:10 a.m. The sun was rising at about 5:40 a.m give or take. I was thirty-seven at the time. I was delivering newspapers near a wooded area around the local university in Victoria, BC, Canada, located near the UVic area. There is a wooded area that surrounds the entire campus, and I was southwest of it facing north. I was one block away on a parallel street. I was doing the paper route at the time due to emergency money being required due to my girl-friend breaking her leg, and being unable to work. I was on med-ical disability as well at the time, but the paper route was [supplementing] my income."

B. said the street he stood on was at a higher elevation than the grounds around him, so he had a good view of a nearby street where an owl began to make a ruckus. He said, "The owl was really squawking, and making quite a lot of noise, and I could even hear it through my headphones. When I took them off, I could have sworn the bird got louder. I was curious what was go-ing on, so I stopped delivering to the block I was on and quickly whipped around the block to where I heard the noise. I had no idea what was going to happen next.

"When I arrived, the bird was no longer making sounds. In fact, it was so silent. I slowly turned my head to the right, and this was my field of vision. I do not want to sound flakey, but I had been told how to encounter what I saw by someone who deals with hidden, occult creatures. I had been hoping for about a year to encounter something, and I was practicing quite frequently. So this was an end result of hard work, I guess you could say.

"As my eyes became adjusted to the dark forest, I no longer felt alone. In fact I felt I was looking 'into' the trees, or the earth realm. It went completely silent, and it felt like I was in a big vacuum."

Readers may recall this same phenomenon of eerie silence and a simultaneous feeling of distance from normal reality, known as the Oz Factor, from an earlier story. B. continued, "Several creatures had stepped towards me all at once, but one of them, the one in the center, stood out the most."

B. described the characteristics he had documented in a drawing.

Notice how his one leg is bigger than the other? That's because he was stepping into my world. I wonder if I was doing that to him. He was about four feet tall. [The others were] really tall and skinny, or small and fat. Some of them were even bent sideways like an upside down "U." Feet on the ground, and their head pointing to the ground. Very unusual. They were all staring at me, but the one in the [illustration] felt like he asked me a question. Like, what are my intentions? I could still see the forest behind him, or half of it. It really looked like two worlds had overlapped. Both worlds looked transparent.

I replied in my mind and heart with the intention of peace. At this point, I was really uncomfortable, so I decided that [the encounter] had to stop. I threw it out there that I was not going with them, and stepped backwards. Kind of how Van Helsing steps back from Bela Lugosi in *Dracula*.

The vacuum sound vanished, and so did they. I raced home, and drew the [picture]. I have no idea what they were, but judging by the conical hats, and pointy ears, they were earth creatures. Possibly elves, gnomes, or sprites. They were black, and had an off-white glow around them. Their eyes were like strobe lighting/pulsing, and they flashed the entire colour spectrum. Even colours I had never seen before. Possibly infrared, and ultraviolet?

You could call it summoning because I did actively seek them out, and was inviting them through intention. I knew from what my friend told me that it wouldn't be a hostile situation, but to be cautious, and don't accept anything. Food, etc. He also told me that you have to be in the right place in your mind and heart in order for it to work. I would say that the elves and myself were indifferent, but were willing to trust. I however, didn't want to go past what we encountered.

I have felt them attempt [to contact me again], yes. Usually at sunset I feel a bit uneasy. I'm not out in the early morning anymore, but I do still feel like there is a link available if I was to pursue it. I'm pretty good at opening and closing my reception to it all. Like a big steel door that I open if I want to see through the veil.

I was curious as to from what tradition B.'s friend—the one who advised him about how to act in an encounter situation—had come. B. said, "As for my friend, he is a Huna shaman trained by elders in Hawaii. He's also got Masonic lineage. He is of Scottish descent. That's about all I can really say about him because that little info really covers his area, and is about as much information as I'm comfortable in sharing. I was not under the influence of any medications, at this point, I was off all medications for three years. I'm not a drug user, or someone who was influenced in any way. Stone cold sober at the time."

B. also mentioned that he felt he had an innate ability to see these creatures. He said, "I've been poking at other realms as far back as I can remember. It's like turning a light switch on and off, and I generally keep it offline most of the time due to it being a little too much. It's when I actively seek out and invoke stuff, it quickly appears."

THE OLYMPIC WOOD ELF

The author's rendition of a wood elf

Not all elf reports are as detailed as B.'s, nor are most people as prepared for such an encounter as he felt that he was. I received another report of unknown little forest beings from someone who said he'd been contemplating whether he should contact me for about half a year and finally decided it was worth a try. His experience occurred in the fall of 2016 in the Olympic National Forest in the state of Washington, an area better known for its many sightings of Bigfoot. The writer, a man in his early thirties who wished to remain anonymous, wrote:

"I don't know what you could even call it, exactly, except some kind of Ent or wood elf, or skinny, creepy being that is a walking small tree thing. I have a photo. It would really help me if you know of other people seeing this kind of thing. I have had an extremely hard time going out alone during the day and would like to have some closure. I have loved the outdoors all my life and have a lot of anger about not feeling safe. That is my own stuff, I guess, but even if just one other person has had something like this I will feel some sense of relief."

I think he might have found B.'s report helpful. The creatures described by B. aren't exactly the same as the "wood elf" encountered here but may have proved an illuminating comparison. Alas, I never (to my knowledge) received an answer to my reply. What interests me most here is that, although I have no reason to believe these two gentlemen had any acquaintance with one another, the sightings were only two years or so apart and located in surprisingly close proximity to each other. The Olympic National Park lies just across the Strait of Juan de Fuca from Victoria, capital city of British Columbia. Perhaps there are more reports of weird little creatures from that vicinity, just waiting to be heard.

Although elf reports may be rare among my personal emails, encounters with elfin entities aren't terribly unusual in our forests or other wild areas—or even where we live.

OSHKOSH GNOME KING

Wisconsin author and former university English professor Patricia Hodgell, for instance, wrote about seeing a small, pointy-headed, man-like being she called "The Gnome King" in her grandparents' horse barn for my book *Strange Wisconsin*. It was autumn 1959 and she was eight years old, she said, on the day she noticed the shadowy figure staring at her with red eyes, one dark hand grasping the rung of a ladder visible inside the open door of the old building. She described it as a "black, squat silhouette with a pointed head or perhaps a hat," and clearly remembers thinking, "This is 1959. This moment is real. I will never forget it."[2]

Tiny, odd people or creatures, especially with pointed hats or heads (a mystery in itself), are truly the stuff that worldwide legend is made of. Moreover, old and new legends of various pint-sized creatures of the Americas bear great similarity to older tales of "little people" in Europe, the British Isles, and almost every other place a person could think of on this planet. As Ted Holiday and Colin Wilson aptly note in their book, *The Goblin Universe*, "There are many sorts of fairy or nature spirits, ranging from the tiny *Ellyllon*, which function within the cell structure of vegetation, to the wandering *Sighes*, Elohim or Trooping Fairies whose illusions and paranormal hoaxes are an intrinsic part of the flying saucer story. . . . Although no longer invited to hunt for fairy gold, we are asked by technical-looking people to step aboard a space ship from Venus and examine the crew headquarters."[3]

ALIEN GRAYS AND UFOS

This mention of the flying saucer story, of course, brings in the view held by many other researchers that all the wee folk, including the short-statured, bug-eyed "grays" often associated with UFO visitations and interactions, are just variously flavored tidbits from the same Otherworld-creature stewpot. John Keel is another investigator who came to the same conclusion. In his classic *Complete Guide to Mysterious Beings*, Keel wrote, "In case after case, the percipient reports seeing a bright light which comes closer and closer, suddenly changing into an apparently solid object or entity. Much of our UFO and religious lore is based upon the appearances of such lights. They turn into angels, fairies, hooded beings, grays, ugly monsters. . . . They transmogrify."[4]

I've personally seen those bright lights on a couple of occasions, one of them with two other witnesses. Neither of the basketball-sized, white spheres turned into anything, although I had the eerie sense that they could have and that they possessed some level of sentience. When such anomalous lights take up lodging in a particular outdoor area or human structure, they often become the source of local legends that may involve monsters, ghosts, UFOs, or supernatural little people. The term *fairy lights* is probably one of the oldest references to glowing anomalous forms.

NATIVE AMERICAN LITTLE PEOPLE

To search for legends that may be related to the above southwestern Canadian sightings, the most logical place to look would be the lore of that region's indigenous people. Readers will recall the special mound burials given ancient Tennessee pygmy people in chapter 5. According to a 2006 paper on Native American mythology regarding little people and giants, as many as 85 percent of over three hundred tribes sampled claimed ancient traditions concerning Little People. The same paper notes many similarities in the various tribes' beliefs about Little People, such as their preferred location near water. Paper author Frederick Harris wrote: ". . . springs, bogs, swamps, riverbanks, caves behind falls, ice sheets, and large islands prove very popular because they link and reconcile two main elements of American Indian folklore, water and stone. The sound of flowing water disguises the voices of Abenaki and Salish little peoples, while Micmac little people were created from watery sounds."[5]

Few places on earth could claim such a perfect blend of water and forest terrain as the Pacific islands off southwestern Canada and Washington State! If the little creatures sighted by B. and "anonymous" are indeed guardians of water and sacred wood, they should feel right at home near Victoria and the nearby Olympic National Forest.

There was another similarity that struck me between those two cases: both creatures impressed the eyewitnesses so strongly that afterward, neither man felt safe walking their favorite wooded paths alone anymore, to the point that they were distressed and even angered at the loss. We shouldn't be surprised. The modern, Westernized world generally sees elf-like beings as cute, benign creatures suitable for exploitation as cookie hucksters (Keebler) or North Pole toy factory slaves toiling for the jolly, humanlike über elf, Santa Claus. (Remember the line in Clement Clarke Moore's classic 1822 poem, "A Visit from St. Nicholas," or "'Twas the night before Christmas"? "He was jolly and plump, a right jolly old elf, and I laughed when I saw him in spite of myself.")

But diminutive humanoids have also been widely and historically considered tricksters—spirit beings more likely to be naughty than nice to those who irritate them.

CHILEAN CAVE CREATURE: GOLLUM COME TO LIFE?

The term *Little People* is usually applied to either firmly supernatural, tiny but humanlike creatures or to certain groups of indisputably flesh-and-blood—but smaller than usual—modern *Homo sapiens*. Mark (last name withheld), an adventure guide and writer from Iowa, has seen and experienced the effects of something small and animated that didn't fit neatly into either of these categories at two locations, caves in Mexico and Iowa. His description of the cave dweller reminded me of Gollum, the creepy, near demonic character in Tolkien's fantasy novels *The Hobbit* and the *Lord of the Rings* trilogy. Mark even caught an accidental photo of what he says could be the creature in the Iowa location, shared here.

Cave in Maquoketa State Park,
COURTESY OF MARK@MAINSTREAMADVENTURES.COM

Several people had encouraged him to write me about his experiences, he said. I interviewed him by phone and we shared several other written conversations. He also took part in an extended conversation with members of the Facebook group Unknown Creature Spot, not long after his Iowa encounter in mid-June 2017.

The first incident occurred on a spelunking trip he made to the state of San Luis Potosí, Mexico, in 2002 with a colleague and a local guide, Rico. Their initial destination was the Cave of the Swallows, the world's largest known cave shaft, which is considered the ultimate place to BASE, or BASE jump (an acronym for the jump platforms: Buildings, Antennae, Spans, and Earth). The daring sport involves taking a flying leap off one's choice of platform and deploying a parachute at the right time in order to land safely below.

Mark and his companions survived a day of jumping 1,400 feet down into this cave and then struck off on a two-day backpack trek through the jungle to explore a different cave in Aquismón, where, Mark said, things began to get strange.

It was a several-day trip through the cave. During our trip through, we kept seeing a thing dart in and out of the flashlight shadows. An upright, walking thing about waist high. None of us got a great look, as it would run off as soon as we shined a light towards it. I felt it was stalking us as we made our way through. Not in a [menacing] way, but we felt it was more out of curiosity. Some of the passages we took were extremely tight; crawling room only, and we could hear the creature behind us. We would stop to listen and it stopped right away as well. On our trip, we had gear disappear. Several wrappers, a lighter, a candle, goggles.

Nothing of real value, just shiny things. Several times we would catch a terrible smell at the same time we heard something coming. It reminded me of rotting from a dead animal.

We had a set of night vision goggles, and through the goggles we saw the creature run into the shadows and hide behind a ledge. We could see movement through the goggles, and Rico told us that the movement was the breath of the creature in the cold air. This was very strange to me, because it showed intelligence that I doubted it had. Somehow it seemed to know that we had night vision lenses. Or else why would it have hidden and waited us out? It was so dark in this room, it had no reason to think we could see it. You could not see five inches without light. So that left me confused and still sticks in my mind to this day.

If you're wondering why we didn't just walk over and look behind the ledge, it was because we were about thirty feet up overlooking a large room at this point. We waited for about thirty minutes and it stayed put and waited for us to continue on our path. At one point, my buddy fired off a flare and he saw it.

Mark said it was about the size of a four-year-old human, perhaps three feet tall, hairless and bald, and a very pale color. It seemed to have some muscle definition, he said, but looked more like a packrat than a savage. He said it appeared humanoid with no tail and long-fingered hands. "The eyes were not visible," said Mark. "It was always quick. The feet were more like humans' with narrow toes."

Mark also noted that Rico, the guide, said he had no knowledge of the creatures. They wondered what the creatures would find to eat in the cave and speculated they might scavenge in the jungle.

"They followed us the whole time," he said. (Mark wasn't sure whether they were stalked by a single individual or by several of them in turn.) "We did not feel threatened but we definitely had things stolen. The locals wouldn't talk about it; they may have thought it would be bad for business. I feel there are real possibilities for the discovery of these things. If only we'd had traps or recording equipment."

After over a decade had passed, Mark still thought about the hairless cave creature but did not expect to see one again—especially not in the US and most especially not in his home state of Iowa. He did see something very similar to the original Mexican humanoid, however, and although it wasn't an obvious "shorty," it was close enough to shock him. He ran across this second creature in mid-June 2017, in Maquoketa Caves State Park, a location he considered safe enough to bring his young daughter. The park is about thirty-two miles south of Dubuque, covers 370 acres, and boasts thirteen caves.

"It happened pretty fast," he said. "My daughter and I were alone and had pretty much the whole park to ourselves. It was early on Tuesday morning. I was about fifty yards away from my daughter inside the lower Dance Hall cave, just exploring and climbing around. I was taking a picture of the cave and something just popped up between my daughter and me. It was tall and skinny with a really long neck and long arms, too. It was completely naked. I snapped the picture and took off running toward it, thinking my daughter may be in danger. I had to watch my footing, looking down and back up again, and it was gone just like that. My daughter never saw it."

Mystified as to how the creature could have disappeared from view so quickly, Mark wracked his brain for an answer. "There are no passages in that area for it to run into, but there are plenty of places to hide and wait me out. With my daughter there and my adventure team not with me, I did not pursue the creature, just got out of there. A couple of days later I went back with my team and explored the cave top to bottom, every [nook] and cranny, and found nothing. Not even a footprint, which makes sense because it's almost all rock. I have explored every passage in those caves and never seen anything before or after that day. But it will never leave my mind."

It was especially puzzling, added Mark, because the passages from that cave all become too narrow for humans as they progress deeper into the earth. "But perhaps," he said, "this creature can squeeze like a mouse can under a doorway. I have many theories about Iowa's caves, that they are all somehow connected into a larger system. One system has been explored for forty years and no end is in sight. I believe in subterranean creatures, but [such creatures] being in Iowa and at this park makes zero sense. This is the most visited state park in Iowa, so there should be lots of other sightings. How this thing just appeared and vanished so quickly, I will never understand. The nearest passage is quite a distance from where [this photo] was shot; a cheetah could not have covered the distance in that time. Which means it either vanished into thin air (not likely) or there is another system in this cave that I do not know about (not likely). I'm very thankful I was able to snap the picture I took."

That photo does appear to show a bald, thin-necked humanoid standing in an otherwise empty spot. This creature and the shorter Mexican one seem more goblin-esque than elfin in appearance, but what they truly are may be anyone's guess. Mark said a small, partially mummified skeleton displayed on the reality TV show

Destination Truth with Josh Gates (season three, episode five) came very close to a match with the cave creature's anatomy. A crew member of Gates's show stumbled upon the tiny mummy in an old mine in an arid region of Chile. It's difficult to say whether the strange remains have anything to do with the two humanoids Mark glimpsed, but are interesting in their own right.

MINISCULE MUMMY

In 2003, Atacama Desert researchers in Chile uncovered a well-preserved, six-inch skeleton that most press sources and some researchers dubbed the "Alien Mummy." It did look truly weird. The Lilliputian marvel presented a contorted face, a pointy head, and two missing ribs. Scientists from various fields of study were quick to point out that these features combined with the small size might be characteristic of a human fetus. Strangely, closer study and DNA testing did not support the pre-birth theory. The skeleton was shown to have a single, developed tooth and some other growth indicators that pointed to a female child of age six to eight years!

Others suggested the wee one might have been affected by progeria, a disorder that causes premature aging, or by some rare form of dwarfism. At this writing, there was no conclusive evidence as to the strange child's origins, other than that she was no more than some decades old and that she tested out as mostly human. The "mostly" part was due not to aliens but to about 9 percent of her DNA having been eroded or obscured by weathering and other ravages of time. That is common, say scientists, and 9 percent is a figure well within normal parameters of test results for remains found in similar situations.

Regardless of the final diagnosis, it's probably safe to say that little Ata, as she came to be known, wasn't a link to Mark's hairless goblinoid. Ata was at least three feet shorter than what Mark glimpsed in the Mexican cave, and probably not able to get around on her own. And there was still nothing at the site to indicate her parents looked at all unusual. Her DNA, without getting too technical, showed that Ata's mother was from somewhere in that vicinity of Chile. Ata's story may not be over; the IFLScience site says, "thorough genetic testing is still ongoing . . . researchers have pledged that further results will go through the appropriate channels and be published in an accredited scientific journal."[6]

EL DUENDE

Although Ata didn't pan out as a likely relative of the cave creatures, another possibility may be found in regional folklore. A 2016 article by David Bowles on the website Medium notes that people throughout Mexico, Chile, and other countries of the southern Americas tell of a small, furtive creature called the Duende, or some variation of that name. The Duende is generally described as a darkly mischievous entity that requires food offerings from those who cross its path or live near its lair. Its appearance and habits may also vary from place to place. One widespread version describes a small man with a battered red hat, backward-facing feet, and no thumbs. Those who meet up with this odd creature are advised to hide their thumbs, or the Duende may bite them right off their hands.

The red-hatted Duende seems more like a fantasy, modern-era folk story than a reportable cryptid. I would declare the Duende a dead end in the search for small mystery folks, if not for another variation more similar to the creature that followed Mark and his crew. Local legend dates it back to pre-Columbian times. That indicates something native to the area, although later versions of the legend eventually blended with European tales of dwarves, elves, and other undersized humanoids. But Bowles says of this older legend, "The *Nahuas* ("Aztecs") believed in the *ohuihcan chanehqueh*, 'those who live in dangerous places,' [which were] magical and hostile sprite-like beings that could cause illness and misfortune to anyone who wandered into their realm."[7]

The disturbing part of Mark's sightings, I think, lies in the fact that even a cursory study of world folklore will reveal that small, often malevolent humanoids have been said to exist in every part of the world. And in most of those stories, the humans who interact with them are likely to wish they hadn't. Native American traditions are especially rich in lore of stature-challenged beings.

PUCKWUDGIES AND MENEHUNE

One of the presently best known, most widespread examples of legendary Native American little people is the entity known as the Puckwudgie (variously spelled). The tradition is especially strong with the Wampanoag and Algonquian tribal groups. The Native Languages of the Americas website informs us that "*Puk-wudgies* are usually described as being knee-high or even smaller. Their name literally means 'person of the wilderness' and they are usually considered to be spirits of the forest. In some traditions, they have a sweet smell and are associated with flowers. Pukwud-gies have magical powers which vary from tribe to tribe but may include the ability to turn invisible, confuse people or make them forget things, *shapeshift into cougars or other dangerous animals* [emphasis mine], or bring harm to people by staring at them."[8]

I find that part about shape-shifting into cougars or other dangerous animals (bears? Dogman? Bigfoot?) especially intriguing. It seems to lend credence to the idea that all mystery creatures may be cut from the same otherworldly cloth, something to keep in mind in any study of unknown humanoids and animals.

Even Hawaii has a hidden tribe of diminutive ones, the Menehune. The Menehune are much like the Puckwudgies, except that they get to live in a tropical paradise. One would think that the idyllic habitat would make them happy and carefree nature entities, and according to the understanding of one Hawaiian native, that is true. The twenty-two-year-old neuroscience student was interviewed for the University of Southern California Digital Folklore Archives in 2016 and gave the following description:

"Menehune were natives of the Hawaiian Islands and were really small in stature. They have been known to look like little elves or fairies, but not really fairies, more like trolls, and they lived deep in the forest away from civilization. They have been known to trick and mess with the tourists who come to the islands for vacation, like they tend to play practical jokes on the tourists, like they would misplace your things while on your stay or they would pull your hair. They would also pinch or poke you. Mostly just silly stuff."[9]

Folklorist Jan Knappert discusses a slightly darker take on the Menehune. In her *Pacific Mythology: An Encyclopedia of Myth and Legend*, she refers to them as brownies or gnomes, and says they live in the Pu'ukapele Mountains. According to Knappert, they can be helpful to humans when approached with respect and appropriate gifts, but if offended can use their magical skills to cause death.

CANNIBAL DWARVES AND PYGMY PRINTS

Another indigenous little being with a bite is the cannibal dwarf, as revealed by the Arapaho of the western plains. According to their accounts of ancient beliefs, these legendary dwarves wreaked havoc and devoured people in ancient times until a brave tribal hero learned how to kill and eliminate them.

The elimination of the dwarves, however, may not have been thorough. In his 1961 book *Abominable Snowmen*, Ivan T. Sanderson discussed small, strange footprints that revealed the path of something with "little, man-like feet but with very pointed heels." He noted the small makers of these prints lived in forests and in the lower valleys where climates were milder, and they lived in small family groups and spoke a crude language. Sanderson added that ". . . literally thousands of the little pigmy type are alleged to have started turning up along—perhaps appropriately—the Mad River Valley about 1950."[10] It had been suggested that the prints might be those of a large porcupine species, but Sanderson argued that the big porkies left long claw prints while the Mad River Valley prints did not. He said, "These tracks clearly show five toes—not sharply incised claw marks—all of about the same size and arranged almost straight across the front of the feet."[11]

Anyone who has looked at castings or photos of the larger prints believed to be those of Sasquatch will recognize that description of the toes. And it is possible that these smaller tracks, rather than belonging to an entirely different tribe or subspecies, might be left by juvenile human (or Bigfoot) individuals.

But there are legions of other strange creatures spotted from ancient times to the present in Mexico, Chile, and neighboring countries. Often, however, they are described as similar in size and build to the cave creatures we discussed earlier, but having fur like mini-Sasquatches. Albert Rosales included several different sightings of what I call the Chilean Shortsquatch in his far-ranging collection *Humanoid Encounters 2000–2009*.

SHORTSQUATCH

A trait that can make identification of small, hairy creatures even more difficult is that some apparently have wings, making them resemble humanoid, oversize bats. It's possible that some of these sightings actually *are* just misidentified big bats, but consider this May 7, 2000, incident in Santa Elena, Chile. In his book cited above, Rosales recounted the unsettling experience of thirty-three-year-old G. Alejandro Canales.

Rosales said that Canales was walking home late that night after tending the rabbit pens he kept at another location, when he discovered something lurking in the darkness that seemed more interested in him than in his rabbits.

As the man made his way through an unlighted alley shortcut, he felt something big flutter onto his back. He screamed and tried to shake off the unseen assailant as he grabbed for his flashlight. What the light revealed was unimaginably frightening: a pair of shining, golden eyes accentuated a mouth brimming with fangs, and its furry, hominoid body clung to the man's back with the aid of bat-like wings. It emitted a foul stench. When the flashlight beams hit its face, the creature suddenly released its grip on him and flapped away into the night.[12]

This hairy, winged humanoid sounds like a pint-sized version of the "Batsquatch," a flying wolflike beast of Tacoma, Washington, and countless other winged humanoid creatures reported by eyewitnesses around the United States, from West Virginia's Mothman to the Jersey Devil of the Pine Barrens of New Jersey. It's hard to say whether the small size of this Chilean creature means it is a juvenile, a subspecies of the Batsquatch, or something entirely different. It also reminds me of a Mexican bedtime bogeyman, El Cucuy, or the more menacing, blood-sucking creature known as El Chupacabras throughout Mexico, Chile, and the American Southwest. It begins to look rather like this myriad of cave dwellers, small forest people, and short furry flyers comprise an aerial and terrestrial population in whose glowing eyes we humans are the giants that must be kept at bay. If so, it makes their prickly yet inquisitive behavior toward humans a bit more understandable . . . especially when some of them are also actually human.

TRUE HUMANS OF MODEST STATURE

There's something about a small creature acting fiercely or even just behaving in an unanticipated way that is unnerving. And tiny terrors need not be actual creatures nor even haunted dolls named Chucky to inspire our outright horror. We have a lamentable habit of fearing and mistrusting other people who don't conform to our personal standards of "normality." This means that folks who seem extremely short to most humans may attract unwanted attention, leading them to seek reclusive lifestyles. There are many places where hidden abodes of little people have been rumored to exist: Florida and New Jersey are two such states. One of the most colorful, however, lies near a lake just southwest of Milwaukee, Wisconsin.

LEGEND OF THE HAUNCHIES

As discussed above, little people who band together and live in groups or colonies may be misunderstood and even feared. One legendary community of reclusive little people is said to exist on a road aptly called Mystic Drive on the north shore of Wisconsin's Big Muskego Lake, inspiring a growing body of urban folklore whose reputation has become gigantic. The colony is said to be hidden near a cornfield just off the rural lane. It's called Haunchyville, and its mysterious and understandably irritable residents are known as the Haunchies.

Although I've never discovered the origin of that name, *Haunchies* is a great moniker if you wish to inspire fear and make people leave you alone. It rhymes with *raunchy* and conjures up images of a big, dripping haunch of meat. Who would want to mess with that?

The Haunchies are extremely elusive, as most people who have tried to find them will agree. I've been to Mystic Drive, driven its narrow road, and photographed a few strange little sheds with abnormally small doors without seeing anyone shorter than myself. (Of course, I'm five foot one and might risk being mistaken for a Haunchy there myself.) Police patrol the street and exact heavy fines from those who stop and trespass, but an even greater deterrent is the dreaded black pickup truck. This legendary vehicle is driven by a large, shotgun-wielding man who keeps the windows rolled down to take quick aim at loiterers missed by local officers.

If extremely provoked, the legend continues, the Haunchies will rush out of the cornfields wielding small baseball bats or garden spades and charge at intruders. They guard a secret entrance to a series of underground caverns, it's said, and no one knows what they keep there. Some claim the Haunchies have hanged at least one unfortunate trespasser who got too close to the cavern entrance.

This may all sound far-fetched, but there are people who insist, some tongue in cheek and some dead serious, that Haunchyville is more than a fable. I received the following letter from Bruce W. Foltz of Chicago, in February 2014, and it is published here for the first time. Readers may judge its veracity for themselves.

Dear Linda, "The Haunchies" of Muskego Lake were real, very real! Myself and two friends had an encounter with them many years ago in the late 1980s or early 90s. One of my friends has since passed away. But my other buddy, Bob [last name withheld], does remember parts of this strange encounter and it was extremely real and frightening! It was much like you described in your book *Monsters of Wisconsin*.

It was a warm night . . . all you could hear were the many night crickets. We think it was close to the fourth of July, and we were lost after spending the evening at a flea market near Muskego, Wisconsin. For some strange reason [we] found ourselves on Mystic Drive. We heard what we thought were firecrackers and then realized it was a gunshot blast from a rifle. We were being followed by a black-colored truck.

Then from out of nowhere, these strange, odd, little men started running out of a cornfield on the left side of the road. Each time the truck would fire a shot into the air, another little fellow would seem to appear! They were what we call midgets, and they were not happy to see us. We could see them fairly well because the moon was full. They carried sticks and clubs and shouted in angry voices, "Get out of here! We don't want you here! Did you come to laugh at us? Get out!"

Linda, we were really horrified . . . we were not going fast and we tried to holler out of the window, "We're just lost," but they kept hollering at us, "We've heard that one before, get the hell out of here! Go away!"

These odd little men kept coming closer to our car, chanting. I can't remember for sure how many came running through the cornfields but I would guess around eight or ten. At this point we were in a panic and looking for a spot to turn around (the truck was still behind us). We came to a "dead end" area that was blocked off by sawhorses and guarded by little men who carried sticks and threw rocks at our car. There were also little stone-like houses or sheds. Some had lights on inside, others were dark. We could NOT believe what was happening. Our driver made a quick u-turn and we passed the black truck and [my friend] hit the pedal. None of us looked back.

After driving for maybe five or six minutes we saw a police car sitting alongside of the road. We pulled over and told him what was happening on Mystic Drive. He looked at our car with a flashlight and then he gave us directions to the nearest highway and told us to "just go home, get going, and be thankful you're all okay."

I don't know if the Haunchies are still around today but I can tell you they were there that summer night many years ago! I have never gone back to the Muskego area and never will. But I have a dear friend who owns a small business in Muskego and he told me, and I quote, "No one talks about them, the Haunchies . . . we want to forget about them," and so do I!!

Unfortunately for that business owner, this type of legend is seldom totally forgotten. I've spoken at Muskego's public library several times and always had a good crowd with high interest in the Haunchyville legend. I wrote about it in several of my books, and the entry in *Weird Wisconsin* (2005) includes brief accounts from contributors who more or less echo the experiences of Bruce Foltz. Here are a few partial quotes from those accounts, selected for variety and for further exposition of the legend:

"I'm from Bay View, and the legend of the Haunchies has been around since I was a kid. Supposedly, the Haunchies live in the woods around the lakefront in Grant Park, and Sheridan Park around Bay View, Cudahy, St. Francis, and South Milwaukee. They wait for the big people (that's us) to park their cars and make out. Then they attack, wielding little knives. . . ."—Zatty3

"I first heard the story growing up in Greendale about thirty years ago. We were told that the area was once home to a group of midgets who had worked in the circus. Years later, after the area had been abandoned, a teenage couple parked their car in the cornfields to make out, and they were attacked by the 'little creatures' that left scratch marks on the roof of the car. The teenagers were found dead, mutilated in the car."—Rich

"The whole Haunchyville thing is completely outta control—there is nothing there . . . this myth got out of control in the eighties . . . it's just a made-up rumor. Now about some of the stories I've heard. There's one about there being a large, large man guarding the entrance to Haunchyville, who's the only 'normal-sized' person there. I've also heard that there has been a massive killing back there."—Jess[13]

I included these stories and comments because they incorporate so many of the earmarks of modern legendry. There's location migration, as we learn the Haunchies have also been seen in other parts of the greater Milwaukee area such as Bay View, Cudahy, St. Francis, Grant Park (which is already allegedly haunted by other things), and even Oak Creek, where a werewolf-like creature chased four people on a longtime haunted lovers' lane, East Fitzsimmons Road. It's easy to see how these stories can perpetuate themselves.

An alternate view posits that such sightings areas are linked through some unknown, anomalous energy source. When I consulted a map, I couldn't help but notice that the sites lie inside a narrow band that stretches due east from Big Muskego Lake to the shore of Lake Michigan, about ten miles end to end. For extra weirdness, I could add another upright canine sighting made at an uncomfortably close range by a middle-aged woman in Rainbow Park near the Root River Parkway in 2007. And heading due west of Big Muskego Lake it's only about twenty miles to the Kettle Moraine State Forest, home to Bigfoot and dogmen. The idea that this concentration of oddness should center on a lost colony of ninja warrior little people *almost* begins to make sense.

More sensible, still, is the rumor that the Haunchies were retired circus performers merely seeking peace and privacy. This idea does hold a little more water. Southeastern Wisconsin was once a popular winter headquarters for various circuses. Delavan Lake, less than an hour's drive southwest of Big Muskego Lake, was an off-season home to so many circus performers that one Delavan cemetery has special markers for their graves. The city itself hosted what was originally called the National Clown Museum for many years and is now known as the International Clown Hall of Fame and Research Center, located in Baraboo, Wisconsin. Delavan's town square still features oversize sculptures of a clown, elephant, and giraffe, and the bones of a circus elephant lie at the bottom of Delavan Lake. The lake was also once surrounded by ancient, animal-shaped effigy mounds, a number of which have been preserved on the grounds of Lake Lawn Resort, which was owned by a circus family for a time. Two of the mounds, just to add a dash of irony to a story about little people, sheltered the remains of two skeletons over seven feet tall: giants that also possessed double rows of teeth.

But I have more specific information than that. An area artist and personal friend of mine remembers visiting some "special people" who lived in a secluded neighborhood on the lake. She recalls a lady she knew as "Auntie" serving cookies barefoot, and that Auntie's feet were covered with thick hair or fur and had claws instead of toenails. My friend thought Auntie had once worked as a sideshow performer. I believe this lakeside community may have been one of many small enclaves of people who either retired from their jobs as circus attractions or lost their employment as the circus gave way to more modern forms of entertainment. My friend said they lived quietly and that their neighbors didn't bother them. (This was decades ago, and I doubt Auntie and the others are still there.)

Backing this idea of the circus folk hideaway is the fact that there are other places around the country where groups of little people with their own colorful, legendary names are said to have spent their showbiz retirement years. In New Jersey, there's the mythical village of Midgetville, which *Weird U.S.* authors and editors Mark Moran and Mark Sceurman call "the Holy Grail of *Weird U.S.*, our *El Dorado*."[14] Moran and Sceurman have checked many possible locations and consider a group of small houses in New Jersey's northern Morris County the likeliest candidate for a true community of retired little people. It lies in a wood on the former estate of Alfred T. Ringling, of the famed Ringling Brothers Circus. Moreover, the property was intended specifically as a winter home for performers.

Moran and Sceurman also include a sampling of letters from folks who say they either knew about the little people or encountered them in various locations. Many of their reports feature the same elements mentioned by the Wisconsin contributors: little people wielding baseball bats, rocks, and knives; road signs set at low levels; tiny cottage-like dwellings; and visiting vehicles riddled by shotgun blasts. They also reveal the extent to which this urban legend (possibly rooted in historic fact) has spread, with write-ins from eastern Maryland, Virginia, California, Pennsylvania, Kentucky, Florida, and even Salt Lake City, Utah, where mysterious small folk are called "hobbits" and are considered very dangerous despite the fact that their most common method of turning away unwanted visitors is to pelt them with fruits and vegetables.

We do know, of course, that there once was an actual human variant or hominin also nicknamed "hobbit," the very small people discovered in 2004 in a cave on the island of Flores in Indonesia. Presently extinct, they're now known as *Homo floresiensis*. Scientists assumed they started out much closer to the size of most humans in that time and place and gradually became smaller due to limited food resources on the island. A study released in June 2016, however, showed that, in fact, their ancestors were probably even tinier![15]

It just goes to show, I think, that we humans are versatile and unpredictable in our physical designs, and that we will naturally always have with us these special extremes of our kind who will want nothing more than to get away from the rest of us.

CHAPTER 8

Phantom Quadrupeds and Other Nonconformist Canines

IN MY STUDIES of unknown, bipedal canines, I've often noted that your understanding of what you see is not always what you finally get. You may be looking at something that appears to be a wolf, dog, or wolf-dog hybrid standing on its hind legs (not a supernatural act, just a bit unusual) and then realize that due to its glowing red eyes, unearthly utterings, and ability to pop in and out of view like a will-o'-the-wisp, the thing you see is—only mimicking a natural canine animal.

The same is true for unknown canines on all fours, and the same tip-offs—red eyes, creepy growls, impossible actions—indicate that you may only be seeing a knockoff of a real canine. In recent years, I seem to receive more and more reports of huge canine animals whose appearance and behavior scream that they are anything but natural animals. I don't know whether that's due to an increase in such incidents or if it simply means more people are willing to report their weird encounters, but it's a definite trend.

INDIANA'S PENDLETON SPOOK POOCH

I recently received a letter from an Indiana man whose experience with such a quadruped has stayed with him for nearly four decades. Wayne Highsmith had thought what he and a friend saw in Pendleton, Indiana, in 1980 or 1981 was some type of "hell hound," for lack of a better term, and wrote to me in late 2017 to see whether there might be some other way to frame his experience. I will leave his detailed report mostly as he wrote it, with minor edits for clarity and brevity. He wrote:

My story isn't a long one but it remains a most singular event. For what it's worth, here goes.

When: Late summer of 1980 or '81, in the evening.

Who: Myself and my best friend, Mark. We were both 19 or 20.

Mark was visiting me at my house in Pendleton. It was a warm late summer day and very sunny. We decided to bicycle down to Falls Park and hang out (and check out the ladies, of course). Sitting on a hilltop directly overlooking the park was an old, dilapidated Victorian home that everyone in town claimed was haunted though I was never told why. An elderly caretaker would drop by every day or two to check up on the place and he was the only person I ever saw on that property. He was, however, your classic "curmudgeon," lol, and was nasty to anyone who even stepped into the driveway. But it was Saturday evening and he wasn't there, and Mark and I decided to go for it and venture up there.

The place was Spooksville, to be sure. Creepy spiders everywhere, loose shingles, broken windows, the works. We tried the front door first and it was, as expected, locked. We walked clockwise around to back of the house and on to the back porch which was actually located on the right side, from our perspective, of the house. Nothing.

That's when things took a turn. We stepped off the back porch and began to walk back to the front when I stopped and said to Mark, "Hey, we didn't try the back door." We turned, rounded the corner to the side porch, and there it was! On the very spot on the porch where we had been standing mere seconds earlier! The thing looked rather like an oversize Rottweiler on steroids. Except for glowing red eyes! Its bark was utterly unearthly! Its teeth were large and exceptionally bright white.

The thing had us dead to rights. I don't know why it didn't pounce. We were no more than seven to eight feet away. The rest happened real fast. I half stepped backward and yelled, "M-Mark! RUN!" We quickly bounded down the driveway and took off on our bikes.

When we first left the porch, we never took but maybe a dozen steps when we turned and went right back. Only a few seconds had passed. If that thing had come from the back of the house, it would have immediately seen us. It couldn't have missed us! Why would it have ignored us, waltzed up on the back porch without barking or making any noise, and then turn aggressive only when we just happened to turn around to walk back??

The dog itself: Totally black in color with very smooth hair. Extremely large and muscular. It had large glowing red eyes that were terrifying! But its ears weren't like most of the ones I've read about. They were large but flopped forward. For some reason, the whiteness of those teeth struck me. Maybe the contrast with the solidly black fur. Unfortunately, I didn't check out its legs and paws. I'd seen more than enough already. Its overall size was roughly that of a large English mastiff.

Yet, despite the glowing red eyes, the large size, the blood-curdling sounds, and the show of aggression, it did NOT give chase as they usually do in the accounts I've read (although, on that day, I think we'd have outrun it!).

Linda, I wish I had more to offer. Our encounter wouldn't exactly make for much of an entry in one of your books without a heap of embellishment. Mark and I had no "supernatural" events in our lives before that damned dog, and we've had none since. Mark says he still sees that thing in his dreams. Better him than me. So there you have it for what it's worth.

I spoke to Wayne by phone soon after receiving his account and told him I was happy he had told only what he could remember, without embellishment, and that I would not add to nor sensationalize it. But I did have some minor questions to fill in a few gaps. I wanted to know if they detected any odor from the creature, and he said there was no smell. Phantom creatures often—but not always—leave an aroma of sulfur. I also asked for a more detailed description of that "utterly unearthly" bark, and he replied that there was no howling, just the barking, and that it continued for what he felt like was a lengthy time for any animal to make a continuous vocalization. He described the bark as "low and guttural."

Another question I had was whether he was able to see the animal in various positions, but he said no; when they first saw it, the creature was already sitting in place, facing them, and continued to look straight at them. The whole thing happened very quickly, he added, since he and Mark immediately turned and ran.

He also emphasized the dazzling whiteness of the creature's teeth, especially in contrast to its "solidly black" fur color and the glowing red eyes. All of this puts the Pendleton Spook Pooch squarely in the realm of phantom dogs similar to the UK's Black Shuck, which has haunted old mansions and crossroads there for centuries, and of other entities that have shown up in people's homes. I have often referred to these "things" as bedroom invaders. They have basic traits in common besides their scary faces. They tend to shun grand entrances, appearing and disappearing on two legs, and display tall, pointed ears people liken to those of the Egyptian god Anubis or to a tuft-eared lynx. Wayne emphasized that the ears of the creature he saw were large but drooped forward. Also, by the way it was sitting he could make out a short, pointed tail.

Names for this type of manifestation include hell hound, devil dog, demon dog, pooka, and gytrash, among various other appellations. I feel they may best be explained as some other type of entity or projected energy masquerading in the form of one of the earth's natural creations.

I asked Wayne whether that old house was still there. He replied that it had been remodeled over the years, but it seemed to him there had been a steady turnover of occupants. I doubt anyone will find that surprising!

CALIFORNIA PHANTOM HOUND

In late September 2017, I received a letter from a California man named Garrett F. Aziz who works in the field of renewable energy and who had a very unusual set of encounters to relate. So unusual, in fact, that he finished his message to me with a sworn statement that "under penalty of perjury the foregoing, and any other additional information provided in the future is true." He was also very candid about the fact that he once smoked marijuana regularly, but was emphatic that it never gave him hallucinations. Still, the tale he tells is definitely not based on what most of us would call the real world and indeed stands squarely in the realm of the fantastical.

Even though this type of experience is becoming far more common in contemporary reports of encounters with unknown creatures, I thought hard about whether such an unusual event should be included in the book. It occurred to me, however, that part of my goal was to search for elements of lore and legend and that this experience—which was very real to the eyewitness—contains clear mythic elements. He was awake, not dreaming, and a companion also witnessed the second encounter. Besides that, we *are* talking about unknown creatures as a main theme of this book. Some of these beasties may be weirder than others, but they are all by definition unknown. Garrett began by describing the location of his first encounter about fifteen minutes north of Middletown—Lake County, California—also the county where some local legends originated. Here are his own words, with some editing for spelling, brevity, etc.:

This occurred about two years ago [2015]. I live in a lower mountain, rural community. However, we do have a population of 5,000, and there are neighbors here and a golf course. Our county has 75,000 people and is much more rural and less dense than the community in which we live. Sasquatch has been a common occurrence here since the 1960s. Native Americans in the area speak of giants being buried here and also about the little men and other entities who reside inside Mount Konocti (a dormant volcano), and if you are on the mountain at night time, [the belief is] they will take you.

There were also historical accounts from local native people in the early nineteenth century of underground caverns below the lake [populated] with unknown beings. Calpine, one of the world's largest geothermal companies, occupies the entire mountain range off my back porch. They have huge tunneling equipment, and Blackwater Military Contractors [private military services providers] have been seen frequently for decades.

Next to our property we have a small "fairy ring" or grass circle, and a very large one approximately twelve to fifteen feet in diameter. During spring, not only does the grass grow much taller and look totally different (much more bright in color), there is a ring of large mushrooms that only grow on the perimeter of the circle as well. It is without a doubt an energy vortex/portal. This is where I believe the dogman came from, about 75 yards from my doorstep.

It was around 10:30 p.m. to 11 p.m. or so at night. I let my dog out to go to the bathroom. She is a purebred Chinese shar-pei, which is the equivalent of a Chinese wolf as her breed has no ancestry to other canines that geneticists have been able to track.

She acts much more like a wolf in her caution and standoffishness compared to a normal domesticated dog.

I stayed on my front concrete deck and let her go run off to do her business. As usual, I was looking up at the stars. I felt a very powerful presence watching me. I moved my head down from the stars to eye level, and ten feet away was an all-black, GIANT dog on all fours. Looked like a Doberman pinscher, but Great Dane dominant and all black. When it was on all fours its eyes were level with mine, and I am five feet eight inches tall. I've had close family friends that owned very large Great Danes, and none of them were ever that tall. Moreover, this seemed to be a Doberman pinscher but its head looked more like a Great Dane and had no brown markings.

It was absolutely psychic, or telepathic. I've felt the energies of many different entities both in waking and dream time, but this being emitted such a force that it nearly knocked me back. I could feel its raw power. I didn't feel fear, but it was many times stronger than any human or other being I've ever met. Its eyes looked directly into mine, and I felt it pierce my soul and scan me while emitting this frequency/power/energy. This lasted for ten seconds, then it abruptly broke eye contact with what seemed to be a slight head nod and it took off. I had no fear, nor concern for my life. The dog had no collar, and I knew it was not a terrestrial dog—size alone dictated it couldn't have been a common house dog—not to mention its exponential telepathic and energetic strength. I am a lover of all dogs, even aggressive ones, and I will always approach them. This entity was not a dog, domesticated or wild . . . but something else.

I then called for my dog and didn't see her or hear her. Then a minute later I hear her panting. This entity was copulating with my dog. [Author note: !?!] The weird thing was that this time, it no longer was all black and Great Dane dominant. It now looked like a typical Doberman pinscher and was very large. The entity had shape-shifted. It made eye contact with me too while doing this lovemaking to my dog. I dared not disturb them so I left them to do their thing and kept reviewing the entire situation and feelings and thoughts of what had just happened. A few minutes later my dog came back and I didn't see that entity again that evening.

That is a lot to unpack—on many levels—concerning the appearance and actions of this decidedly unnatural canine, but since Garrett has more to tell, I'm going to continue with his story and discuss it all later.

HAWAIIAN FLYING DOGMAN

Garrett's second encounter occurred while he and his family were vacationing in Hawaii at a resort on the Napili-Honokowai coast. Again, he noted certain local legends he had heard about the area. Probably most pertinent to this encounter are the Menehune we discussed earlier, which are small dwarflike people often known as tricksters, and the mo'o, shape-shifting dragon-lizards. Both are widely portrayed in ancient and present Hawaiian culture. The mo'o are water dwellers and guardians of freshwater springs and may appear as humans—usually female but sometimes male.

Owls also figure prominently in Hawaiian legendry. The Internet Sacred Text Archive site says, "In a legend from Maui, Pueo-nui-akea is an owl god who brings back to life souls who are wandering on the plains. The owl acts as a special protector in battle or danger. . . . The universal guardianship of the owl is expressed in the saying attached to it, '*A no lani, a no honua.*' (Belonging to heaven and earth). . . . Many stories are told of escapes from imminent danger due to an owl."[1]

Garrett noted, "Sasquatch and cryptoids are experienced on the islands as well. We also had a Sasquatch experience [on] the most recent trip to Maui but he/she/they did not visibly show themselves, rather made a thunderous crashing sound in the empty riverbed thirty feet from us to respond to our calls. It was a very nice and greatly appreciated response."

This second experience began two months after his California encounter with the morphing, huge black dog. Garrett wrote:

I was now [at time of second sighting] in Maui with my family. Earlier in the day, my cousin's boyfriend (Michael) was talking with me at lunch on how he is adamant that Sasquatch is real but he is a "dumb animal'" and doesn't have psychic powers and is only physical. This deeply hurt me and I kept sharing information about why he should reconsider his position. At the end of our conversation, I told him, "If you really think they're just animals then ask them to come to you in your dreams tonight and you will know for sure I am telling you the truth." When I said this he was a little off-put and thought twice about it, but he then agreed. (Michael has had ET/reptilian experiences since he was a boy, so he is open to all this, but didn't believe Sasquatch was as I claimed them to be.)

I must admit Michael and I were drinking alcohol at lunch, had a few drinks in the evening, and smoked marijuana that evening . . . I've stopped smoking cannabis, but the point is that I was a daily smoker for half my life and I've never hallucinated from it. [The National Institute of Health and other medical information sites say some people do experience hallucinations from cannabis, depending on other factors.]

So it was around 11:30 p.m. or so, we were on the balcony on the fifth floor of the condo (the same evening when he and I had the Sasquatch convo earlier in the day). A brilliant bright light with long tail [like a] shooting star shot across the sky and caught both of our attention. All of the sudden the shooting star went from traversing the sky to taking a sharp ninety-degree angle right towards us as if it was a comet. I was speechless, as was he; it truly looked like something was about to crash very near us.

Approximately thirty-five yards diagonally upwards from where we were on the balcony, the shooting star became a bright white flash and out of it [flew] a white owl. The white owl flapped its wings twice and began to glide away from us towards the other condo on the other side of the property (approximately 200 feet to the other condo across the way). As if the previous wasn't enough to question reality, as it flew further from us, it grew exponentially in size and its color went from white to an orange/orange red. It was now what looked like a giant fruit bat or flying fox with wings, and it continued to grow and morph as it got further away.

It then became reddish brown in color and gigantic in size with a huge wingspan and looked like a bipedal dogman with wings. At this point in its transformation, I knew it was my friend that had visited me two months earlier. In my mind I asked to see its face, [and] at that moment it turned its head forty-five degrees so that I could see its elongated snout and eye. He looked identical to Anubis but his coat was reddish brown and he had a wingspan that looked like that of a dragon . . . wider than he was tall.

The dogman with wings was now at the other condo and its

wings were equivalent with the width of the banister/balcony railing. Later we took a measurement, it measured twenty-six feet wide! I know this sounds ridiculous, but these are facts that we were able to measure. I would have guessed seven feet tall, but based on the wingspan measurement, which we know for sure, he was conservatively nine feet tall, likely nine to eleven feet.

The dogman then flew over the condo and we have yet to see him again. We felt he appeared through an aerial vortex above the property but [I have] no proof on that. Both Michael and I looked at each other, he was kind of freaked out a little and still doesn't like to discuss it to this day. I on the other hand enjoyed it. Michael enlisted in the military and held top secret clearance for some of his assignments, he is not easily frightened. He felt the raw power/energy I spoke of before but it resonated as fear in him.

Immediately after the dogman with wings was gone, I asked him and he immediately asked me what we each saw. We both explained the exact same experience. When I returned home from the vacation it was apparent that my dog was pregnant. I kept two, my brother has one, and a close friend has another one of the puppies.

Well. My first statement to this gentleman was, "I want to see those puppies!" Garrett told me that they look no different from normal dogs, although they are "magnificent." He also feels they are in tune with "another level" of reality, and that they are loving, conscious beings. He said, "They act more like psychic wolves than domesticated dogs."

He also felt they were conceived for a certain purpose he chose not to share. He did share photos of the puppies and gave permis-

The puppies that the witness says were sired by a spirit dog,
COURTESY OF GARRETT

sion to include the photos here. As he said, they are magnificent but look no different from normal dogs.

Garrett did not have extensive knowledge about Hawaiian mythology before these experiences, but the parallels between the apparition-like creatures he saw and the various legendary phenomena that exist in Hawaiian culture are evident.

There is the owl, a protective figure that helps wandering souls, and there's also the shape-shifting mo'o, similar to Garrett's "flying dogman," known for guarding sources of fresh water as mentioned earlier and worshipped as a goddess or god. What these things mean personally to Garrett and his friend I will leave as their private business, but the animal forms they perceived certainly fit island legends, as well as many ancient archetypes (pictorial forms of feelings and instincts universal to all humans) of unusual creatures.

This just may turn out to be a key in the search for links between myth and modern experiences and encounters. Animal
symbolism expert Patricia Dale-Green says in her *Lore of the Dog*,
"The nature of the dog archetype is revealed by examining the
part played by dogs in myth, legend, folk-lore, fairy-tale and
primitive beliefs, for it is into these that the archetypal images are
externalized from the deepest layers of the human psyche."[2] Were
the black dog and owl actually manifestations of old and ancient
images that come factory installed in each of us?

Garrett's Northern California experience, where he perceived
the black phantom hound paying romantic attention to his dog,
evokes the widespread, ancient, and mythic notion of supernatural entities mating with creatures of the physical world. The Zuni
of New Mexico have a story-myth about a human priest's daughter who is made pregnant by the sun, for instance.[3] An ancient
myth in parts of China that dates back to at least the third century
CE tells of the dog hero P'an Hu, who was believed to have married a human princess and thus became the ancestor of many people in some southern areas of that country.[4]

Seen in this light, Garrett's experiences begin to seem less odd
and more like something inherent to humankind. But there is
another whole category of unusual canines that also come with
ancient pedigree but are nothing anyone would wish to see up
close.

CHAPTER 9

Dire Dogs

IN JULY 2016, I received this polite letter from a southern Wisconsin man, aged fifty-one at the time, who wishes to remain anonymous. I've noted over the years that there seem to be a disproportionate number of creature sightings along the border between Wisconsin and Illinois. And when I say "creature," I mean Bigfoots, dogmen, and . . . something else. That "something else" is not a usual dogman or wolfman (as if either of those could actually be considered usual), nor is it the apelike humanoid Bigfoot. I'm going to give it its own name here, but first read what this eyewitness had to say about the frightening enigma he saw at a spot that is at dead center and about five miles north of the Illinois-Wisconsin line.

THE DIRE DOG OF ROCK COUNTY

Dear Ms. Godfrey, my name is [held on request], I am a lifelong resident of Beloit. I've been a truck driver for many years in this area. The reason for my correspondence is on Saturday night, July 16, 2016, about midnight I saw a strange animal cross the road about fifty or so feet in front of my car. I was on State Hwy. 81, headed eastbound in Newark Township, Rock County, about ten miles west of the Rock River. I first saw the creature after it had crossed the road. It was a full moon so I had a decent view.

The animal was on all fours. The front legs were much longer than the hind legs. Its head was large, and it was very large in the chest and shoulders area. My first thought was that it was some sort of mini horse. Then, maybe a small, disproportionate moose without horns. It ran in a sort of hop-along way. Kind of a gallop but not fast; actually, it seemed awkward. It ran across the road from the south to the north. It came from an area that has a saw-mill surrounded by a hardwood patch of woods. It was heading north where there is an open field and a several-acre patch of thicker woods, about two-tenths of a mile west of Newark Road.

The witness said that it never looked at him or even turned his way, so he was only able to get a side view of its head, just enough so that he could see the snout was "prominent" and the ears pointed. He also noted a curled, bushy tail but couldn't see the feet. He added, "I felt curious at the time of the sighting. I had just seen a raccoon cross in front of my car shortly prior to seeing this creature. I had a feeling like it just didn't make sense, but I didn't feel spooked."

He said that he tried to research the creature online, and the dogman was the closest thing he could find—and yet it was not quite the same as this powerful canine that ran on all fours and was roughly the size of a mini-horse. I have received similar reports over the years and was never sure what to do with them mainly because they lacked the key feature of the dogman—upright stance. They also seemed larger and burlier than most reported dogmen descriptions, and less eager to exchange eye contact with human witnesses. Often people would say the creature's head looked too large for its body, and that it acted aggressively by trying to ram the side of their vehicle.

Sometime in the past several years, I realized my reports of this creature had reached critical mass as encounters increased. I had been calling them "quads" for the simple reason that they walked on four legs. But the name suddenly seemed too mild and generic for what people were describing, not even close to doing them justice. And there was no way to distinguish between them and the more usual dogman type that is frequently observed dropping down to four legs whenever it likes. So I began casting about for a more fitting name.

Some aspects of their appearance reminded me of the *Canis dirus*, or dire wolf, a wolflike species that scientists estimate went extinct about twelve thousand years ago, a mere flash in the pan for supposedly extinct animals. They were widely spread over North America, but the best cache of their remains is in California's La Brea asphalt, or tar, pits where several thousand specimens have been found. This means we have quite a good idea of what they looked like; the *dirus* part of their name means "fearful" and was evidently well earned.

They weighed up to 150 pounds, with an average body length

of four to five feet, and were not overwhelmingly larger than today's eastern gray wolf—perhaps about 25 percent bigger. But their skulls were massive, with bones designed to support huge muscles for biting and chewing, along with stronger, larger canine and slicing teeth. They had shorter legs and wider bodies than our modern gray wolves.

Their coat textures and coloration were probably much like contemporary wolves, however, and the fact that at some sites they were found buried with other canines such as coyotes and wild dogs opens the door to the possibility they interbred with the early forms of man's best friend. That may have provided the shot of genetic diversity needed for some of them to survive extinction in isolated places. It's also possible these larger, big-headed dogs are simply an otherwise unknown species that seem to be roaming closer to populated areas. Whether they are ancient creatures that somehow survived although thought extinct or hidden, unknown canines, or something else, I think they have earned a name of their own. I call these no-nonsense behemoths "dire dogs."

The author's rendition of a dire dog

LEGEND OF THE HEAD CHOMPER OF NAHANNI VALLEY

Some think that these creatures already have a modern name: Waheela. One of the most frightening canine-related legends ever told is a story from Canada's Northwest Territories, where gray wolves can grow to startlingly large proportions and where any relict dire *wolves* might think themselves in predator heaven. Ivan Sanderson wrote a 1974 article for *Pursuit Magazine* about some hunting friends of his, including a man he identified as Frank, and Frank's unnamed Native American chum. The pair were exploring some of the most rugged areas near the Virginia Falls. While the two had split up temporarily for some hunting recon, Frank encountered a massive "wolf" with shaggy white hair. It stood three and a half inches at the shoulder. He emptied his gun at it, hitting the creature in its flank at a distance of about twenty paces, but it just turned and walked off. His friend then returned, and when Frank recounted what had just happened, his friend also turned and began walking out of the valley. Frank followed without protest.

Frank's friend told him what he saw was not a wolf but a wide-headed "something else." Sanderson said the animal was "probably the cause of the now age-old legend of the Nahanni Valley which has for many years been called the 'Headless Valley' because a number of prospectors and others known to have gone up it have either failed to return, or have been found in their cabins or sleeping bags with their heads bitten or torn off."[1]

Remember the above description of dire wolf skulls with their extra-large slicing teeth and super-sized chewing muscles? Frank's friend also informed him that these wide-skulled canines were "loners" with thick tails, paws that splayed outward, and that they usually kept to the northern tundra. Native people of the area called them Waheela, said Sanderson, adding, "and they insist that it is indeed a 'dire wolf' of some kind."[2] There is also a creature of the western plains with the looks of a hyena-dog hybrid that the Ioway people called Shunka Warak'in, or "carrying off dog." A preserved, mounted specimen exists in a museum in Ennis, Montana. And Sanderson's article also discussed an even older and larger carnivore, the Amphicyon, which looked like part dog and part bear. But as the incidents continue to pile up, I believe the dire wolf is the closer match to today's reports, and also has the advantage of a much more recent date of believed extinction.

It might seem far-fetched to imagine such a creature chasing around southern Wisconsin and many other states, but notice that Sanderson's quote ends with "a dire wolf of *some kind*" (emphasis mine), meaning perhaps there are other *kinds* or subspecies of surviving dire wolves. It did live successfully in a wide variety of habitats thousands of years ago. Perhaps there is a southern subspecies of a dire wolf survivor, prowling modern woods and roadways alongside its more gracile cousin, the dogman, while sticking to four-footed locomotion. In that case, I think the term *dire dog* suits it even better. But don't take my word for it; I have a large collection of reports, more than can be included in full here. A few have been seen in other books—some readers may recall a 2007 story from an Oconto, Wisconsin (near Green Bay), couple detailed in *Monsters Among Us*. They were driving in a snowstorm when a huge, dark, doglike creature began to lope alongside their car, shouldering into it as if trying to ram it off the road. It was so tall on all fours that its head was visible in the passenger side window. Luckily, the creature hit a tire and flipped into the ditch. Oh, for a video! But most of the following reports are published here for the first time. I will start with a couple of other stories from the Green Bay area.

WHITE DIRE DOG

The year 2007 seems to have been an active one for dire dogs. I had another report from the northeast corner of Wisconsin that occurred in March of that year, just a few months after the Oconto SUV-ramming encounter. As in that incident, this one was also seen by more than one witness and marked by bad road conditions. One of the witnesses wrote:

"There were three of us driving back from Sheboygan to Madison at about two in the morning last March. It was an exceptionally foggy night, visibility on [State Highway] 151 was very poor. I was driving, my serious lady friend was asleep in the front seat, and my good friend was asleep in the back seat. They both heard my sharp intake of breath as I saw a giant, white animal-like figure standing in the middle of the road, only appearing through the fog as my car was barreling in from about twenty yards away.

"I locked up the brakes and swerved around it, my tires squealing the whole time. The animal just calmly stared right at me, right into my face as I did this; it never moved. Standing on all fours, it was about the size of a bear, but had a wolflike head and ears. I've never seen anything like it, and my two passengers both witnessed it as well. We've been wondering what we saw [ever since], and reading your article, it is good to know there have been other sightings of the creature. After reading the *Green Bay Press*

Gazette article about bearwolves, this animal pretty much fits the description."

It's hard to imagine any wild animal standing in the middle of a road, not budging, as an automobile skids right at it. Again, I have to wonder if the creature's strategy was to force the car off the road. The comment about the bear-wolf is also interesting. That's a name that was coined by some hunters in Wausau, to describe an animal they had seen that looked like a wolf but had the bulk and body size of a bear. Most witnesses are adamant that it is not any kind of a bear, just the size of one. A telling difference between bear-wolves and what I'm calling the dire dog is that the dire dog is seldom observed standing or walking on two legs—although we don't know what dire dogs do when we're not around to observe them. The white fur is also a bit unusual, and makes me think of the possible Waheela encountered in Canada by Ivan Sanderson's friend.

As for the location, if they were on State Highway 151, that would place them somewhere between Fond du Lac and Madison, about a seventy-mile stretch that would take them past the Horicon National Wildlife Refuge and then the Beaver Dam Lake area, about two hours from Green Bay. And I have still another story from that general east central part of the state in 2007.

KNUCKLE-WALKING DIRE DOG

It was a clear, cold November evening in 2007 when a fifty-two-year-old woman and her seventeen-year-old daughter drove home from an event in Green Bay, headed due west on State Highway 156 to Clintonville. The young woman's sister, Kim, wrote to me on behalf of her sis and their mother, since both requested anonymity, and they had carefully reconstructed their memories of the event. Kim said that the two women were about eight miles from Clintonville sometime around ten p.m., a CD playing softly in their Dodge Caravan as they kept a sharp eye out for deer on the road. The area was mostly rural, with scattered houses set back from the highway lined with bare trees. The traffic was light to nonexistent, and neither woman had any drugs, alcohol, or medications in her system.

Suddenly, a large animal appeared about one hundred yards in front of the car on the passenger side and began to amble across the road. Kim wrote that according to her mother and sister, "It was walking at a medium-slow pace across the road. Looked like a hyena but MUCH larger. [It was] walking on all fours, on its knuckles and the fronts of its hands/paws." It had long front limbs, she said, similar to those of an ape, and its "shoulders" were very broad. The back legs were shorter, closer to the ground and similar to those of a large dog, while the front limbs were more like those of a muscular human, said the two witnesses, who also said that even on all fours it stood as high as the top of the van.

Kim added that they said it did not seem to be bothered by the fact that a car was headed straight for it. Her mother managed to slam on the brakes and she and Kim's sister then watched the animal continue across the road. They estimated it weighed at least 250 pounds, and described its fur as gray and brown, fairly short and with a "wiry" texture.

The women had a good look at the creature's head as it was lit by the van's headlights. Although the creature seemed in no hurry, it did take enough notice of the van to turn and survey the women as they sat there in the car. That move gave them an even better look at the creature.

Kim said they described the head as shaped "similar to that of a wolf, but the snout seemed much wider and the head itself was larger and covered with shaggy fur." They couldn't see its teeth but observed black claws on the front paw that was visible to them. Its eyes reflected yellow, said Kim, which is a normal canid eye color. They couldn't tell if there was a tail, because the creature's back end was "quite shaggy," said Kim, adding her mother and sister were afraid of what they saw.

Kim also mentioned that she was writing me because she had attended a university classroom talk I'd given in Oshkosh a couple of years earlier on the topic of Wisconsin Gothic literature. She also said that she later learned a family friend described an encounter with what she called "the weirdest-looking wolf she had ever seen" on the same road where Kim's sister and mother had their encounter, and described it in exactly the same way they did. The friend hadn't been told about Kim's family's sighting. "We don't talk about it much," said Kim.

LAKE MILLS DIRE DOG

Only about twenty miles from the State Highway 51 sighting near the Horicon Marsh, and about a year earlier, in January 2006, two people in a Chevrolet Cavalier almost hit a large, shaggy animal. The witness didn't give me her name but wrote via my former site BeastofBrayRoad.com:

"I had always wondered what the heck we encountered on County Road A on our way to Lake Mills one night, but [your] site makes me think that what we saw wasn't at ALL what we thought it was. We were traveling home from Watertown taking

County Road A. Not too far off from where the other sightings were (on Navan Road), my husband had to suddenly stop as we almost hit a large shaggy creature. It was as the others [on the website] had described it.

"My husband had considered it a wolf but I had my reservations, having seen wolves up close, and a wolf wouldn't reach the hood of our Cavalier. It took one look at us (it had unnatural yellow eyes) and took off extremely fast. We had nudged it slightly with the car before it took off. It gave me an odd feeling; like it wasn't at all a coyote or wolf. I don't even think those two are seen around that area anyways. Any insight into this would be great because that particular sighting has always bothered me, and I can't help but look any time we travel County A at night."

This sighting is yet another great example of a large, shaggy creature remaining implacable despite an approaching automobile. The description of it reaching the hood of their vehicle is also very common in this type of report. In addition, they were within miles of Aztalan State Park, a prehistoric Mississippian village active about one thousand years ago that is one of Wisconsin's most important Native American archaeological sites. Restored remains of its giant, earthen pyramids, burial mounds, and the stockade fence that once surrounded it can be seen by visitors today, and many have told stories of experiencing phenomena such as apparitions of prehistoric people, odd sounds, music, and light phenomena. Perhaps dire dogs should be added to the mix.

THE RED-EYED MONSTER OF
RUSK COUNTY, WISCONSIN

People driving through the far northwestern parts of Wisconsin expect to see bears, deer, even an occasional wolf passing through the heavily forested land. The twenty-year-old maintenance technician "J" and his uncle, however, knew that what they saw as they returned from bow hunting north of Ladysmith in Rusk County was none of those things. J's wife first told me the main story in an email, and then I interviewed J at some length for the details. It was in fall 2002, he said, at either the end of October or beginning of November, just after dark, as he and his uncle drove home after their day in the woods.

"There was a little drive by the Hubbard Town Hall," J told me. "Our headlights shone into the field next to it and it was standing there facing right at us, forty to fifty yards away. It was the size of a horse, real stocky and muscular. We could see it plain as day; the eyes reflected red and deer have yellow [eyeshine]. Its head came down in a snout and it had a muzzle more like a Lab than a German shepherd. It was very hairy with matted hair covering its head and body. We could not see ears—it kind of shocked me. It seemed very solid. I felt it was just challenging us like a dog will stare at you. It wasn't moving. After maybe three minutes it turned and walked real slow on all fours and disappeared into the woods. I don't know how to describe it, it didn't move like any other animal.

"We were silent at first, then looked at each other. It had a beard but it wasn't real long, almost like a goat's. The hair there was four or five inches long in the shape of a beard. It had a presence; I almost felt like it was evil or something."

He added that in 2006, four years later, the family found some strange tracks by their cabin, some miles from Hubbard. They were seventeen inches long and eight inches wide, barefoot and humanlike but the big toe was "split" and there was a claw mark in front of each toe. He said his aunt took photos but wasn't sure how they came out. And four years after the fact, there is no way to know whether the footprints came from the creature J saw. All in all, I can't be sure this was a canine. The red eyes are usually more indicative of a Bigfoot, as is the absence of ears. The "beard" also sounds more apelike and less canine. It was on all fours, and the size fits the generally stated dire dog estimates, but Bigfoots are also known to run on all fours. Either one would be at home in those northern forests, bogs, rivers, and lakeshores. At any rate, it was definitely not a member of the normal "up north" menagerie and therefore deserves inclusion here.

GREAT GRAY DIRE DOG OF
KENOSHA COUNTY, WISCONSIN

It was a spring break never to be forgotten—but not for the usual reasons. In February 2006, a man I'll call "K" wrote:

Ok, here's our event. It was on a Friday evening sometime in March 2004, whenever spring break was for the university. Myself and two friends were going to Las Vegas for the week. Since we were going with another friend from Chicago, we decided to fly out of O'Hare. Our flight was at like five a.m. so we decided to head down the night before. We left Whitewater early that evening, took [State Highway] 12 to Lake Geneva and then got on

Hwy. 50 to Kenosha. [The next turn would be] I-94 to Chicago. I was driving my '97 Chevy Cavalier along Hwy. 50.

Just as I was approaching the top of a little hill on the road (not sure exactly where), something flashed in front of my car. I hit the brakes quick, but it was too late. I thought I should have hit whatever it was, but there was nothing. No thud, no clunk, nothing. Beside the fact that I should have hit it, my friend "A" and I knew whatever it was, we had never seen anything like that before. The other friend, "R," was on his cell phone and didn't see, but yelled at us because he thought we were playing a joke.

The reason this thing was out of the ordinary was its features. For one, it was taller than a large dog. We thought at first it could have been a dog, but the size was tremendous. Another was its coat. It had this long, grey, thick coat that just flashed as it crossed my headlights. And finally, I don't know how it moved so fast to get past the front of the car. My goodness, it was there, then gone again.

The whole rest of the way we tried to explain to our friend what we saw, but he wasn't buying it. Even when we got to Chicago and told our other friends, they thought we were nuts. I know I saw something, just not sure what. After our trip, we tried to find any information on loose animals or other sightings, but nothing.

Just past that final turn the three young men would have taken to go south on I-94, and before the city of Kenosha, lies the community of Pleasant Prairie. The trio didn't know that there had been two sightings of odd canids in Pleasant Prairie, one in 1983, and one four years after their own encounter, in 2008.

BIG POOCHES ON THE PRAIRIE

A man named Jason, who was fifteen in 1983, decided, along with a friend named Charles, to camp in the woods near a farm pond in Pleasant Prairie. He wrote:

I was familiar with the area from hunting there. I had to talk our parents into letting us camp out but there were some in-laws of my brother who lived close by so if anything happened we could go there. My father dropped us off and we fished the pond that evening and fell asleep that night, but nothing unusual happened. The next morning we got up and were fishing again when I started to walk around the pond. There, standing by the water was the strangest-looking animal I have ever seen. It was about six feet long with dark brown fur. It had doglike characteristics but was not a dog; it was very large.

I stood maybe ten feet away from it; it was staring at me and I was staring at it. In one quick move it went off through the woods moving so quickly and gracefully it was amazing. My friend Charles never saw it. I was in shock at what I had seen, and needless to say I left right away. I told my dad what I had seen and he looked at me like I was nuts. After that look, I didn't speak of it again. I went home and looked at every animal book, but it resembled nothing in the books. I basically shut up about it due to people thinking I was nuts or had mistaken it for something else. I can honestly say it was so strange to see that animal—or whatever it was—and getting so close to it. It looked as though it could have done me in quickly if it had wanted to. I am an avid hunter and fisherman but what I saw that day will stick in my mind. My father brought up this incident recently and he thought I should tell it.

Jason and Charles are not the only ones to have reported an eerie creature in this part of southeastern Wisconsin. Another Kenosha County man emailed me about a creature more puzzling than scary that he and an also unnamed friend saw in June 2008. He wrote:

"This past summer, my friend and I were driving up and down random streets in Pleasant Prairie. We ended up going down Bain Station Road which already gives off a rather creepy vibe just driving down it. It's that kind of forested area seemingly in the middle of nowhere with a narrow road where you'd be afraid to stop at night. Out of nowhere, an animal ran across the road in front of my car, and we looked at each other not quite sure what the animal was. It was about the height of a small deer, but it was very dark, furry, and resembled a large dog or coyote. We now realize it wasn't a coyote because the ones I see running across Green Bay Road are generally fairly small and reddish in color, and the ones living by my house are grey and also pretty small. This [an unknown canine] is the only thing we could think of it being, because we have lived here our entire lives and haven't seen anything like it."

My thought about this second sighting is that perhaps a coy-dog might be the culprit. A coyote that mated with a large Irish setter, Afghan hound, or other large dog could produce something very unusual and much bigger than your average Wile E. Coyote. I doubt it was a deer, since even a small deer is usually taller than a large dog. But the encounter does support the previous story of another quadrupedal canine sighting in the same area.

DIRE DOG OF MILWAUKEE

Bay View Park in Milwaukee is normally a serene stretch of paths along the Lake Michigan shore, perfect for a walk with pets or friends. It turned out to be something more than that one evening in mid-fall 2015. The eyewitness asked that her name be withheld, so I'll refer to her as "E." She wrote:

This happened on Monday evening, November 2nd. My boyfriend and I were walking our dog along the lake in Bay View Park (in Milwaukee, Wisconsin). It was about ten p.m. We didn't encounter anyone else out walking that night but I had a very strange feeling, which was out of the ordinary because I walk in that park every day. I was raised to never ignore feelings like that and I was uncomfortable enough that I insisted we walk more quickly so that we could exit the wooded area. I actually have goose bumps now as I write this.

Anyway, there is a staircase leading up from the lake trail to the trail at the top part of the park. There is a bluff along that entire stretch, which is very tall (more than 100 feet) and very steep (nearly a 90-degree angle), but it's not very wide. You don't often see deer or any animals besides squirrels on that side of the park because there isn't enough coverage for them. Anyway, as we were exiting the wooded area, there suddenly appeared a rather large animal in front of us. It was about thirty feet away from where we were standing, but there was a street light directly behind it so we got a fairly good look at it. I was surprised to see such a large animal over there due to my description above of the terrain.

At first glance I thought it was a deer, due to its size and shape. It was thin, gaunt and had spindly, long legs. It was on all four legs, not upright, but it also had a hunched or arched back and appeared to be moving very awkwardly. It resembled a greyhound dog, but scruffier. I know it was not a coyote because it was substantially larger and did not resemble one anyway. The shape was very distinct, especially against the light.

We had clearly startled it. It ran out onto the path from the woods and continued up the path in front of us until it ran back into the woods. It was probably only a ten-second encounter. However, the way that it moved was very disconcerting. It appeared disoriented and it was more of a stumbling canter than a run. It also appeared to continue looking at us as it did so. I'm trying to think of a way to describe how it moved because that was definitely the most disturbing part. Imagine an inebriated dog trying to pick up a slippery toy and run at the same time.

Anyway, the uncomfortable feeling I had leading up to this encounter suddenly washed over me like a wave. I immediately was filled with an inexplicable feeling of terror. It was not something I am used to. It didn't feel right. I was extremely uncomfortable and immediately knew we shouldn't be there. We crossed the street and headed home, but we had to walk along the top of the bluff (where we saw it) to get there. I could sense that it was still over there (across the street, in the woods) and that it definitely was aware of our location.

"N," (my boyfriend) and I wrote down our observations of what we thought it looked like, without discussing it first, so that we wouldn't alter each other's memory of it. Our descriptions were identical. I hadn't gotten a good look at the feet, that's why they just fade out. Also its face was hard to see because it was in shadow. But I am confident that its shape is accurate, as we had a very clear view of it against the streetlight.

The only difference is that N noted how loud it was and I couldn't remember that part. I have no idea what this creature was. I have been looking up reports and it seems to resemble some of the descriptions for the Beast of Bray Road, but I haven't found any reports of sightings in this area.

I didn't see it move quickly, though. It sort of staggered but it kept looking back at us—it did seem very aware of us. Although, the woods it disappeared into are located in almost a 90-degree angle so clearly it must be rather agile. I have been too afraid to walk my dog in that part of the park at night ever since.

She did finally take her dog out there again—before nightfall—and realized that the sighting spot had occurred directly across the street from the St. Francis Seminary Woods Cemetery. (See chapter 5, Haunts of the Werewolf.) She said, "That was the first time I made the correlation to the Seminary/cemetery . . . and once I did, a strange sensation came over me. I have a feeling that the creature was not just passing through, if that makes sense. I stuck around for about twenty minutes playing fetch with the dog and at one point became so uncomfortable that I leashed up and we went right home. Based on how strangely the creature was moving and how it seemed so very aware of my presence, I have a feeling it was choosing to go on all fours. I'm not entirely sure what I am basing that notion on, but that is my gut reaction, and it typically does not lead me astray."

I think that E's Spidey senses were right on target. This creature neither looked nor behaved like an average canine, and there have also been upright canid sightings in many south Milwaukee area parks. Their attraction to the parks may simply be that they are part of a wildlife corridor leading to the Lake Michigan shore and then on to Chicago and Indiana around the Great Lakes. Perhaps that helps explain the opening to our next story.

FLORIDA'S TWO-TIMER DIRE DOG

Just as dire wolves once lived in all corners of what is now the United States, my so-called dire dogs seem to have an equally broad distribution. A Florida business owner who asked for anonymity wrote me in 2012 about two Florida sightings—his own and his brother's. He was thirty-three at the time of his own sighting, which occurred between Ormond Beach and Daytona Beach along State Road 40, between one and two a.m., under a bright moon. He described seeing an upright, seven-foot-tall, hairless canine. Hairless dogmen are quite rare among the reports sent to me, but the oily, pink skin described by the witness is typical of the mite infestation known as mange, which can be very debilitating—the animal may have been sick. It also had pointed ears, long claws, dog legs, and glowing eyes, reported the witness. "The eye shine looked demonic," he said. "It didn't feel like it was of this earth."

Since it walked upright, this hairless creature may not exactly fit my dire dog label, but I included it because of his brother's sighting that same year, which did fill the bill. The brother was thirty-one at the time and worked as a manager in the food industry. He saw a huge quadruped run across the road in front of his SUV *twice* in one night as he and his fiancée drove near the border of Lake and Polk Counties. It ran across the road in about a stride and a half, the man said, and it was big enough so that its back was as high as the hood of his vehicle.

This creature was definitely not hairless. It had grayish-black hair, a long tail, and it took up the whole width of the road as it crossed at Highways 192 and 27, said the man as he described his brother's sighting. Surprisingly, it ran toward the east into a more populated area. It later crossed back in front of him, and this time his fiancée also saw the creature.

MORE FLORIDA FREAKISHNESS

I have personally vacationed on the beaches north of Destin, Florida, and never saw anything stranger than the usual tourist crowds. But in 2013, a fifty-four-year-old retired military engineer saw what he called a "honking big wolf" near a private lake in that area. The man was out for a morning run when the creature dashed across the road in front of him and entered some brush. The lake happens to be less than half a mile from a massive military range, a location characteristic which I've noted in previous books often seems to be associated with sightings of cryptids. The "wolf" was eight feet long, the man estimated, and it ran with great fluidity on four legs. He now runs that path only in the afternoon. His wife, who wrote out his report for him, told me:

"The crazy part (but not if you know my husband) is that he chased after the wolf and ran to the bush where the wolf had disappeared seconds before. No sign or sound of any creature. Of course the lake was adjacent to a . . . swamp."

He described the creature as approximately a German shepherd shape but longer and thinner, she said, adding, "WAAAY longer and WAAAY thinner. We are originally from the South-west, and he says [it was like] a Mexican gray wolf crossed with a coyote, but huge. He says it wasn't shepherd color. It looked like it had guard hairs. Stupidly crazily long tail. He said, 'You just don't see tails like that on a dog.'

"My husband has raised dogs and is very familiar with them. He says that the really disquieting thing was it looked back over its shoulder at him. He said it was very creepy. Again, you are talking about a middle-aged, very fit former military engineer. He is not prone to fish tales . . . he's a 'just the facts' kind of guy. He said that the way it moved was just wrong, the way it looked back at him was just wrong, and it was just creepy. He's a hunter and has been around animals. 'Creepy' is not a word he would typi-cally use to describe an animal. He said it was not a dog, not a coyote, and not a wolf (not shaped right). It moved too quickly, and absolutely silently. We live in a subdivision with a wide green space around it, attaching back to a river/swamps and a half-million acres. Elephants could move around in there and no one would know."

I think this is a very solid sighting, with a trained military observer and hunter witness who has a close, daylight view of the animal. This creature differs a bit from other possible dire dog sightings in that it sounds less bulky than most, but its estimated eight-foot body length still describes something "honking big."

UNKNOWN IN UTAH

A Utah man named Grant Tuft wrote me in 2012 about an un-identified canine he encountered in Utah in 2003:

I heard you on the *Ground Zero* radio program tonight, and from what others have described I may have seen one of these wolfman creatures. I have only told my wife what I saw because I didn't know if anyone would believe me. Here's my experience: In 2003 I was attending college at Southern Utah University in Cedar City, Utah. I was majoring in physical education and special education. I was working on becoming a teacher and a football coach. I had the opportunity to coach football at a local high school while I was going to school. The school I was coaching at was Enterprise High School in Enterprise, Utah, about forty-five miles from where I was living.

Enterprise is a small, very rural town. We had played an away game on a Friday night in mid-October. The team didn't get back to the school until about 1 am and I still had to make the forty-five mile trip back to Cedar City. The road that connects the two towns is just like one would expect a rural country road to be: no lights, no houses, and no businesses. It's beautiful in the day but can be spooky at night, and when you're the only car out on the road, it doesn't help. There are a lot of deer in the area and also a herd of wild horses.

I was about halfway home that night, not speeding because I didn't want to hit a deer and the road was very winding. I had my brights on and up ahead on the left side of the road, I could see something walking just off the shoulder of the road. I slowed in case whatever it was ran across the open road. At first I thought it was a big dog, but as I got closer I knew there was no way it could be. It was huge. I don't really know what to compare it to in size. I guess a bear would be a good comparison. If it stood upright it would have been easily over six feet tall. I know it wasn't a bear because it didn't look like a bear or walk like a bear. It walked like a dog.

As I was getting closer I was thinking, why is a dog in the middle of nowhere? My interest was piqued so I slowed more to get a look at this huge dog. It had thick black or brown fur. Not thick like a bear's but more like a golden retriever kind of shaggy. Its head was huge. Not like any dog or wolf I had seen but you could tell it resembled a canine. As I was almost up to it, it turned and looked my direction and that scared me. My skin crawled and my hair stood up. Its eyes were red! Like a stoplight. As I passed I was looking at it and it looked directly in my eyes. At that point I hit the gas and sped away from it as fast as I could.

I don't know what it was, but I know it wasn't a dog, a bear, or a wolf. I can see it in my mind's eye to this day, and the eyes still give me goose bumps.

Well. If there were ever a sighting description that sounds like a dire dog, this would be it—huge head, thick fur, size of a bear. And with its red eyes, dark coat, and bold, purposeful stare, it invokes yet another reminder of phantom dogs of England.

UNCANNY IN KANSAS

A report from west of the Mississippi revealed a slightly different-looking quadruped than we've seen here before, one with a possibly different origin that relates to a familiar legend. The eyewitness, who requested anonymity, sent me an email in 2015 that read:

Hi Linda! I talked to you on Art Bell's show for a moment . . . I'd like to share [my story] with you for your research as long as I can remain anonymous because the Skinwalker legend really freaks me out! I saw something I can't explain ten years ago [2005] in northwestern Kansas. I thought you might be interested just because I don't think the area is usually associated with this kind of activity.

I was driving about seventy miles per hour on I-70 after dark near Ellis, Kansas, and something very large ran in front of my car. It was running very fast, a full-on gallop, really, maybe about forty miles per hour and passed right in front of me so I got a very good look. It was simply too big to be even a huge dog, something like eight feet long, and was gray/white and had thin fur on its body. I didn't see its feet but the overall impression was that it had dog or wolf paws.

There was no snout like I've heard others describe, but the face was more flat and did not look right. It looked like an exposed skull, no fur, and I could see lots of giant teeth but no eyes. It reminded me of something out of H. R. Giger's art. [The late Giger was a Swiss artist well known for his paintings of biomechanical-looking fantasy creatures.] The way it ran did not seem bipedal like a running human. It ran like a big, powerful animal and was covering large amounts of ground with each stride. It was the most uncanny thing I've ever seen, and I did not even consider stopping or turning around for another look even though I'm usually the brave and curious sort. I was all alone in basically the middle of nowhere with no other cars anywhere and I did not want to tempt fate!

I feel I may have seen a Skinwalker. It definitely felt like a bad omen. The only rational explanation I can possibly think of is it could have been an Irish wolfhound, bigger than anything I have ever seen, that had been hit by a car. But the speed it was moving just seems impossible for a dog, let alone an injured one. I have

heard about the Skinwalker from a family member who has very
unique connections to the Navajo, so I definitely believe in the
power of Navajo beliefs. One interesting tidbit you may already
know: He told me the reason Native Americans are so reluctant to
speak about the Skinwalkers is they believe if you bring the subject up, you may be one of them!

I can understand the reluctance of this witness to have his
name known. Over the years, I've noticed that huge and/or bipedal canines spotted near Native land areas do seem to be something apart from what most unknown canine witnesses describe.
They are usually much larger, more muscular, and more humanlike in form. They may have red rather than yellow-green eyeshine, and often bring a deep feeling of dread to those who see
them. I think I will just let this witness's assessment of the creature stand.

NEBRASKA NEMESIS

It's striking how many sightings of these very large, "dog but not
a dog" creatures occur along roadways. This Nebraska sighting
incorporates an extra feature—what appears to be interference
with the automobile's electronics system. The driver wrote to me
in September 2014 about an incident that occurred about twenty-
five miles west of Omaha:

> I was reading American Monsters and I thought you might be in-
> terested in my weird encounter in late summer or early fall of
> 1996. I was driving home from working second shift at a food

plant in Columbus, Nebraska. It was around 12:30 or 1 a.m. I was driving a Buick Skyhawk wagon, a very reliable car that gave me zero problems until my wife of that time hit a tree two years after this event. As I began to drive up out of the Platte River Valley five miles north of my hometown of David City, the car shut off as I was doing at least sixty miles per hour.

My response was a normal WTF utterance when the [engine and the] headlights, which had also shut off when the engine quit, came back on and I was startled to see a huge, doglike animal running in front of me, looking back over its right shoulder, tongue hanging from its huge mouth. I hit the brakes and looked at the speedometer because I was expecting to hit this horse-sized dog, but it was staying fifty to sixty feet ahead, loping along at forty-five miles per hour by my speedometer. It was russet in color, had pointed upright ears like a shepherd, and darker fur at the massive, bushy tail's tip.

As I coasted behind it, it pulled away, looked over its left shoulder, and veered into the oncoming side of the road. At this time, my headlights went out [again] much like a switch was thrown, coming back on in a couple seconds, accompanied by my car's engine restarting and immediately racing since I, in my freaked out state of mind, had the pedal fire-walled. The horse-sized dog was nowhere to be seen, and since only open pastures lined the road I would have expected it to still be visible.

I made the last five miles home in record time and I did not sleep well that night. I have never seen anything like this before or since. One more thing: during the minute-long encounter, I had the strangest feeling it was looking at me, not just at a car behind it. But when I mentioned earlier I was freaked out, it was because I thought the car had suddenly crapped out in the middle of the night. I felt no fear while watching this huge animal loping along in front of me. I was unsettled afterwards, but never felt threatened during or [right] after the encounter.

Situations where an automobile's electrical system suddenly fails as it approaches some kind of anomalous entity or light are more often linked to phantoms, gray extraterrestrials, UFOs, and the like than they are to unknown upright canines or huge quadrupeds. But the car's electrical sputtering hardly seems coincidental in this case, given the facts of the animal's intense behavior, its extreme size, and the observer's *strange feeling* that the creature had looked back to focus upon *him* rather than to gauge the danger of a vehicle coming right at it. Astute readers may have noticed similar thoughts among other witness comments mentioned here. I wonder whether a "strange feeling" was the last thing experienced by those hapless campers in the Nahanni Valley before their heads were liberated from their bodies.

OHIO'S SACRA VIA DIRE DOG

Marietta, Ohio, is home not only to the Washington County Fairgrounds but to the remains of a massive walled city built around 200 BCE to CE 500 by the Hopewell culture. Now called the Sacra Via ("Sacred Way") Park, it is situated where the Ohio and Muskingum rivers converge, and its earthworks and other features included a huge burial mound and a flat-topped pyramid. It is also now the site of a large burial ground dating from the Revolutionary War.

The woman who sent this report in about her sighting in this highly sacred area said it happened in late May or early June 2012 as she and her then-boyfriend drove home from the Washington County Fairgrounds. She boarded her horse at the grounds, she explained, and was often there late to take care of it. The time was about 10 p.m., she said, and they were traveling past the Sacra Via Park, heading southeast when he suddenly hit the brakes and asked, "Did you see that?" 'See what?' I asked. He was obviously shaken. I will also mention he was not a believer in the paranormal, weird happenings, and such. Very much a skeptic. Neither of us are what you would call easily flustered or spooked. I hold a bachelor of science degree in psychology. My boyfriend at the time was a manager at a heating supply company."

The couple pulled over to discuss what had just happened, as her boyfriend, a hunting enthusiast, described seeing an unrecognizable, deer-sized animal with a canine head and face. He said the color was also similar to that of a deer, and it moved extremely fast. He wanted to leave immediately, but she insisted on circling around the area in case it might still lurk nearby. Visibility from surrounding streetlights was good, and she noted that neither of them consumed alcohol nor were they using any type of medicinal or recreational drugs. Her boyfriend refused to discuss it from that point on, and if he ever took her to the horse barn, he avoided Sacra Via Park as much as possible.

That's not surprising; something with the head of a dog and the size of a deer—but faster—and seen at close range could definitely shake a person's worldview. It's impossible to say whether the nearness of that ancient "sacred way" complex had anything to do with the sighting, but again, nearby holy places are one of the things that often show up in concert with weird and giant canine creatures.

MONSTROUS IN MISSOURI

Missouri is best known in the cryptid world for a Bigfoot-like creature nicknamed Momo that was first spotted, according to local legend, in 1971 in Pike County. But there are other large animals to be found in the Show Me State, as well. This one was spotted in 2013 by a school bus driver whose bus happened to be empty at the time, near Fulton in Callaway County, about halfway between St. Louis and Kansas City. A relative of the driver contacted me, and I talked to "L," the driver, by phone. She estimated it was only forty feet away from the bus.

"I saw the strangest creature I ever saw in my life," she said. "It was too big for a dog, with beautiful muscles and golden eyeshine from the setting sun." She spotted it standing on all fours not far from the road, she said, between the guardrail and some flattened grass, as she drove up a hill. She had the impression it was sunning itself, and estimated its weight as up to two hundred pounds. "It was the size of a Shetland pony," she said, and was covered with gray and black short fur. "The face was what got me," she said. "It looked super intelligent."

She continued, "Its ears were short, pointed and on the side of the head. Its face was a cross between animal and human, with a nose that was a cross between a pig and a Doberman, with a snout that was long but snub-nosed. Its legs were muscular but thick, like a gorilla's with a big thick chest and a tapered waist. Its face was scary-looking, all gray. Its hindquarters were a darker gray. It stood sideways to me so I had a full shot of his side and head as I passed. I've had an Irish wolfhound, and this was bigger. It was not a dog, wolf, or bear. I look every day now."

L's cousin, who first wrote me about L's experience, added, "She was even using phrases that other witnesses use, like, 'At first I thought it was a dog but no . . . it was way too huge to be a dog,' and 'it was put together funny, not built right for a dog—enormous or otherwise' . . . things like that. She even said the eyes scared her [how many times have I read that?] and to quote her exactly, 'This thing looked like it was smarter than I was.' L is my cousin . . . she does not drink or take drugs. She's [at time of writing] sixty-four years old and I've never known her to lie or tell crazy stories in all those years. If that's what she said she saw, she saw it."

Both women asked me to keep them anonymous, but they felt the creature should be known to the world. Any unidentifiable canine the size of a Shetland pony is surely worth remarking upon, and I ask readers to take note of yet another example of those strangely compelling eyes.

EERIE BY LAKE ERIE

A Pennsylvania woman wrote me in 2016 about a sighting she had in 2012 in the far northwestern corner of her state, not far from Lake Erie. I've often noticed the Great Lakes seem to be something of a weird creature attractor, and perhaps a wild animal corridor as well. This particular sighting included *five* witnesses. The one who wrote said:

> Back in May of 2012 I was a senior in high school in my area of Pennsylvania. It was senior skip day and my class decided to go to Lake Erie for the day. We piled into cars and drove up, spent the

day there, then headed back home. On the way back my car got a little lost but we got ourselves on the right road again. There were five of us in the car, two guys, three girls. I was in the front passenger seat. We were on Route 18, which is a highway that leads through neighboring towns.

It was dark, we were on an area of the highway that was surrounded by field and forest on either side, no houses in sight, around 10:15 p.m. We were laughing and going over last-minute homework when something huge ran in front of the car. My friend braked hard so we wouldn't hit whatever it was. It was on four legs and had matted, dark colored fur and a tail. No one saw the head to know what it looked like because it happened so fast, but let me just say, we grew up here our whole lives and we have bears, coyotes, but no wolves. It was too big to be a dog, didn't look like a horse, and we knew it wasn't a bear. We all asked each other if they saw the same thing and everyone agreed they did. No one wanted to believe it was really there so my friend booked it back to our school since we were all scared. The rest of the way back to our school parking lot, no one said a word until one of my other friends in the car said, "What we saw tonight—tell no one; they'd think we're crazy if we did. We know what we saw but let's never speak of this again."

That night we all agreed to never speak of it and I haven't until now. I don't know what we saw that night four years ago, but since then, if I'm on any back roads at night with friends, I always keep a lookout for what? I don't know.

I asked the woman a few questions, such as the exact location, but didn't hear back from her. However, a few moments of research told me this occurred in the far northwestern corner of

Pennsylvania. Route 18 runs mostly north–south about fifteen miles east of the state line with Ohio and, as she said, on up to Lake Erie. It is not a big wilderness area, but there are plenty of lakes, rivers, and wildlife areas to serve as habitat. That is all the more likely since bears were known to be in the area.

It would have been better if the head—which usually tells the tale—had been visible, but the fact that the group agreed to keep the encounter to themselves makes me believe they really did see something on four feet, and that they were very lucky the car was able to brake in time.

NEW YORK DIRE DOG OF THE CORN

Judging from what many who send me reports say, it seems that a higher proportion of dire dog witnesses prefer to remain anonymous than those of any other cryptid I've studied. I believe it's because these creatures are much less well known, making witnesses more fearful than usual to tell people what they saw. Here is a typically reticent gentleman, and as always, I completely understand! He wrote:

Firstly, I apologize for using a pseudonym, and because I am concerned with privacy. This is the first time I've been on your site, and incidentally, [you are] the first person with whom we've shared an account of our experience. We were traveling through the western New York region (near Medina area) at around ten p.m. about two years ago [2012]. We were taking the country roads as opposed to the thruway, and decided (stupidly) to stop alongside one of the many farm fields dotting the rural countryside. [Note: Medina is in the western corner of New York and, as in the previous event, also lies close to Lake Erie.] I was curious to get a look at a variety of corn my girlfriend told me about. Apparently some farmers grow a type of corn solely intended for animal consumption (it hasn't been approved for humans) and it's un-sweet with large, tough kernels. It was late summer and the weather was nice, so "why not" was my thinking.

I approached the peripheral edge of the field by a section where the drainage ditch wasn't too steep. My girlfriend remained by the car on the other side of the narrow road, which was bordered on both sides by the cornfield it intersected. It must have been a clear night because the field and its rolling contours were easily visible. What we saw next is difficult for me to express; difficult because I find myself in a sort of tug of war between what I saw and how I see the world. What I saw doesn't fit into my general worldview.

My girlfriend says she first saw it leap across the road, and I saw it running at a frightening rate of speed across the barren section of the fields. It seemed to be covering absurdly long distances in mere seconds. And it was large. To me, it looked like a hairless wolf on steroids with an enormous (almost horse-like head). It made absolutely no sounds that I heard, and as it traversed the field, it barely seemed to touch the ground. Its four legs looked parallel to the ground when stretched at full-stride. I was so taken with what my eyes were seeing (like not knowing at what I was looking and in that moment thinking, "That can't be real. I'm misinterpreting what I'm seeing"). It was hypnotic. My girlfriend claims she was screaming for me to get in the car, while I continued to watch the thing run, beginning to realize that if I'm judging its speed correctly, it could change directions and be upon us in several seconds. My girlfriend says that only after she said my whole name sternly did I acknowledge her and rush to the car.

I still don't know what we saw. Since I'm not given to supernatural explanations, I've wondered if it was possibly a wolf-type dog (perhaps a hybrid) that I hear farmers use to guard their fields. My girlfriend insists it was no dog or even wolf—its size and speed completely preclude that possibility in her opinion. It never snarled at us, but being that I was so utterly transfixed by it, my girlfriend maintains that I was oblivious to the danger we were in (she actually said a prayer after discussing the event).

I am reluctant to offer guesses of its dimensions. I scrutinized it from a distance while it trekked across a barren section of land so it is difficult to get a sense of scale . . . maybe seven to nine feet (?), I'm really not sure, but it was the largest "dog" I've ever seen. Its snout was too pointy to belong to a Great Dane, so I'm at a loss.

I've considered calling a commercial farm from there and simply asking if they use large dogs to patrol their fields, or if they've heard of that practice being employed by any other farms in the area. Honestly, it seems unlikely just because of the potential for lawsuits if it attacked a stranded motorist, and the lack of any predators in the area—who would steal some stalks of corn meant for animal feed? But who knows?

Who knows, indeed? This dire dog account concludes the sampling I can fit in this book, but I think it's enough to show there really do seem to be sufficient reports of these quadrupedal canines the size of a small pony with forceful gazes and no apparent fear of humans that they deserve their own category. The term

dire dog, I'd like to emphasize, is simply my name for these creatures and in no way means I believe they must be related to the
extinct dire wolf. Most descriptions make them seem larger than
were the dire wolves, and closer to the much longer extinct Amphicyon (bear dog) in body and head size (190 pounds, up to eight
feet body length). At any rate, there do seem to be a fair number
of these muscle-bound dashers in different parts of the country
and I'm sure they don't care at all what we call them.

CHAPTER 10

Black Mystery Cats and Inconvenient Mountain Lions

MOVING ON TO A DIFFERENT ANIMAL ENTIRELY—not only are there huge mystery canines running around the Americas, but there are great mystery cats as well, and some of them are hard to categorize (no pun intended). Researcher Loren Coleman says that large mystery cats with manes—normally only seen on African lions—have been spotted around North America in modern times. One showed up in in western New Brunswick, Canada, on March 1, 1941, said Coleman in his *Mysterious America*. Described as a grayed, yellow-red color, it sat calmly on a logging trail as a team of horses approached. Coleman wrote, "Its 'length of hair was such as to make the neck appear to be thicker than the head.'"[1] Two families fishing by a waterfall near Elkhorn Falls, Indiana, on August 5, 1948, saw another maned lion right there in America's heartland. Other sightings ensued in that area for years, as documented by Coleman and other sources. Sustained sightings always suggest a breeding population which would require a number of lions, and that seems unlikely according to most government wildlife officials. Others have suggested that maned great cats in the Americas are mutations or lingering remnants of a long-extinct American lion that did sport a full-fledged mane. But the most puzzling trait of some mountain lions is their color.

COUGARS: THE IMPOSSIBLE AND THE LEGENDARY

Mountain lions are the largest cats of the Western Hemisphere, and they once ranged freely from Canada to South America as top predators. They still inhabit a huge area within North and South America, but industrialization and human population growth have eaten sharply at their numbers since the early 1900s. The decimation has been partly redressed by protective laws, and the elusive felines known as cougars, panthers, and pumas, are coming back. Eyewitness reports are on the rise all over the US, some even describing highly controversial black-furred big cats. But many government agencies seem loath to admit the success of their carnivore conservation programs, assuring many credible cougar eyewitnesses—especially in areas where the animals have long been declared extinct—that they are mistaken.

I personally know of people who have seen both tan and black great cats on their own properties in Wisconsin, only to be told by wildlife officials that, no, they did not see any such things—especially the black ones—because these animals are not officially recognized as living in the area. That irritates the eyewitnesses, to say the least. We'll talk much more about the black "panthers" shortly. But first, we must touch upon some background lore to gain a footing in this wild world of fearsome felines.

ARIZONA *CHINDI* AND THE CORONADO CAT

We know that mountain lions and lynx have stalked this continent for millennia, showing up in Native American legends right along with other catlike beings. An Associated Press article dated February 9, 1941, in Racine, Wisconsin's *Journal-Times Sunday Bulletin* reported a truly weird specimen of the unknown, catlike variety, allegedly spotted by several groups of people near the Little Colorado River east of Winslow.

The first witnesses were a pair of white hunters who saw the creature in late summer or early fall 1940. Their sighting was followed by that of two young Navajo men and then an eighty-four-year-old Navajo elder named Hosteen Nez. Every witness described the beast as a sort of dog-cat. They all agreed the creature's movements were catlike, and that its dark coat was patched with white in the manner of a domesticated cat. The ears were catlike, they said, but the animal was the size of a medium-weight dog and its tail was short. The article noted that Nez declared, "it must be a 'Chindi,' evil spirit of someone who died by violence."[2]

There is also at least one phantom mountain lion legend in Arizona, noted briefly in *Phantom Felines and Other Ghostly Animals* by Gerina Dunwich. The legend says this creature stalks travelers who leave the main road after sunset in Coronado National Forest east of Tucson. The story notes, "Its presence has been described as 'heavy' and 'negative,' and persons who have witnessed this apparition while hiking or jogging through the area have said it appears to be angry."[3] This area would be a couple of hundred miles south of the *Chindi* sightings near Winslow. Might the Coronado Cat be another example of a *Chindi*?

Legends about the *Chindi* are usually ascribed to Navajo traditions, which define them as a malevolent type of ghost composed of everything negative that had been contained in its original human form—from bad habits to evil thoughts and criminal acts. That's why the Navajo usually recommend people avoid encounters with it at all costs. Also, the *Chindi* may appear in any number of guises that are not at all catlike, ranging from a butterfly to a wild pig.

Prolific author on paranormal topics Brad Steiger tackled the *Chindi* in his book *Shadow World* as he related the experience of two men who had been hunting in an unnamed southwestern state. One of the men was a longtime landowner in that region and had learned a lot about Navajo legends. As he explained it in Brad's book, "Some say that the thing that watches over this patch of ground is a *Chindi*, a kind of guardian spirit that can shapeshift into any form it wishes to punish those who would violate the wildlife of this land. Not only can it assume any form, the *Chindi* can inhabit any living thing in its path of retribution."[4]

Please note that according to Steiger's description, the *Chindi* could not only assume any form—presumably including a panther of any color—but could even dwell *inside* any living thing. All of this seems to be an active and presently practiced Navajo belief as well as ancient legend. While the *Chindi*'s ability to shape-shift also seems related to Navajo Skinwalkers, it's different in that, unlike the Skinwalker, a *Chindi*'s main causative agent is not a human manifesting through occult practices, but an unknown spirit entity. I would probably tread lightly, then, in applying the term to just any old strange animal. But the *Chindi* is a good example of Native American tradition that supports the longtime, local existence of large, catlike animals. Just for comparison's sake, it is also somewhat similar to an Australian tradition that probably has little direct association with contemporary black or tan "panther" sightings but illustrates another concept of a feline spirit entity known as the evil spirit cat.

EVIL SPIRIT CATS

In all of these old traditions of "conjured" animals, the shaman works with or battles an unknown or nature-related spirit force that shows itself as a powerful animal—such as a great cat. Australia may lie far from the US, but the principle is quite universal. This example comes from the Aborigine people known as the Aruntas (among other spellings) as described in Ernesto de Martino's *Primitive Magic: The Psychic Powers of Shamans and Sorcerers*. The paragraph from de Martino's book that caught my eye read, "When a bad wind rises up from the west, the witch-doctors gather in a circle and watch the wind approaching. If they see evil elements in it, the ones that have the form of large cats and are called '*erintja ngaia*,' they begin throwing *ngankara* stones at them, afterward battering them to pieces with their sticks. Then they show the dead *erintja* only to their colleagues."[5]

In this case, the large, evil spirit cats thought by the shamans to inhabit windstorms are perceived as a dark side of nature to be neutralized before they can do any harm. And then the dead great cats are kept hidden from the people, perhaps as another means of protecting humanity.

Researchers and investigators of unknown animals often lump all these spirit-like mystery "cats" in with obviously paranormal animals such as phantom black hounds, since they share characteristics such as black fur, glowing red eyes, great size, and a habit of lurking in graveyards. A question I'm frequently asked is whether human rituals designed to raise or bring forth supernatural forms might be the true cause of such sightings. *Raising* is the usual term for bringing something from another realm or world into this one, and this belief is present in most shamanic, tribal religions around the world, anywhere unexplained creatures are found. Theoretically, this could account for some sightings but seems unlikely to be able to account for all reports of anomalous or out-of-place animals. But there are other possibilities that lie closer to modern legend than to ancient religious practice.

WILY WAMPUS

A feline-related creature known as the Wampus Cat may be seen as a widespread, traveling Native American urban legend best known in the southern US east of the Mississippi. As I noted in my book *American Monsters*, the name has also been co-opted as an alternative for *Bigfoot* in some places, but is most often understood to resemble some type of large mystery cat or cat-human hybrid. And its legend is usually told in a version similar to a Cherokee tale that began with a curious human, as many legends do.

As the general story goes, the men of one Cherokee tribe held medicine circle meetings with no females allowed. An inquisitive woman hid near their circle one night and was found out. Her punishment was to be turned into a half-woman, half–great cat creature condemned to roam the forests, swamps, and bayous. I've seen different descriptions and minor plot twists for Wampus Cats elsewhere, very much like today's urban legends. As in those legends of Crybaby Bridge or the hitchhiker ghost, the fact that it's not attributed to known persons, places, or time means it is not to be placed in the same category as the contemporary sightings of natural cougars and other great cats. And as far as I know, cats in modern sightings also do not display any *human* female attributes. There is one more creature, however, that we can probably call ancient myth due to its depiction in rock paintings and artifacts. It is also a bit more specific to the particular sightings flap we'll be examining here.

PATHS OF THE WATER PANTHER

Probably the best-known feline-like, legendary creature found in Native American lore and tradition is the water panther, or Mishipeshu. Spellings of that name vary so widely that I'm going to use the simpler term *water panther* when I can. The traditional being is known from Canada throughout much of the northern half of the US, and probably beyond. According to Native-Languages.org, the water panther is also known as the Great Lynx, Water Lynx, Night Panther, Matchi-Manitou, Underground Panther, and Underneath Panther.[6]

The author's rendition of Mishipeshu,
the North American water panther

Samples of shapes of ancient animal effigy mounds as found in
southern Wisconsin, depicted by the author

The same site describes the creature in detail: "The Water Panther (or Water Lynx) is a powerful mythological creature something like a cross between a cougar and a dragon. Water Panther is a dangerous monster that lives in deep water and causes men and women to drown. The legends of some tribes describe Water Panther as the size of a real lynx or mountain lion, while in others, the beast is enormous. Water Panther has a very long prehensile tail which is often said to be made of copper. Details of the monster vary from community to community, but in many stories, Water Panthers are described as furry, with horns or deer antlers, and a sharp, saw-toothed back."[7]

A variety of such myth-related creatures are portrayed in Wisconsin's unique, ancient effigy mounds. These are raised earthwork designs often one hundred to two hundred feet in length and created between 500 and 1200 BCE by people of the Late Woodland era. Their meaning and purpose are now debated by anthropologists and archaeologists, but those that remain are still held sacred by most Native peoples. Many depict stylized but sophisticated animal forms, and the lynx and panther both show up frequently. The panther mounds are also known as water spirit or lizard mounds (the latter probably incorrectly) due to their long tails.

These panther mounds are especially numerous in southern Wisconsin, where, as mentioned in the first chapter, Native American tradition claimed Geneva Lake had long been the site of epic battles between thunderbirds and the various water monsters that battled over sea and sky to keep the world's elements in proper balance. Historian Paul B. Jenkins published a book about the region's lake monsters, *History and Indian Remains in Lake Geneva and Lake Como, Walworth County, Wisconsin*, in 1930[8] that documented the Native American belief that the water panthers emerged into this world from underground fresh water springs.

More recently, author Patty Loew says in *Indian Nations of Wisconsin*, "There is some evidence that the tails of panther effigies often point to underground springs—entrances to the underworld, in the Ho-Chunk oral tradition."[9]

Three miles south of the city of Baraboo, Wisconsin, lies the beautiful Devil's Lake, surrounded by Wisconsin's largest state park. The lake was once ringed by a variety of effigy mounds, which over the years have been mostly plowed over for farming with a handful remaining off the lake's north shore. These include panther and bear mounds and an eighty-two-foot-long effigy known as the lynx mound. There are also some unique human-shaped mounds in nearby Man Mound State Park, with some wearing buffalo-shaped horns that may indicate depictions of shamans since buffalo headdresses are still used in ceremonial activities.

These human-shaped mounds may represent a widespread Native American legend of a warrior hero named Red Horn. His story is also told in a rock painting site in an Iowa County cave. According to Robert Birmingham and Leslie Eisenberg, authors of *Indian Mounds of Wisconsin*, "Among these stories are accounts of *epic giants* [emphasis mine] as well as the death and rebirth of Red Horn, himself."[10] It is true that bones of very large people, some with high, inclined foreheads and double rows of teeth, have been found in certain Wisconsin mounds, as well as in other states. But that is another story.

There were literally thousands of these mounds that in their heyday transformed the landscapes of lakeshores in southern Wisconsin. The mounds undoubtedly meant many important things to their makers and portrayed subtle beliefs about which we can only guess, but the presence of the panthers and lynx shows us that these animals were important to those who lived here before the European settlers arrived. It's also safe to assume, I think, that the Native American water panther figures were originally inspired by the cougars and lynx living in the area. But there is even more to learn about their importance.

Native-Languages.org explains that among certain northern tribes, "lynx are seen as dangerous but also powerful, and many communities considered them one of the *spirit animals* [emphasis mine] of the Midewiwin medicine society. . . . The Mohave tribe, who lived outside the natural range of the lynx but close enough to be aware of its existence, accorded great spiritual significance to lynx and believed that dreaming of a lynx would bring a man special hunting powers."[11]

I believe this explanation of Mishipeshu's spirit powers and of its status as a spirit animal, combined with its links to sacred springs, show that the water panther was not intended to describe nor explain out-of-place black cats prowling around modern barnyards. But the present-day sightings of black mystery cats along with the more usual tan cougars are as astonishing as the remains of their earthen portraits created around a millennium ago.

BLACK PANTHERS: THE DARKER SIDE OF GREAT CATS

Naturalists and zoologists consider the black great cats seen around most of the United States to be so impossible that they usually label sightings as cases of mistaken identity or products of human imagination. Of course, many witnesses also describe tan-colored cats, but great felids of both fur colors have begun to take back much of the turf lost before they became legally protected. A 2012 study published in the *Journal of Wildlife Management* bore this fact out, according to the *Milwaukee Journal Sentinel*, as it "showed 178 cougar confirmations in the Midwest and as far south as Texas between 1990 and 2008." It continued, "While confirmed sightings of Midwest cougars were sporadic before 1990, when there were only a couple, that number spiked to more than 30 by 2008, the study shows."[12] As always, only confirmed sightings were counted, and the many reports that did not include footprints, scat, or clear photos or videos were not.

But the findings were definitive. As the *Journal* paper stated in its opening abstract, "Seventy-nine percent of cougar confirmations occurred within 50 km of highly suitable habitat (i.e., forest areas with steep terrain and low road and human densities). Given the number of cougar confirmations, the increasing frequency of occurrences, and that long-distance dispersal has been documented via radio-collared individuals, our research suggests that cougars are continuing to recolonize midwestern North America."[13] Add in another decade of population increase since that study was done, and the actual numbers could be several times the stated figures.

It should come as no surprise, then, that tan (and black) panther sighting reports can easily be found in a simple online search in states such as Wisconsin, Illinois, Indiana, Pennsylvania, Ohio, Michigan, Arkansas, South Carolina, and many more. The paper cited above noted fourteen American states and Canadian provinces where sightings were confirmed by wildlife experts. There are doubtless many other locales that have not been officially confirmed and perhaps never will be.

WHEN IS A PANTHER NOT A PANTHER?

The chief problem with many sighting reports is that according to zoologists, black "panthers" are not panthers, mountain lions, catamounts, or any other members of the felines known scientifically as *Puma concolor*. They are actually dark-colored, or melanistic, jaguars (*Panthera onca*) or leopards (*Panthera pardus*), which today have a much smaller range of habitation than do mountain lions. But both are often called panthers by their many eyewitnesses.

Do these conflicting opinions on the possibility of dark-furred panthers mean the creatures must be spectral entities or visitors from another world? Does it consign them to the Land of Out-of-Place Animals, as wanderers lost from zoos or private collectors? And what about other feline misfits such as the red-eyed "lynx-dog" reported in Alberta, Southern California, and Florida? Before I am forced to dub myself queen of rhetorical questions, I'll add that, in my book *American Monsters*, I discussed reports that came to me from all three of those places, as well as New Hampshire, of what people described as hybrid dog-cats. There was also a newspaper article dating from 1824 about a brown-furred, sheep-killing creature around Trenton, New Jersey, that was said to equal a large dog in size but had a catlike head, long tail, and unidentifiable footprints. And in January 1954, a similar animal nicknamed the Beast of Bladenboro wreaked havoc on dogs and livestock in North Carolina.[14]

It didn't seem likely to me that all these strange predators should just pop up as lone mutants all around the country, especially since these incidents were only the ones I'd actually *heard* of. I believe the true extent of their range at present is unknown.

We've looked at the legends and ancient myths. Now, in hopes of teasing out the true nature of animals so reclusive that people often believe they must be either phantoms or misidentifications, it's time to look at the great multitude of reported encounters of black and tan cats in all the wrong places.

NEWFOUNDLAND BLACK PANTHER

Our neighbor to the north, Canada, has its share of black-furred, great cat sightings. And yet, its frigid pine forests are not a known habitat for jaguars or leopards, even though some subspecies such as the snow leopard can live in colder climates. A 2017 article in CBC News detailed recent reports of "black panther" sightings in Newfoundland in the town of Deer Lake on Glide Brook Road and Pynn's Brook Road, made by two women who came forward separately. They each described seeing a large black cat with "rounded ears, a muscular cat body and very long, thick, rope-like black curled tail."[15] The article mentioned other panther sightings in the previous ten years around west Newfoundland but didn't reveal the color of those animals.

As usually happens in official investigations, authorities discovered no definitive proof that the women had seen black great cats in Canada. But the article implied that area residents tended to believe the women rather than wildlife authorities. One perplexed local journalist, Gary Kean, asked the CBC News reporter, "What are they [eyewitnesses] seeing to make them go public?"[16]

BRITISH BLACK CATS

Perhaps what the women were seeing is the same thing others have glimpsed as far away as the UK, where neither cougars, jaguars, nor any other big cats are native animals, but where they have been reported consistently for years. Online British publication *This Is the Lake District* posted one such report in March 2003, of a sighting near Lancaster, England, between Cumbria and Lancashire. The story said two motorists along the M6 motorway saw the large, black feline coursing rapidly across an open field at about 3:45 in the afternoon. The reporter quoted one of the motorists' recounting of the surprising sight that met her eyes as she glanced to her right.

She said, "'I saw a big black thing and thought: That looks unusual. Then suddenly it started pounding up a hill faster than I have ever seen any animal running. It had a huge, huge stride. It was at least twice as big as a black Labrador and was very muscular. There is no way you could mistake it for a domestic animal.'"[17]

The woman, age thirty-eight, notified Terry Hooper, a field naturalist and UK police forces wildlife consultant, who at that time kept logs of such incidents. Hooper, who has also published numerous scientific papers on wildlife and history, informed the witness that someone else had also very recently spotted what sounded like the same animal while driving along that highway, and that two more sightings of a large, black great cat had occurred in nearby Kendal not long before that. He speculated the warm spring weather was drawing them from their lairs, since black, panther-like creatures had previously been seen in three other area locations, as well.

Hooper told the reporter that with so many reports reaching his desk, he felt the creatures must have been living in the area "for some considerable time"[18] in order to have achieved such a population, and stated that police did have evidence such as "sightings, photographs, plaster casts of tracks, livestock deaths where it was suspected to [be caused by] a large cat, like a puma or panther . . . and they get in touch with me."[19]

But where did these animals come from? I thought that if Terry Hooper had found any answers in the UK, perhaps they would also apply to the appearances in the US and Canada. I contacted him to find out what he had learned by keeping the registry. He told me, "We have reports of black leopards (panthers) going back many years and sightings have been seen by police officers as well as naturalists and not to mention a few very skeptical ex–game hunters from Africa."

He added that they also received many reports of tan cougars or pumas that showed up in a wide variety of locales, but noted, "With the panthers I used to get twenty to thirty reports each year that could safely be said to be accurate and true—most witnesses were within ten to fifteen feet of the cats in question. But people tend to joke about sightings still, as they never see the evidence and have no interest, either. There are people who still call cat sightings 'urban legends.'"

Hooper officially retired as a police consultant in 2007, but he still pays attention to reports. He said, "Sightings tend to be constant, but the problem is people have only [three] options when it comes to reporting what they saw: police, newspapers or one of the very fringe groups out there. Most think the police will laugh (they do take it seriously—'ABC' appears in some police call record books and does not stand for 'Alien Big Cat' but 'Another

Bloody Cat!'). In some areas they get a lot of reports and issue standard advice based on what I sent out many years back. I used to be answering the phone from eight a.m. until 10:45 p.m. or later, and eating hot meals or drinking hot coffee was a rarity!"

Hooper does have a strong hunch as to where the alleged population of black-furred, non-native cats in the UK may have originated. He said, "There have been suggestions that the cats are either offspring of cats released before licensing came in with the 1976 Dangerous Wild Animals Act (DWAA), illegal pets or even escapees from one of the old circuses. There have been a few people who came forward to confess to dumping cats in the 1970s—not facing prosecution because it was so long ago. Legal exotic pets were bought and sold with no legislation up until 1976, so you have hundreds of years of private zoos and even people keeping large cats (even tigers) as pets in their houses. No one really knows WHAT was kept as a pet or when until they find a reference from the period."

COUGARS OF THE MIDWESTERN US HILLS

There are many other possible origins for these cats, of course, but Hooper's explanation makes sense for at least some of the encounters, and can probably be applied to some in the Americas, as well. One American sighting occurred on February 27, 2003, and hit the papers in early March—the same month and year the two black great cats were reported on the M6 motorway in the UK. The US sighting took place north of St. Paul, Minnesota, at Forest Lake, near the Wisconsin border, and was just the latest in a string of great cat spottings, according to an article in the *Forest*

Lake Times. The article began, "The legacy of the large and ever elusive black cat continues to grow as there has been another sighting of what is believed to be a black panther."[20]

This time, according to the newspaper, the creature was not running along a highway or at a safe distance in some field. It sat in the backyard of a home as local authorities witnessed it. Police called to the scene confirmed that the animal did indeed look like a black panther with its dark fur and trademark sinuous tail. The creature then evidently slunk off, as there was no description of a chase. The article noted there had been several other area sightings over the past few years, mostly during winter months. No humans were attacked in any of the encounters.

There have been plenty of other black-furred panther flaps in the United States. Michigan is one of the best-known states for reports of black mystery cats.

Residents in the southern part of the Wolverine State reported large, black "panthers" near Muskegon in early October 1990 in two separate incidents. According to the October 4, 1990, *Saginaw News,*[21] one witness, Patty Richmond, was able to get a two-minute video in bright sunlight. The other Muskegon sighting was made by seven children playing in their backyard in early evening. A similar creature had also shown up earlier that year in mid-February near Camden, where the Kenneth Vincent family was able to make a short video of it. Two conservation officials who viewed the video agreed it was "undoubtedly a panther."[22]

Michiganders were probably still a bit nervous from a 1986 incident in Oakland County in rural Milford where many residents believed a "black panther" killed a palomino quarter horse. The *Detroit News* noted, "Sightings of an elusive panther have been reported since 1984 in southeastern Michigan. Two years ago, officers from the U.S. Fish and Wildlife Service confirmed that a panther was on the loose. It was never captured."[23] The paper also noted that the first 1984 sighting occurred in Manchester, about fifty miles away, with additional reports from Coloma, Grand Rapids, and cities in between. Other major clusters of sightings occurred in the mid-1990s, the early 2000s, and continue to the present.

CHAPTER 11

Great Ghost Cat Nexus: Wisconsin's Baraboo River Watershed

CLUSTERS OF SIMILAR CAT SIGHTINGS have occurred in many states besides Michigan. It was hard to zoom in on any one locale to use as an example until I realized one of the best documented and most astounding in terms of sheer numbers exists in the mid–south central area of Wisconsin. This area lies almost entirely within a fifteen-to-thirty-mile radius of the small city of Hillsboro, mostly in the watershed area of the Baraboo River. It's an area familiar to me from frequent childhood visits to my grandparents, but I only recently learned of its abundant feline-osity from former Hillsboro newspaper editor and reporter Steven Stanek.

A few years ago, Stanek became familiar with my writing and began sharing news clips of cougar sightings he has investigated and published in Hillsboro area papers for over two decades. With his full and generous cooperation, we'll use the Hillsboro area as representative of the many American communities where locals

The author's rendition of a cougar-like animal

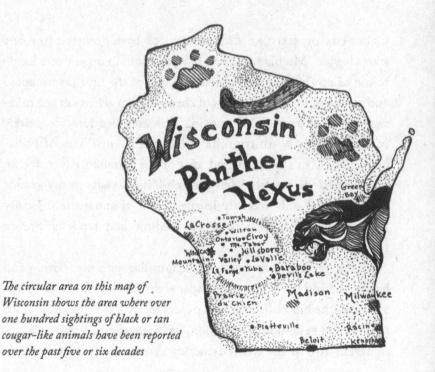

The circular area on this map of Wisconsin shows the area where over one hundred sightings of black or tan cougar-like animals have been reported over the past five or six decades

insist they have observed—and sometimes interacted with—great cats whose existence is usually deemed "impossible" by state wildlife experts. Hillsboro also serves as a great example of the maxim of many investigators of strange phenomena: where one anomalous oddity exists, there very likely will be others.

BIG CATS OF THE WISCONSIN HILLS

It might surprise even many Wisconsin residents to learn that the Dairy State's beautiful central area can be amazingly rugged with deep valleys, high ridges, and ample water supplied by the Kickapoo River. The terrain around Hillsboro, in fact, boasts every necessity for a population of puma-sized cats. Many of the sightings reports come from area farmers who encounter the cats in their fields and barnyards, suggesting the feline marauders are looking for easy domesticated pickings or fast food. It's no accident that Hillsboro lies only thirteen and a half miles from the appropriately named Wildcat Mountain State Park in Vernon County.

Even more surprising, says Stanek, is that perhaps half of the hundreds of sightings around Vernon, Sauk, Juneau, and Richland Counties are of *black*-furred, cougar-like animals, which—one more time—we must remember are not supposed to exist. The rest of the sightings mention the usual tawny buff color most people associate with mountain lions, with a few reported as dark brown or gray. The majority of eyewitnesses have not been afraid to give their names for the record, which lends great authenticity to the entire caseload.

Many of these sightings were made in the countryside closely surrounding Hillsboro, a fact that I find personally discomfiting.

Rock formation near Camp Douglas, Wisconsin,
shows typical landscape of the suggested cougar habitat,
COURTESY OF THE AUTHOR

My paternal grandmother lived in a small house in Hillsboro near the edge of town, and her yard was bordered by a park next to a cow pasture. I spent weeks there every summer as a child, my siblings and I running freely around that park from dawn to dusk, totally unaware that area residents were observing large mountain lions only a few miles away, often near livestock buildings and (gulp) cow pastures.

But I've also since learned that other strange things have visited Hillsboro. For instance, side-by-side UFOs known as Hillsboro's "flying fence posts" made area newspapers well before I was born. Bizarre UFOs may seem unrelated to slightly out-of-place, known animals, but as I mentioned above, many other researchers have noticed and explored this connection between UFO sightings and any type of strangeness at all. Here, then, are the eyewitness stories of an amazing but little-known UFO sighting—along with a few other odd phenomena—that help confirm Hillsboro as a true locus of mystery as they also set the scene for "impossible" great cats.

FLYING FENCE POSTS OF HILLSBORO

It was a front-page story like no other ever seen in Hillsboro. The headline in the February 26, 1948, edition of the *Hillsboro Sentry-Enterprise* read, "Flying 'Fence Posts' Seen Near Hillsboro."[1] At about 11:30 a.m. that undoubtedly chilly morning, two unrelated men at separate locations just northwest of the city heard a mechanical roaring in the sky. The town was not on any regular air route, so the sound surprised them. Both men peered overhead and saw something that looked very different from other aircraft of the time: two white, horizontal objects that resembled giant white fence posts roaring through the air in precise alignment. Farmer Sidney Shear told the paper, "Each was a long tapering cylinder with a slightly bulbous head and a fan tail of light colored gas or mist."[2] Shear's wife also witnessed the objects, which soon began to behave even more weirdly.

The paper said, "While they watched the 'fence posts' sail through the sky, the objects appeared to slacken in speed somewhat and to turn on end so they stood vertically. At that stage, the 'fence posts' appeared to be floating in the air rather than speeding like a rocket or torpedo."[3] The strange craft then continued to move away toward the northwest at a slower speed, still in tandem, still upright, until they were out of sight. Shear estimated the length of the objects at eight feet, but I think that number may have been a typo, since he also said they were "immense" and at "a great height in the sky."[4] It's very difficult to gauge height from the ground, but something that looked immense at a great height would likely be more than eight feet tall. Perhaps he meant eighty? At any rate, he decided to tell the newspaper about it in hopes of discovering other eyewitnesses.

He drove to town and had just described the event to the news staff when his neighbor, Joe Benish, also walked in and declared he was there for the same purpose. The two men excitedly compared descriptions of the objects and their positions, which appeared to be traveling halfway between the two farms, a mile southwest of Shear's property and a mile and a half northwest of the Benish acreage. Benish's eleven-year-old son also saw the craft, so with his father and the Shears, at least four people shared this daylight sighting. There may have been more. The final paragraph seems to affirm this was true, adding that others had also seen the objects and that there was much discussion around town as to what they might have been.

On one of my investigative visits to Hillsboro, Don Benish, now eighty-nine, told me he remembered the sight as if it were yesterday, and pointed out the rolling, wooded valley over which the strange crafts had flown. He had never even heard of UFOs at the time, he said, but he knew it was an amazing event and felt lucky to have seen it.

A VERTICAL CIGAR

Reports of airborne objects often describe shapes aligned horizontally in the sky, which is how the fence posts were first positioned when observed by the two farmers. But when the two long objects slowed down, the article says they "turned on end" and looked as if they were floating vertically as they slowly moved on. Reports of tall, vertical shapes are scarce in UFO lore, but they do exist. A central Wisconsin woman sent a report of something quite similar to the fence posts in February 2017, in fact. Several observers saw a "huge cigar-shaped UFO hanging vertically in the sky" a few miles from Neillsville, Wisconsin, which is less than ninety miles north of Hillsboro. The color of the object was black, and it was large enough that the eyewitnesses, a husband and wife whose names are withheld, thought a friend several miles away should have been able to see it, too. She couldn't, but she did let me know about it.

The Neillsville objects seemed to have been fairly stationary, while the Hillsboro objects were moving. My first thought about the Hillsboro objects was: What possible destination lay to the west of those farms? The easy answer: Wildcat Mountain State Park, with miles of rural hills and valleys between. The park's name conjures visions of mountain lions ranging over some lofty peak, but the truth is a bit less impressive. The 3,643-acre park was named for an incident in the 1800s in which a bobcat (an animal much smaller than a cougar) was killed by a posse of farmers who suspected it was preying on their livestock. The area became known as Bobcat or Wildcat Hill, a title later upgraded to Wildcat Mountain. Ironically, the park and its environs seem to be home to an even wilder variety of cat nowadays, as we shall soon see. But first, a bit more Hillsboro sky weirdness.

THE HILLSBORO AIR DISASTERS

The 1948 Flying Fence Posts spectacle occurred about the same time the cluster of mountain lion sightings began to gain local attention, and only two years previous to another unexpected mystery: the beginning of a fourteen-year string of air disasters over the townships near Hillsboro. Again, Stanek provided much of the following information in a detailed article about the accidents.

These tragic events began with the deadly crash of a Wisconsin National Guard jet witnessed by Sheriff's Deputy Otto Jefson on March 25, 1950. The plane piloted by First Lieutenant Raymond Beaumont dove into a forested valley and exploded into small pieces, for reasons never publically explained.

The next, even more shocking, crash occurred during a thunderstorm on September 14, 1958, taking the lives of four people from River Falls, Wisconsin, and leaving the demolished plane "rolled up like a ball." The Piper Tri-Pacer aircraft was thought by some to have run out of fuel while searching for a place to land in the storm.

Then, on September 9, 1963, a crash that killed the mayor of Streator, Illinois, and two others occurred when their small aircraft fell out of a heavy rainstorm to the ground about five miles south of Hillsboro, upping the area's ongoing death toll to eight. The plane was said to have hit a vertical air squall, causing turbulence like that of a small tornado. The craft then dropped like a rock, straight down on the farm of Raymond Nemec. About half a year later, another plane went down only a mile and a half from the Nemec farm in an equally mysterious manner.

On March 26, 1964, a National Guard F-89 Scorpion jet fighter slammed into a field on the Rudolf Penshorn farm near Wonewoc, missing the barn by fifteen feet while the farm's owner slept through the entire crash. Luckily the two pilots were able to eject and land safely. Penshorn family members said that there was a military cordon around the crash area for two weeks, and that they understood technicians were searching the wreck for possible devices similar to dynamite caps that may have triggered a bomb. The results of the search were unknown, although as far as the family knew, searchers never found an actual bomb.

Stanek's *Sentry-Enterprise* article about the tragic events noted the plane crashes seemed to stop after that fourth incident.[5]

Could there have been any connection between the crashes and the Flying Fence Posts? The Flying Fence Post crafts did not crash and were not identifiable like the ill-fated planes, but their flight path was unusual. To recap, they slowed down, changed from horizontal to vertical positions, and finally headed upright at diminished speed for the Wildcat Mountain area. Did they detect something unusual in the geology or atmosphere of the area that affected local air traffic for years? Perhaps, but the only real association to the planes is that they were aerial.

But the weird nature of the huge, fence post–shaped objects traveling in the sky, the fourteen years of air disasters that included two military craft wreaking havoc over one small community, and then the appearance of animals said not to exist in that geographical area (great cats sporting black fur)—*feels* mythic, even if it isn't.

THE STRANGE RANGE

It may be mere coincidence that this entire area lies just west of one of the most unique geological features in the world, the Baraboo Range. The range, whose westerly edge touches the tiny berg of Rock Springs only about thirty miles from Hillsboro, is made of some of the earth's oldest and most unusual rocks—pink quartzite and red rhyolite (similar to granite but with finer crystals) that are estimated by geologists to be one and a half billion years old. The range measures about twenty-five miles long and up to ten miles wide. That's a lot of quartz, even with a few other minerals tossed in.

My thoughts about the Baraboo Range are those of a layman as far as the science is concerned, but I have to wonder whether such a large formation of quartz might attract or affect such things as, say, UFOs that resemble fence posts, or strange crashes of planes that have just flown over it. The reason I think a possible link isn't entirely off base is detailed in a February 2017 news release I found about a new study showing that quartz crystals are the "powerhouse" of the earth's magnetic field![6] I'm not sure how or whether that powerhouse effect also applies to the Baraboo Range, but with twenty-five miles of quartz bunched up in one massive spot, the idea that it may interact with animals, human-made electronics, and other things in its immediate surroundings seems possible to me.

More to our point, might this huge repository of quartz somehow serve to attract the large numbers of predatory felines that have been observed by hundreds of people in the surrounding area over many decades? It has long been known that birds and butterflies can navigate over great distances by using the lines of the earth's magnetic fields as guidance, tuning in via a natural ability called magnetosensation to "read" magnetic fields. Another recent study published in an academic journal—this one from a Czech Republic university—found that a deer herd menaced by a mountain lion will use magnetosensation to help them know in which direction they all should run so that they will escape in the most efficient way. The study also posits that it's likely the mountain lion shares this same trait of being able to sense and use magnetic field lines. The journal article says, "The authors feel this pioneering study points to magnetosensing being common in mammals. It might even reside in us humans!"[7]

If the quartz formation does help to somehow "power up" the earth's magnetic field in that area around Hillsboro and the Baraboo Range by even a tiny amount, perhaps both deer and mountain lions can sense it, are led to the area, and then stay because it has such abundant food, water, and shelter. I know that sounds very simplistic and perhaps a bit of a stretch, so I asked Louis Proud, author of *Strange Electromagnetic Dimensions: The Science of the Unexplainable*, what he thought of my hypothesis. He thought I might be on the right track but suggested there may be other factors at play in such a scenario: "For example, fault lines, other mineral deposits, underground streams, and so forth. With respect to the Baraboo Range, I would suggest that the area, owing to its high content of quartz and a variety of other factors, features certain unique magnetic and electrical properties that somehow combine to produce what I like to call an 'electromagnetic anomaly zone.' Perhaps the odd plane crashes in the area are partly the result of navigational problems caused by irregularities or disruptions within the magnetic field. As for the UFO sightings, it's been noted that such occurrences do seem to be concentrated around electromagnetic anomaly zones, as borne out by research concerning earth lights, earthquake lights, and other mysterious luminous phenomena of terrestrial origin."

HOME ON THE RANGE

It's true that the community's big cat population may have dwindled a bit during the time cougars were thought extinct in Wisconsin, but Steve Stanek thinks they never totally left. He also disagrees with the Wisconsin DNR's (Department of Natural Resources) website, which says, "Wild cougars probably disappeared from the state by about 1910, but reports again began to surface in the 1940s. These were probably escaped captive cougars or misidentifications."[8]

Stanek doesn't think either of those two possibilities is likely, since he knows of cougar sightings dating back to the 1930s. In an article he wrote for *Fate Magazine* in 2007, he explained that he is acquainted with members of the family of a farmer named John Rogers, now deceased, who had a cougar encounter one summer in the 1930s. The family told Stanek that Rogers had a great surprise as he directed his horses to trot beneath some tree branches along a back road near Union Center, which lies about four miles northeast of Hillsboro.

Rogers was enjoying a pleasant ride in the shade when suddenly, a large black animal he identified as a panther jumped off one of the branches and landed on the back of one of the horses. Luckily, the big cat didn't get a good grip and slid off, giving Rogers no more trouble. But Rogers did get a great look at it in broad daylight from a vantage point that the startled farmer probably felt was a bit too close for comfort.

Stanek wrote, "This story was forwarded by Rogers' grandchildren, and it would appear obvious that what he saw was neither a black lab nor a pet that someone released."[9]

Stanek's files also include at least two sightings from the 1940s. One report was made by Elgin Hooker, who said he encountered a cougar while hunting near Fox Ridge about five miles south of Hillsboro. It was tan with a white belly. The other report from the forties told of a black panther seen by the father of a Viroqua woman (name withheld). It occurred near Towerville, in a very hilly rural area about six miles west of Soldier's Grove, or thirty miles southwest of Hillsboro.

From those dates to the present, Stanek estimates, "There have been literally hundreds of sightings in the Hillsboro-Elroy-Wonewoc area of Vernon, Juneau, and Sauk Counties."[10] He also notes, "The reports of tan and black animals resembling cougars and panthers in rural southern [central] Wisconsin have been nothing if not spectacular. Not mere fleeting glimpses, but close-up observations of prolonged duration make it clear that area residents aren't being deceived by more mundane animals."[11]

BLACK PANTHER GOES FISHING

More importantly, the sightings have continued until the present. One of the most recent sightings, also one of the longest in duration, occurred on May 8, 2017, at a small pond in the Wonewoc area in daylight, when a black great cat was spotted by Cody Revels and Katie Coleman, who had planned on seeing nothing more exciting than a few flopping fish on their lines. At first glance, they took the creature watching them from across the water for a big dog, perhaps a black Labrador retriever. It withdrew, and they continued making their way around the pond, looking for the best spot to fish. They had been there for several hours, paying no attention to the occasional twigs snapping in the brush, when they saw the animal again . . . this time much closer.

Revels said, "I got a really good look at it because it was standing still. I don't know if it had been drinking out of the water or what. . . . It was about the same size as a German shepherd. It was solid black. Its coat was really shiny. Its head was big and round. The tail was real long, not like a regular cat's."[12]

He said the cat took a few seconds to notice Revels was watching him, and when it did, it let out a growling roar. He said that was when he realized it was a cougar, and the two ran for their car, certain they would otherwise be attacked. They continued to watch the animal slink around the immediate area after they jumped back into their vehicle and shot a cell phone video from about one hundred yards. They were disappointed in the results, since the surroundings made it difficult to get an exact bead on its size, but Revels noted he and Coleman had seen it up close and also heard the roar from only a short distance. The video was posted for a time on the *Juneau County Messenger* Facebook page.[13]

There have been many other sightings in recent years. In the summer of 2015, Stanek was especially impressed by a report from area resident David Widner, who provides automobile transport services for the many Amish who live in the area. He was en route to pick up a family between Hillsboro and La Farge one morning, when a large animal popped out of the woods and onto the road, disappearing into the brush on the other side. Widner barely avoided hitting it. He described it as a "big, black cat" with a "long tail."

It's striking to me that so many of the encounters have taken place at very close range without any reports of human injury. Stanek said to me in a phone conversation, "Cats have been living and dying near people all these years, so they have an understanding of us."

He also believes that the variety of fur colors around the Hillsboro hub are due to genetics rather than anything otherworldly. "Jaguars and [mountain] lions have mated," he said. "One website on black jaguars stated that jaguars once roamed most of North America. I believe matings between these cats and cougars probably took place hundreds of years ago, and the black animals seen now are descendants of those matings. Also, some tan lions share jaguar traits such as noticeably large heads." Stanek's theory would also explain the animals with intermediary shades of fur color such as brown, gray, and dark red, as well as the splotchy markings observed by some witnesses.

Lest anyone think all the puzzling phenomena around Hillsboro have been fully brought to light, here are just a few others that have cropped up over the years.

THE MYSTERY SKULL

I find it heartening that some mysteries do find resolution. The Hillsboro Mystery Skull, a fairly recent "discovery," is one of them. The artifact made news in May 2016 after an anonymous Hillsboro man discovered the huge, large-fanged animal skull on his property and did some googling to try to decide what it was.

He thought it most closely resembled a photo of a cougar skull he found online, and brought the skull to the town's newspaper office. The headline for Steve Stanek's article that soon appeared in the *Hillsboro Sentry-Enterprise* read, "Mystery Skull: Is It Proof of Lions in the Area?"[14]

A local veterinarian thought not, concluding that the skull was canine and probably came from an area farm dog. Stanek also showed it to a taxidermist, who compared it to several bear skulls in his shop and declared the skull in Stanek's possession was almost surely that of a bear. A close technical examination proved the taxidermist correct. To cement the skull's ID even more firmly, an area man confessed that he had owned the bear head and had placed it on an anthill he found in some nearby woods to allow nature to take its course in cleaning the skull.

Interestingly, in an almost parallel event in Michigan in 1966, archaeologists found a mystery skull that did turn out to be that of a cougar—at least five hundred years old! It was discovered in a burial site in Saginaw County that also held four human children's skeletal remains.[15]

THE HILLSBORO HAIRLESS THING

Finally, there was the small, hairless, frightful thing found prowling around a barn at the Ed Hora farm in mid-March 1992, when the family pet, a beagle named Andy, brought it to the farmer's attention. Andy managed to subdue the thing and drag it out of a pile of hay by its naked, nine-inch tail. About two feet long and totally lacking in fur, the creature's identity baffled Hora and his family, prompting them to send photos to a zoo for identification.

Close-ups of its anatomy—which included twelve-inch-long legs and somewhat flappy ears—left zoo personnel stumped, as well. Most people around Hillsboro were guessing it was a raccoon with mange, but other experts dismissed the mange diagnosis, saying mange usually leaves at least a small amount of hair, thickens the skin, and has a distinct odor. They gave no alternative reason for its complete baldness, although genetic mutations for hairlessness do naturally occur in mammals.

It gets even weirder. As more people heard of the creature, one man came forth to say he had twice seen what looked like the same creature in June and July of 1991, on a road by his hobby farm near Yuba. Phil Connors of Madison told the *Sentry-Enterprise* that it appeared healthy, was totally hairless, and the only difference between it and the creature on Hora's farm was that the one he saw had larger ears.[16]

And even weirder, because this begins to suggest a resident breeding population of unidentified, hairless mammals in south central Wisconsin, Juneau County Highway Patrolman Jeff Potter saw yet another of the creatures ten years later, on July 18, 2011. It was already dead, and again, no one seemed to know what to make of it. A local reporter, Dianna Anderson, described it as "approximately thirty inches long, weighs between eight to ten pounds. The body is hairless and lite [sic] tan with a leathery feel to it. The body is swine shaped with a possum like tail. The front feet have four toes and the rear feet have five toes. The ears are large and the snout looks kind of like a dog. The animal has long protruding canine teeth hanging out."[17]

Perhaps it was the mention of the protruding canine teeth, but people began asking whether the strange animal might be the legendary Chupacabra, or "goat sucker," a vicious (but unproven) creature famous for draining farm animals of blood in Puerto Rico, Mexico, Chile, and southwestern states of the United States. The Chupacabra became well-known around 1995 but appeared earlier in Puerto Rican and Mexican folklore. Remarkably, this fairly recent legend from another part of the continent had now developed into a new version in rural Wisconsin, even though there was little physical similarity between descriptions of the northern and southern animals.

MYSTERY CAT CONCLUSIONS

I do have an opinion about the Hillsboro cats, both black and tan. After reviewing the many examples gathered here, it seems none of them has exhibited any kind of behavior that could be considered unnatural to their species, or that even hints that this area's great, black-furred felines are of supernatural origins. I agree with Steve Stanek that this seemingly established population of black and tan cougar-like animals can be explained by natural mating between cougars and jaguars, even if we don't know exactly where or how that happened. The area's welcoming hilly habitat, perhaps enhanced by the literally magnetic draw of the Baraboo Range, could have attracted a small but thriving bunch of large, wild cats, some of which are colored Impossible Black. This hybridization may also be responsible for the sightings of panther-like animals with red or gray fur. And their actions as described by scores of witnesses over several decades indicate nothing but flesh and blood animals.

To be sure, there are many other places in the United States and other countries where researchers have come to the opposite conclusion based upon their own sightings reports. But in these cases, the reports include phenomena like vanishing or morphing animals, or sparse habitats that seem to magically sustain a population of large felines. I don't think that one conclusion disproves the other. We seem to have both types of animals—natural beasts and their less natural mimics—among us everywhere in this world. That is a very great mystery in itself.

No matter what the cougar sightings in the Hillsboro hub area may be, it would take an entire book to describe and do justice to all of those reported over the past decades. I feel a separate record is necessary, in fact, in order to convey the enormity of the number of sightings reports—especially those that describe the "impossible" black-furred panthers—so I've included an appendix with a timetable extending from that first known sighting in the 1930s to as close to present as my book deadline will allow.

There is one other unexplained creature reported in the Baraboo Hills in the vicinity of Wildcat Mountain that will not surprise many long-time researchers. It will, however, provide a smooth segue into the next chapter: There are many places in the world where sightings of Bigfoot and black furred panthers occur in tandem.

Pennsylvania researcher and author Stan Gordon mentioned one such instance of Bigfoot plus mystery cats in the April 2017 issue of *The Gate to Strange Phenomena*. He was discussing 2016 reports of Bigfoot around Pennsylvania when he said, "Another mystery beast that continues to be spotted around southwestern Pennsylvania and other areas is what witnesses describe as a 'black panther.' . . . In some instances when there has been a local outbreak of Bigfoot encounters in an area, there has also been an outbreak of black panthers reported at the same time."[18]

The Hillsboro, Wisconsin, area has it the other way around; it boasts more reports of black-furred cats than Bigfoots, but Sasquatch sightings still crop up. In early September 2012, a camper in the Kickapoo Valley Reserve between La Farge and Ontario—prime panther territory—reported seeing a Bigfoot on South Jug Creek Road. The Vernon County Sheriff's Office investigated the site and seemed to take the report seriously, probably because there had been eleven other reported Bigfoot sightings in that county alone over the past three years, according to the September 12, 2012, edition of the *Hillsboro Outlook*.[19]

Reporter Mike Burch added that in 2010, along a farm pond in Champion Valley, he personally discovered "a bunch of long matted black hair in the grass along the pond's shore."[20] He did not have the hair professionally analyzed, but he guessed that it may have been a memento from a black bear passing through the valley. That leaves the hair identification still open in my book.

Burch mentioned another incident that occurred on the same land in August 2012, when an area woman and her granddaughter were riding a UTV past some woods. The girl suddenly asked if they could stop to look at something she saw watching them in the trees; her grandmother replied that she should take a picture instead. The girl clicked away, and the resulting photo showed a hulking, dark figure standing between two trees. The girl explained that this was the "big hairy man in the woods."[21]

All of the Hillsboro area cat sightings lie within easy Bigfoot-loping range of the Kickapoo Valley Reserve and its many nearby river valleys, including several sightings made in 2012, when the above-mentioned Sasquatch reports occurred.

One of the older but most publicized central Wisconsin Sasquatch sightings, known as the Cashton Bigfoot, happened in early morning one day in 1976, when Cashton area farmer Allen Arnold was outside in the predawn darkness, preparing to bring in his cows for milking. On his way to the barn, he smelled an unusual, skunky odor in a nearby ravine. His dog started barking, and Arnold turned to see a six-to-seven-foot-tall creature partly hidden by a cow. As the cow moved away, Arnold said he could see the creature batting at his dog, which ran away without harm. Arnold also left quickly. The dog's head was covered with saliva after the tussle, said Arnold, and later, Arnold found saliva and probable urine stains on the interior barn wall, where it looked like some large animal had been nesting in a straw mound. Arnold continued to hear strange bellowing calls for several weeks, during which he and his wife didn't allow their children out to play, although they didn't feel the Bigfoot intended any harm.[22]

There are many other areas considered richer in Bigfoot legends and encounters. Around the United States and Canada countless Sasquatch reports gathered over many decades by both organized research groups and independent investigators have helped transform this hairy hominoid into the greatest American legend—many would make that *living* legend—ever. And I can personally vouch for the "living" part.

CHAPTER 12

I Saw Bigfoot!

The author's rendition of Bigfoot

YES, I HAVE SEEN what I could not describe as anything but the oversize furry humanoid most people would recognize as a Bigfoot. I haven't said much publicly about my own encounters with this enigmatic creature, but I've come to feel that it would be disingenuous of me to write about strange creatures without admitting my own experiences and sightings. And again, yes, I said *sightings*, plural. I've seen something more than once that fits no other zoological template. These surprising glimpses occurred from some fairly close vantage points, one as near as thirty yards. The incidents all took place while I was totally awake in the daytime, out in the open, with no tricks of shadow or light to blame. Each encounter shook my once familiar world anew.

I've been reluctant to talk about my own experiences for a couple of reasons. First, I'll admit that I knew many people wouldn't believe me. I understand that my sightings might seem all too convenient, seeing that I write books about unknown creatures. But more than that, I still have so many questions about these humanlike beings that bringing up my own meager level of understanding has always seemed premature. Seeing may be believing, but it isn't necessarily comprehending. There's so much we don't know. As I seek to understand creatures whose existence I once thought impossible, my inner journalist constantly whispers, "What *are* they? Why did *I* see them? How do I respond to this knowledge?"

So far, nothing definitive has whispered back. But there are certain facts I can't deny.

For starters, I can say with assurance that within the past six years of this writing, I have experienced multiple close encounters with a large, animate entity. What I saw of this unknown being concurs with most other eyewitness descriptions of Bigfoot across the US and Canada: a large, humanlike primate covered in hair or fur that lives in the wild and cannot be positively identified as any animal known to modern science or zoological classifications. "Bigfoot" is not its only name. It goes by various monikers in different locations and cultures; the second-most-used name today would probably be Sasquatch.

So what's in a name? Everything, it seems, where monsters are involved. I think that for most people, naming them is the first step toward taming them, hence our compulsion to bestow a title upon every beast and booger ever known to mankind. I did that myself, when I named the upright canine of Elkhorn, Wisconsin, the Beast of Bray Road, only to find there were similar wolflike beasts known all over the world, and that like Bigfoot, they had many aliases. I think it is safe to say, though, that Bigfoot claims more nicknames and local lore than any other mystery creature.

WHICH CAME FIRST?

So which came first, the legend or the beast? Legends of tall, hairy humanoids are varied, ancient, and widespread. In the United States, Mark Opsasnick's 1993 booklet, *The Maryland Bigfoot Digest: A Survey of Creature Sightings in the Free State* (self-published and not available for distribution) records an astounding number of cryptid reports from that small state alone between the 1600s (exact years unspecified) and 1983. Maryland ranks only forty-second in size among the American states, but that hasn't deterred creatures of every size, shape, and description from making a home there. I've culled a list of colorful, localized creature names from the booklet, leaving out the many, many entries that identified creatures as simply "bigfoot-like" or "man-like." My main purpose is to show that the area supports a host of legends that have grown around various unknown creatures. So take a deep breath, and imagine meeting up with something called . . .

- The Okee
- Quioughcosughes (No pronunciation guide provided)
- Witch Rabbit
- Cow Man
- Dwayo (or Dwayyo)
- Monkey Man
- Parti-Gee-Ho
- Apple Creature

- Jabowak
- Goblin Damned
- Snarly-Yow
- Wildman
- Snallygaster
- Long Leggity Beastie
- Tommyknockers
- Jersey Devil (type of creature may vary)
- Gyascutus
- Orf
- Laughing Poparina
- Wesorts
- Crisfield Monster
- Eelpoot
- Abominable Phantom
- Swamp Monster
- The Wago
- Sykesville Monster
- The Egg People
- Bunny Man
- Mayberry Monster
- Cyclops
- Green Eyes
- Chalk Point Monster
- Cabbage Head Man

It's a wild appellational ride. I think, however, that at least a few of those names (and accompanying reports of sightings) may be attributed to pioneering newspaper editors seeking readership. Many early, small communities had two or more newspapers, and unknown monsters have always been surefire attention getters—as they are to this day. I've seen Wildman stories in my own local research that were obviously not even close to our conception of Bigfoot.

It's also interesting and a loss to contemporary researchers that, as the general attributes of Bigfoot became better known to the public by the 1970s, most of the local color began to drain out of newspaper articles. The original, inventive nicknames often gave way to the more universally accepted monikers, "Bigfoot" or "Sasquatch." The problem is not just boring sameness, it's that many of those former nicknames—"Cabbage Head Man," for instance—implied specific, if still puzzling, characteristics that could sometimes provide clues. Every time I see that name, I want to know what it was about that beast that reminded witnesses of a head of cabbage.

But back to my own encounters and those of others, as promised.

UNSEEN BUT NOT UNNOTICED

Let me begin by saying that just as in UFO studies, there are different degrees of creature encounters. Some are full-on visual sightings of the Sasquatch, while others lack a direct sighting but report a constellation of evidence and sensory observations that match basic Bigfoot actions and characteristics generally accepted as "Squatchy" by researchers worldwide. The best sightings, of course, include both good visuals and supporting evidence such as prints, odor, or sounds. (Photos and videos are usually not clear enough to be considered proof positive, although everyone keeps trying to find definitive evidence—and should keep trying.)

As noted earlier, I have personally witnessed these creatures behaving in ways very similarly described by countless other observers. Several times I actually laid eyes on the creature, while on other occasions I saw the effects of its actions while the perpetrator remained hidden. For instance, I've watched something huge camouflaged by the foliage of a huge old oak tree twist and tear off a giant branch right in front of me on a still, sunny day; and I was also present when a colleague, Jay Bachochin, got beaned with a flying, rock-hard object hard enough to give him a mild concussion as we hiked a forest trail. Another friend and I were surrounded by the sound of rocks clicking together in at least

*Field near the Kettle Moraine State Forest, Southern Unit, where the author
witnessed what she believed was a Bigfoot in "frozen" position, one of three
daylight sightings in this area. The black, crouching figure representing Bigfoot
(center of photo)* was drawn by the author *as an approximation of size and
position relative to the road and to the ravine-like woods in back left.*

three different locations near us. As we sensibly retreated, the
clicks followed us down the trail from both sides of the path to
the trail's end.

Rock clicking is a Bigfoot behavior often described in stories
and reports, but I had always been a bit skeptical until it happened
to me. I returned to that spot in the southern unit of the Kettle
Moraine State Forest some months later with the same friend,
Corrine Mandera, and another longtime investigative colleague,
Kimberly Poeppey. While there was no clicking that time, something did toss a crab apple *up* a hillside to land at our feet and roll
across the trail precisely where we stood. We had all stopped to
observe the downhill slope, and were directly facing the area from

which the three-inch-wide, red-and-yellow fruit came. We could see other crab apples lying on the ground down below us (none left on any branches), yet we never saw the crab apple thrower. There was very little wind, and no other fallen crab apples stirred in the slightest. There were no crab apple trees on the upward slope behind us. I still have the solid little missile in my kitchen freezer.

As if to confirm that something wildly adept at concealing itself hangs around that spot, a few months later I received a report from a southeastern Wisconsin man named Rick (last name withheld by his request) who had a "no-see-um" encounter in the fall of 2016 during hunting season in the same area of the Kettle Moraine. He wrote:

> It was bow season on a November morning and I was sitting on the ground in a ridge when I smelled something foul. Sulfuric, almost. Something began circling me, keeping twenty feet away and remaining hidden behind trees. It was making grunting noises while throwing sticks and small rocks in my direction. I couldn't get a good look, but I got the impression that it was covered in dark fur and [was] quite tall. Occasionally it would stop moving for several minutes at a time before continuing to circle me. This went on for twenty minutes before it wandered off. All I could do was remain as still and quiet as possible during this encounter. I was a bit shaken, plus I didn't want to frighten whatever it was in the hopes that I could get a good look at it. . . . I haven't even told my wife about this as she would think I was going nuts.

Rick said he wasn't aware of many other encounters with what he presumed was a Bigfoot in this part of the state, but I let him know he was in good company with the many reports from around here I've collected over the decades. I had another recent report, in fact, of an older incident that supports the belief held by many researchers that Bigfoots will throw or shake whatever lies at hand at those who approach their territory.

SHAKE, SHAKE, SHAKE!

A man who contacted me in 2016 lives near the Kettle Moraine area where all these things took place, and he has often hiked the park's trails. He wrote:

> I never really knew much of Bigfoot sorts of creatures in the region. But I sure do recall an incident that I had back in—if I can recall correctly—the late summer, early fall back in 1999. I loved stopping by the Oleson Log Home site located on Duffin Road about one mile south of Bluff Road. Anyways, I just loved to take evening walks and watch the sun go down.
>
> On this one particular evening I decided to take my beagle and my brother's Doberman pinscher for a walk at the Oleson home. I let them run freely off leash. I decided to take them for a walk down the horse trail that passed behind the grounds. It was wide and sort of mowed down, very nice to walk on. We walked north on this trail. As we walked along, we came to a fencerow where the woods began. We could hear the squirrels and birds chirping away. There was no breeze at all. As we walked, I noticed that everything suddenly went quiet. Nothing! It was dead still, no sounds from bugs or animals.
>
> I felt that was very odd, so I was on alert and on guard and

looking in every direction. I knew something wasn't right but I kept on walking and paying closer attention to my surroundings. The trail started to curve to our right in a long, sweeping curve. Before we rounded the whole bend, I noticed that the two dogs didn't want to go any further. I was leery, but tried to get them to continue. They would take a few steps forward, but they stopped and wouldn't go any further. They were very uneasy, so I whispered softly for them to come back, and slowly retreated. I wanted to see what was ahead, but decided to heed their warning. We walked/crept back down the trail toward my truck.

I kept my eyes open. As we approached the trail turnoff at the log home, I witnessed a very strange event. I was looking east down the trail that leads toward the pioneer lime kiln ruins that are about three quarters of a mile away. Where this trail meets the Ice Age Trail, about 500 feet east of the log home, just to the north of this trail junction was one very large tree. Mind you, there was no wind at all; the whole top of this tree was swaying as if it were in a fifty-miles-per-hour wind. It was the only tree in motion. I was like, WTF? It was a big tree. I never did see what was making it violently thrash about. I rushed the dogs and walked a little more swiftly towards my truck. Never run, always walk, even if it's a fast walk. I'm sure it knew that we were there. As I think back now, I still can't help but shake my head in disbelief. I still see it in my mind as if it were yesterday, and that was 17 years ago.

The writer said he did visit the spot again several times without incident until 2014, when another pleasant excursion turned scary. He had only walked a quarter of a mile when all the animals again went silent and he could feel the hair standing up on his neck. He had the distinct feeling he was being watched, he said, and made quick tracks in returning to his vehicle. When I checked out this location on my park map, I realized it was almost back-to-back with the trail site where my friends and I had experienced the crab apple missile and earlier, the multi-located rock clicking.

This man's experience also relates to my friend Jay's having had a rock thrown at his head as described above. At the time Jay received that hard hit on the head, he happened to be shaking a tree. It was my idea, I'm a bit sorry to say, but I'd read that this type of aggressive behavior had also been observed in large primates such as gorillas. The woods were so still that day that I thought waving a few small branches might help stir up some action. Sightings and howls had been reported in this part of the forest, and we agreed a gentle tree shake was worth a try. I went first, shaking a small sapling to little effect. Jay, who is much taller than I am, then rattled the branches of another small tree, taking care not to damage it. That's when an object that seemed to come out of nowhere connected with the side of Jay's baseball cap and fell into the forest floor's leaf covering. We never did find the object, but he said whatever hit him felt like a rock and that it was quite painful, even with his cap on. He didn't seek medical attention although he lost his way driving home from the hike. He may have had a concussion. And although I was turned to face the general direction from which the object must have been thrown, I never saw the thrower.

The incident near the Oleson home, then, has at least one strong similarity with other Bigfoot reports. I don't believe Jay has tried that move again. I can't say I'd recommend it, either. We humans can only guess at what we are actually communicating in these kinds of circumstances—including the practices of returning rock clicks or wood knocks—and we should consider the fact that we may be saying something very different than what we intended!

MORE THAN A FEELING

In many cases, however, the creature leaves little doubt as to its identity.

I can say from experience that it's quite frustrating to hear, feel, and smell—but not see—these things that cannot be explained in terms of known, indigenous animals. I say "smell" because I've also experienced that strong, sometimes "sulfuric" odor the writer earlier described. But even more shocking to my own usual notions of reality were the three times I've seen what appeared to be the same large, black-furred Sasquatch in two adjacent corn and hay fields. That may sound like a lot of sightings of something that's notoriously difficult to spot, but I'd like to note that these visual encounters didn't occur until I'd put in over twenty years of fieldwork and investigation. And none of these creatures showed up when I was consciously looking for them.

Over the years, I'd seen footprints, strange constructions in the woods, and many other tantalizing clues—even a clear look at a hairy foot sticking out from behind a tree that then moved slowly out of view—but had started to think it was my fate to record the sightings of other people and not my own. And as so often happens, it's when we're not looking that the object of our search appears. Most of my sightings and findings have been in or near the Kettle Moraine State Forest, and I've had many reports of Bigfoot in that area dating back to the early 1960s, so I'm going to share from this microcosm of creature interaction to get us started.

In midsummer 2014, I was out for a morning stroll along some roads near the southern edge of the Kettle Moraine State Forest when I noticed what I mistook for the top of a fence post about forty yards away in a hay field. The hay was about four feet tall, ready to be cut, and I wondered idly why the fence post was in the middle of a field where it would need to be moved for harvest, and why it was pitch-black in color. I had often seen sandhill cranes nesting in the tall grass, but this knobby thing was nothing like them. I glanced at the actual wooden posts surrounding the field and realized they were shorter: the color of gray, weathered wood; and much smaller in diameter than was the black post. I glanced back at it more carefully, observing that it was rounded on top and had a furry texture. Immediately, the "post" slowly began to lower itself straight down into the hay. It was the same sort of movement a human would make to drop into a crouch.

Its face was shaded by the sun's position, but I observed no ears as surely would have been visible on a bear, deer, dog, or coyote. And since this was an impromptu walk, I did not have my phone or other cameras with me. I backed up slowly, then headed home for a camera. By the time I returned, the creature was nowhere to be seen.

The second incident happened that fall in an adjacent field, separated from the first field only by a deep kettle, or round depression left from the last glacial age. I was driving very slowly, perhaps twenty miles per hour, because there were often turkeys, cranes, herds of deer, and other animals browsing in it—so many that my husband and I had nicknamed it "the wildlife field." The ground was mostly bare except for a thin layer of cornhusks and stems that remained after the harvest. But as I scanned the open space for animals, a large, completely black tree trunk about thirty to forty feet out from the kettle forest tree line caught my eye. It was oddly shaped, with a thick "branch" bending upward on one side, and a rather lumpy baseline where the bottom of it met the pale, scattered chaff of the field. I kept slowly rolling on by, puzzled.

As in the case of the out-of-place fence post, I was musing that this was an odd place for a farmer to leave a stump. As soon as that thought occurred to me, I remembered there had never *been* a stump in that spot. I'd been driving past that field for twenty-odd years and would surely have remembered something so prominent. I slammed on the brakes and threw the car into reverse, but I wasn't quick enough. In those few seconds, whatever it was had completely disappeared.

Where could it have gone so quickly? It had to have bounded down into the brush of the kettle in just one or two springs, or I would have been able to see it running. It was much, much too large to have been a turkey, and too black, chunky, and contorted to have been a deer. A black bear would have been most unusual in that far southern part of the state, although lone bears have been known to pass through Walworth County on occasion, but I think a bear would have just loped off and remained in sight. It certainly wouldn't have frozen in position out in the open. Bears are also very easy to recognize by their gait and size, and have prominent ears.

There was only one creature I could think of that matched the color and size of the lumpy black thing in the cornfield. Moreover, there are some good precedents for thinking the "stump" may have been a Bigfoot, based on its behavior. The annals of Sasquatch reports include many descriptions of Bigfoots caught out in the open that, rather than risk a run for it, "play statues" by freezing in place until the observer looks away. I've received at least one such report from near Spring Green, Wisconsin, where a couple visiting the area admired a lifelike statue of a Bigfoot on someone's lawn, only to discover the property owners had no Bigfoot statue, and afterward, there was no trace of the alleged artwork the pair had seen.

When I thought of it this way, I realized that the branch-like thing could have been a partially upraised arm, and the lump's lower edge might have been formed by the creature's two feet. The extreme speed the animal would have required to disappear in literally the blink of my eye has also been noted by many other Sasquatch witnesses.

My third incident happened late that winter in that same field, even closer to the road than the "stump" had been, and just at the edge of that same wooded kettle. This time my husband was driving as we slowly passed the wildlife field. I was watching from the passenger side when I noticed a large branch at the edge of the kettle making odd, vigorous up-and-down movements rather like the motion of a pump handle. But something behind the branch was forcing that movement. It was tall, human shaped, and completely black.

I could see its arms applying force to the branch's movements. Its dark form showed up plainly because the trees in that kettle were white with snowy frost. I immediately yelled to my husband to stop the car, but he had pressing business at home. I returned as soon as I was able, but of course the branch was still and the tall black form was nowhere in sight.

I made a brief site check for tracks around the kettle later in the week after getting permission from the landowner. Two colleagues helped me check the kettle and its perimeter, but any traces or prints had been erased by changing weather conditions by then. I did think the branch I saw moving had been removed, but couldn't be positive which branch it was. And what was the tall dark form? Despite its humanlike form, its uniform color and the way it moved that branch made me sure it wasn't a human, and as in the first two cases, the process of elimination ruled out any other known denizens of that field.

I'm not sure why, after two decades of mostly unsuccessful attempts at seeing an unknown creature, the sightings finally began for me. It wasn't as if no one had ever reported sightings in the area of those fields. A former neighbor in his early seventies who had barely even heard of Bigfoot saw what sounded like one to me in autumn 2015—on his own lawn. He lived on the edge of a deep kettle slope that formed a series of kettles that led to the fields just discussed.

He mentioned it to me about a year after the event as we chatted outdoors one day. He said it was near dusk when he heard something rattling his garbage can and, figuring it was a raccoon, went outside to have a look. He saw nothing by the can, but almost immediately, something huge and black furred that he couldn't readily identify lunged past him and leapt down into the adjacent kettle woods. "Man, was that thing fast," he added. Shaken by the strange animal's nearness to him as it powered into the trees, he had quickly gone indoors, he said, and remained so troubled that he had never told anyone—not even his wife—about it. He had seen me on a documentary TV show and figured I wouldn't laugh. "I just didn't know what it could be," he said, adding it was not a bear, dog, deer, great cat, or any other animal he could think of in the area.

IOWA SPRINTER

The brash, speedy movements of the creature that bolted for the kettle in my cornfield sighting and whizzed past my neighbor in his yard may sound unlikely to those unfamiliar with Bigfoot lore, but are actually common observations in sightings of Sasquatch. Bigfoot seems able to intuitively or intelligently calculate the risk involved in showing itself as it gets from point A to point B. A good example may be found in this 1974 account sent to me on Facebook in 2014 by an Iowa man I'll just call by his first name, Jack. He said he had seen something "Bigfoot-like" in late summer 1974, about six miles northeast of Mediapolis, Iowa, while on his way home from riding motorcycles with a friend. He wrote:

> On my way home, I was going down a dirt road close to [my house]. The road is flat, then becomes hilly. As I crossed a creek and came up over the first hill, I saw something dark, huge, and unbelievably fast. [Author note: almost exactly the same as the description my former neighbor gave in the previous encounter.] It ran down a fifteen-foot embankment across the dirt road, and jumped the fence in what seemed like five strides.

The witness slammed the motorcycle to a halt, turned it off, and pursued the creature on foot. He had lost sight of it, but could still hear it crashing through the woods "like a bull elephant." He said that after chasing the creature for about forty yards, his skin became sweaty and tingly and his instinct told him to stop right there. Terror-stricken, he turned around and ran as fast as he could, hopped back on his bike and tore off for home, where he kept completely mum on his experience. He didn't have far to go, as the sighting area was directly across the road from his parents' house. That was the last time he entered those woods, he said, and toted a gun whenever he went out on other forested properties in the area. He added that he still ponders the experience daily, and has never been so terrified of anything before or since. He has continued to keep the incident mostly to himself, he said, for fear of being called a liar or worse.

Jack added, in response to my questioning, that the creature ran so fast, he couldn't give me a fair estimate of its size or weight. "It was big," he said. "What scared the crap out of me was when I heard it running in the woods. It had to be massive."

What surprised me most in Jack's account was that when he saw the creature, he got off his bike and *ran into the woods to give chase*, even though he could see how fast and big it was. This may sound like something no one would ever do, but it does happen sometimes that curiosity trumps fear. I was present once when my colleague Jay Bachochin did exactly the same thing. It was nighttime, and he, another colleague named Sanjay Singhal, and I were enjoying an after-dark campfire on the deck of a former residence of mine after cooking a few aromatic hot dogs. Again, this was in the general area of the southern Kettle Moraine State Forest, and I'd had a few unsettling happenings in my own yard—the most recent being the evening when something tossed a small rock at my husband from *up* out of the kettle bramble as he hammered nails on a deck very close to the steep kettle edge. I'll describe the other incidents later.

But that evening we were just enjoying the peaceful setting in the cool, still air. We saw a possum rummaging about twenty feet below us as it found some tidbit from the cookout and ran off with it. As we sat and chatted, I became aware of soft scraping sounds beneath the deck. I didn't say anything until I saw my dog's ears flatten and he began a low growl. I asked the guys if they heard something and they both nodded. By then my little Lhasa apso was creeping across the deck on his belly, and when he reached the edge, he erupted in a barking frenzy. At that point, something that sounded both huge and bipedal tore out from under the deck and began to crash through the woods.

Luckily I had my dog on a leash, but both my colleagues were free to run, and Jay did—right after the escaping creature. He didn't get far—the kettles are filled with brambles, rocks, logs, and thick brush that can barely be negotiated by a human in daytime, much less at night without even a flashlight. In moments, he came staggering back, defeated by the foliage, while the "thing's" footsteps grew fainter as it sprinted easily through the brush. Jay stood catching his breath as he explained, "I knew I had this one chance to try, to finally see the thing I've been pursuing. I had to try." We understood.

We did spend some time trying to figure out some mundane explanation. We ruled out the possibility that it was a trespassing human, partly because he or she would have had the same difficulty getting through the rough terrain in the dark as did Jay, and partly because we couldn't imagine why or how any person would want to clamber up the steep wall of the kettle in order to crawl under my deck and just listen to us talking. The only other remotely likely possibility would have been a deer, as the rough size and weight of a grown buck or doe would have been close to what we estimated the intruder must have measured, but again, the idea of a deer sneaking out of the kettle, crawling silently under the deck right beneath us and lying flat, then crawling out again—in a split second—before struggling to its feet and bounding into the undergrowth just doesn't seem feasible.

THE BIG BRANCH

These were not my first brushes with the big hairy man, as some of my First Nation friends call Bigfoot. Readers of my blog and of my book *American Monsters* will also recall another incident, in which I watched something twist and then tear away a living oak branch from about forty feet above the ground in another nearby kettle in the summer of 2012. The creature hid itself well behind the very luxuriant foliage of the large tree, so I did not see it. Still, I had no doubt as to what it had to be. This was confirmed less than an hour later when my friend Sandra Schwab and her then twenty-one-year-old daughter (and skeptic) Natalie joined me for a photo session in that kettle, and Natalie saw a huge, beige-gray creature "striding" (her word) behind another bank of dense shrubs nearby.

I know exactly how all this sounds to most people: impossible. I'm acutely aware.

It also seems strange to me that despite my work investigating sightings of upright canines that look for all the world like classic werewolves, I've had far more success in glimpsing tall, sturdily built, hairy hominoids. I guess the unknown creatures neither know nor care why I should see Bigfoots rather than upright canids. I think it probably has something to do with the fact that I

happen to have lived near a state forest known for Bigfoot sightings. It probably also helped that I was always looking at tree lines
in fields as I passed. Most people never even think of keeping an
eye out for unknown creatures; the general population considers
Bigfoots and dogmen to be no more than legend, myth, halluci-
nation, or outright fiction. Legendary they may be, but *legend* is
not synonymous with *untruth*.

HAIRY MEN OF THE ANCIENTS

Bigfoot's pedigree and the beginning of what some call the beginning of its legend may reach back to ancient Sumerian literature
in the *Epic of Gilgamesh*, dating from about 2100 BC, in fact. The
epic's hero, Enkidu, like Sasquatch, is covered in fur or hair and
appears as half human, half animal, but he walks erect and inter-
acts with humans in ways no animal could.

In a 2016 article in *The Atlantic*, Edward Simon says Enkidu is
"the prototypical pre-human, a liminal man-beast, not quite wild
and not quite tame. . . ."[1]

Some say the Bible's Old Testament also alludes to a Sasquatch-
like entity in the twenty-fifth chapter of Genesis, in the story of
twin brothers Jacob and Esau, the sons of the Hebrew patriarch,
Isaac. Jacob, the younger brother, was a quiet man and something
of a homebody. He likely spent much of his time tending and
studying his father's great herds of goats, since he later displayed
great knowledge of animal husbandry by selectively breeding certain characteristics of the flocks owned by his father-in-law,
Laban.

Esau, the firstborn of the pair, grew up to become a skilled hunter with a rather unusual appearance. According to the book of Genesis, Esau from birth was large, smelly, and entirely covered with red fur![2] Even though the text doesn't infer that Esau was anything but human, he has recently gained a reputation in some circles as having been related to Bigfoot. I'm not sure Esau's story bears this idea out, however.

It's true that his birth certainly seems to have been the result of some very special process; their mother, the previously barren Rebekah, conceived the twins only after Isaac prayed that God would grant her the gift of children, as Genesis 25:21 informs us. Isaac was sixty years old when his sons were born. But while Esau's extreme hairiness is also noted, neither of his parents expressed any dismay at his appearance. In fact, the text tells us the baby was also called "Edom," which meant "red" and may have been considered a fond nickname just as people with that hair color are often called "Red" today. Edom was a pun, as well, since it referred to not just his reddish fur but later, to Esau's fondness for a stew made from a type of lentil that turned reddish brown when cooked. This stew, of course, was the prize for which Esau carelessly traded his birthright, a short sighted act that led to Jacob receiving their father's deathbed blessing instead of Esau, the rightful heir. Esau's descendants were called Edomites, and some think that today's Bigfoot is descended from them.

Skeptics of this theory note that unlike Bigfoot, Esau wore clothing, spoke intelligibly, used tools, and married a number of human women who bore him children whose appearance wasn't noted as unusual, and whose humanity was never questioned. Perhaps folks of the time even considered the auburn, shag carpet a good look for Esau. What they did not think, as far as we can tell, was that he was anything but human.

Esau's appearance could even have been due to a case of congenital hypertrichosis, a genomic disorder in which a person's entire body is covered in thick hair from birth, just like Esau's, and stays that way. It seems a plausible explanation, since Esau and Jacob were obviously not identical twins. Hypertrichosis is quite rare, however, and has been shown to run in families.[3] Yet there is no hint in the Old Testament's carefully delineated genealogies that Isaac and Rebekah had any red-furred ancestors. Of course, the divine intervention that resulted in Rebekah's conception of the twins could have thrown a literally wild card into the family's gene pool, but that's hard-core speculation.

Connections have also been suggested between Esau and the offspring of the oversize beings the Bible refers to as Nephilim. These Nephilim were the result of relations between the "sons of God" (widely believed to be fallen divine beings sometimes called Watchers) mentioned in Genesis 6:2, who came down to earth and mated with beautiful human women, or "daughters of men." The offspring of these unions, the Nephilim, were said to be part divine, part human giants known for heroic exploits. One very popular theory proposes these swashbuckling, tall people—rather than Esau—were the ancestors of the modern Bigfoot, a creature that appears giant-sized compared to most humans. But although the Nephilim were large, some as tall as nine feet according to the Bible, they weren't necessarily covered all over with fur.

Whether or not Esau or the Nephilim and Bigfoot were ever related genetically, they are still linked mythically. Musings about the red-haired beings, giant offspring of heavenly beings and *Homo sapiens*, and the possible origins of upright, forest-dwelling hominoids are hotly debated. And giant skeletons (some of them redheads) are still being discovered in ancient burial mounds around the world.

On the other hand, Bigfoot's modern status as campfire-tale star, coupled with ever mushrooming numbers of sightings, has increased general speculation that there must be some natural species of humanlike ape (or apelike human!) as yet unconfirmed by science. And if Bigfoot is, as many insist, a procreating, flesh-and-blood creature, we may then assume from the increased sightings that either its population is increasing or it's spreading into populated areas, just as coyotes and bears have begun to do. Of course, increased sightings and reports also may simply be due to the fact that there are more people out there actively searching for them, and many eyewitnesses who once would have kept quiet about sightings now feel emboldened to share their experiences publicly. I've often wondered, if Bigfoot is not a flesh-and-blood creature, how do so many people (including myself) see it and report such consistent behavior and appearance?

Some have proposed that Bigfoot is a manifestation of "spirit" or unknown electromagnetic energies, and that it may interact with human consciousness to achieve its form. If that were true, might the mass media depictions and merchandising of this "legend" in books, film, and TV have given us the universal, preconceived notions of Sasquatch that enhance its ability not only to appear solid but to show up looking just as we have come to expect?

It's anyone's guessing game, but as wild as these ideas may sound, I'm far from the first or only person to come up with them. As mentioned earlier, many other researchers have pondered the apparent associations between beasts and legends. Pioneer cryptozoologist Ivan Sanderson titled his 1961 book, *Abominable Snowmen: Legend Come to Life.* The History Channel had a four-season hit series called *MonsterQuest: Legend Meets Science.*

Neither of these titles, however, was saying the creatures literally came to life from spirit-energy embodiments of widespread legends. Both Sanderson's book and the *MonsterQuest* series suggest Bigfoots are unidentified, mortal, flesh-and-blood beasts that could be detected and perhaps even captured, given enough teams of outdoors-savvy hunters and scientists with all the latest technology. To our knowledge, such a successful conclusion has yet to happen. Or at least no conclusion authorities will acknowledge is presently known.

But there are researchers who dare to consider the fact that Bigfoot, dog men, and such just don't behave like ordinary—if ultra-reclusive—animals would be expected to behave. The late Texas researcher Rob Riggs in his excellent book, *In the Big Thicket: On the Trail of the Wild Man*, noted that Bigfoot or Wild Man–type sightings "are associated with the mysterious energies that sometimes manifest as light forms. These lights . . . also have *a peculiar relation to the consciousness of the observer* [emphasis mine]. We have speculated that these energies may be evidence of a form of non-localized consciousness and as such constitute a sort of field of psychic energy that may be as much a part of our natural environment as the air we breathe."[4]

But if that's true, then that field of psychic energy may not be compatible or in sync with our own psychic energy. No matter what "they" are, we just don't know how harmful this wide array of creatures might be to us. A growing contingent believes all monstrous creatures are demonic, engendered whenever one of the hybrid Nephilim died and left its spirit on earth to inhabit life forms other than humans. (For a thorough treatment of these biblical origins, I often recommend biblical scholar and Semitic languages expert Dr. Michael Heiser's *The Unseen Realm*.)[5]

And let's not forget there may be some supposed monsters that turn out to be solid and natural animals not averse to scarfing an occasional people burger. All of these possibilities come with their own caveats, especially for those who would go physically chasing upright unknown creatures in their own wooded domains. Although there are some encounters with creatures that behave in a benign or even friendly manner, my reminder is that we always need to take care, be aware, and be as respectful as we would of any wild thing.

Perhaps ancient lore can help with that. With such a wide array of creatures in this world and perhaps partly out of it, and so many possible ways to interpret them, myth and legend may be more than just interesting stories we read to give ourselves chills. Think of the folk knowledge shrouded inside this book alone. We now know, in a straight-to-the-gut kind of way: teens shouldn't park on lonely roads near cemeteries, and you must never pet a dog with glowing red eyes or drive your horses under tree branches where black cougars are seen. Also, it might behoove us to simply let the Bigfoots be and let sleeping dogmen lie.

In the monster hunt's final endgame, the *stories, the scriptures, the legends* themselves may be the real treasure hunted by every culture hero—these tales may be subtly disguised handbooks for survival in what Dr. John Napier and other renowned researchers have called a "goblin universe."

Until science or major events show us otherwise, it's probably not a bad way to go.

Appendix

**Unknown, cougar-like cat sightings
from the 1930s to the present, in the immediate area
around Hillsboro, Wisconsin**

This timetable of sightings of tan or black great cats in the central
Wisconsin area around Hillsboro is representative rather than ex-
haustive. There are other sightings not recorded here for various
reasons, mostly that they have occurred or been reported after the
deadline for this book. For simplicity, I've used the word *tan* universally for any of the usual lighter shade terms witnesses use—
such as light brown, tawny, deer colored, etc.—to denote the
normal, known range of mountain lion fur coloration. Descriptions for other, more unusual coloration, such as black, dark
brown, very dark, etc. will use the words of the witnesses. The

term *panther* may be used when citing the words of a witness or to denote a great cat of panther-like appearance.

1930s: On a summer day on a road between Hillsboro and Union Center, John Rogers saw a black cougar jump out of a tree and onto the back of one of the horses in the team he was driving. The cougar slid off the horse and presumably ran away.

1940s: Near Fox Ridge, a squirrel hunter named Elgin Hooker reported seeing a tan cougar.

1940s: Near Towerville in Crawford County, a Viroqua resident said her father saw a black panther in a valley.

1950s: In autumn in Mount Tabor, five miles northwest of Hillsboro, farmer Bob Sake observed two gray lions cross a field as he watched from the yard of his home. Two other relatives had seen one similar animal in a berry patch a few weeks before the incident.

1950s: In the Fox Ridge area, a farmer (name withheld) saw a huge, black great cat leap over the hood of his car in one bound as the man turned into his driveway. He said it was five feet long, not including the tail. The family heard nearby screams at night for about a week.

1957: In the summer, Hillsboro area farmer Harlan Urban saw a brown animal in his hay field with a head four times the size of the head of a large tomcat and a long tail the thickness of a pitchfork handle a day after his neighbor's calf died from severe and unusual predation wounds.

1958: Near Valton, Sauk County, Lester Degner and his brother David saw a brownish-black panther the size of a beagle—but with long legs—numerous times across the valley from their farm. They believed it had a den in a nearby rock cleft.

1960s: West of Hillsboro, in the daytime, Rachel Novy; her husband, Martin; and Carl Hill heard their small dog barking and saw a tan mountain lion that had evidently clawed the dog across its face. The cat ran away and the dog recovered.

1974: Near Valton, Sauk County, Lester Degner was walking through a wooded area when he saw a long tail hanging down from a tree. Immediately a brownish-black great cat he had seen numerous times before (see 1958 entry) jumped down out of the tree and ran off.

1979: June, rural Cazenovia. Joe Decot and two family members watched an enormous black cat they said was larger than any dog run across a field only one hundred yards away.

1980s: In autumn, in the intersection of Hickory Road and County Highway F, Randy Evans was outdoors with a flashlight, "shining" deer when his light revealed two black lions the size of collies, with yellow eyes and long tails. They were rearing up at each other, seemingly at play. Evans had also seen a tan, cougar-like creature "sometime previously."

1987–1988: In winter, two and a half miles south of Hillsboro, Mike Thomas saw a huge, black great cat while hunting deer on his land.

1987: In autumn in Mount Tabor at dusk, Bob Jackson saw an animal bound across the road in front of his car, well lit by headlights. He described it as black, about the size of a black Lab, and with a long tail.

1988: In autumn, two and a half miles south of Hillsboro, Mike Thomas's wife, Susan, and their son, along with several guests saw a large, great black cat chasing their dog through their yard, yowling as it went. (No mention of the dog's fate.)

1988: Jon Bohn and two relatives hunting pheasants by the Baraboo River between Hillsboro and Union Center saw a black great cat sitting fifty yards away as it leapt at something unseen in a field and ran out of sight.

1989: In Valley, eight miles due west of Hillsboro, a married couple came home after work one day and saw two tan cougars at a pond on their property and watched them long enough to be sure of what they were.

1989: In autumn, on Eastman Road near Valley, Donna Baldwin, who was accompanied by two four-year-old children, encountered a tan, three-foot-long "lion" drinking from a creek between her and the house. She threw a rock at the animal and it hissed and walked away.

1990: In early summer on Pine Avenue, two miles west of Yuba about seven p.m. just after a thunderstorm, Carol Franke saw a large, tan cougar "bigger than a dog" drinking from a road puddle ahead of her car. She had to slow almost to a stop to avoid hitting it but the animal remained until it had finished drinking and then ran off. Franke noted the road was well lit from the post-storm sun and she had a close view.

1990: July. In German Valley just east of Hillsboro, Art and Mary Greisen saw two large black panthers making their way through a field at a distance of two hundred yards from their home, and also heard what they presumed were the screams of these animals at night.

1990: August. Six miles northwest of Hillsboro, university professor Sharyn Richardson observed a tan great cat she believed to be a young cougar about sixty feet from her home. Formerly part of Florida panther studies, she used binoculars to see this Wisconsin animal clearly during the daylight sighting.

1990: August. Farmer Jack Delaney near German Valley Road just east of Hillsboro reported a tan cougar measuring about three feet from nose to rump, sniffing along edges of a mowed hay field. He believed it was the animal that had recently killed all of his chickens.

1990: Date unknown, La Valle. Barbara Bengston stepped outside her home to say good-bye to guests and saw behind them a very large, dark or black great cat climbing down a tree headfirst.

1990: Date unknown, rural Wonewoc, an anonymous couple and their daughter saw a dark gray, cougar-like animal not far from their house.

1990: In autumn, Raese Road between Hillsboro and Union Center, Robert Roth encountered a dark charcoal gray "lion" on his farm.

1991: Date unknown, County Road C near Chicken Hollow west of Hillsboro. Ed Chalupecky was driving when he saw an unknown cat that was "huge and black, 5½-6 feet long, with a 3-foot tail." It jumped over a fence and then remained in place, watching him. Chalupecky had multiple sightings of other great cats in the years following this incident. (See additional Chalupecky entries for 2000, 2011.)

1991: Date unknown. On a sunny afternoon, Irene Hiner was driving near Hillsboro, heading for town when she saw "a big black cat" fifty feet ahead of her as it walked across someone's yard toward the Hillsboro water tower. She said it was bigger than a golden retriever, and that she stopped to watch it.

1991: Date unknown. In rural Yuba, Ron Henderson saw what looked to him like a mated pair of large, tan cougars stride across his driveway.

1991: Date unknown. In Champion Valley, a high school student encountered a tan female cougar with two cubs outdoors, and a colt was killed soon after.

1991: Date unknown. In Champion Valley, the above student's mother saw a tan, full-grown cougar near their farm.

1991: Date unknown. Near Yuba, two teenagers and a woman narrowly missed hitting a large black panther as it jumped in front of their vehicle.

1991: In autumn, in Kendall, Carl and Fern Schroeder saw a large black panther crossing a meadow near County Highway P, about one hundred yards behind their house.

1992: Date unknown. Between Hillsboro and Kendall, a Hillsboro fire chief and a fireman were responding to a call when a large, black cougar-like animal crossed the road in front of one of the trucks, only twenty feet away.

1992: On March 4, eight miles west of Hillsboro at Hidden Valley Resort, Phil Mascione (a retired photographer who specialized in zoo animals) saw his dogs chase what he identified as a black panther.

1992: On April 3, southwest of Kendall near Ember Drive, Rev. Fred Felke and son, Jon, saw a black panther bound through adjacent countryside only 50–100 yards away in daylight.

1992–1993: Date uncertain. In Valley near Highway 82, school bus driver Don Obert saw a "dark brown" cougar with nearly black "splotches" standing in a meadow as he passed by on his bus route.

1993: Date unknown; location undisclosed. An Amish farmer saw two large cougars, one tan and one black.

1993: On May 31 near Yuba, Joanne Brown and Richard Heal saw a large, cougar-like black cat in a meadow several hundred yards away as it chased two deer.

1993: Summer, McKenzie Road west of Hillsboro, sunny day, mid-afternoon. Joe Laskowski was baling hay when a "huge black cat" began crossing the field ahead of him and continued to a nearby creek bottom. He said it was the size of a German shepherd and had a long tail. (See Laskowski also in 1996 entry.)

1993: On October 4, ten miles west of Hillsboro near Fox Ridge, Brian Erickson and Doug Haworth were squirrel hunting in the late afternoon when an enormous black cat suddenly revealed itself in the brush only twenty feet away. They said it screamed and ran in the opposite direction, and that they could see its eyeshine before it turned away.

1993: Date unknown; on Fox Ridge near the same site as the men hunting squirrels, an area resident saw three mountain lion cubs on his property; one was tan and the two others were black. He also saw the mother, a huge black cougar he estimated to measure seven feet from nose to base of tail.

1993: Fox Ridge off County Road C. Francis Haugh saw a tan, great cat as large as a German shepherd in a field about three hundred yards away from where he stood feeding his cows. He shot his gun to chase it away.

1994: In autumn, on Sheep Pasture Bluff near Lyndon Station, Mark Miller was hiking through timber, bow hunting, when he saw a tan cougar through his binoculars.

1994: September in rural New Lisbon. Donna Lipert sat on her front porch and saw one, then another tan cat chase a deer out of the woods by her property.

1995: In spring, north of Hillsboro, Kathi and Roger Sterba were outdoors on their farm when they saw a large, tan cougar walking over a nearby hill.

1995: One autumn morning, near Summit Supper Club between La Valle and Reedsburg, Barbara Bengston and son saw a tan cougar in the middle of the road ahead of their car look at them and then dive into weeds in the ditch.

1995: September in the rural Lyndon Station area. Pat Morris saw a large tan cougar, body four feet from nose to base of tail, walking through woods along her property.

1995: On October 16, in rural Lyndon Station, Pat Roggy saw large tan cougar tracking a whitetail buck through a nearby field in daylight.

1995: On approximately October 23, in rural Lyndon Station, Roggy's son Michael watched a similar or same animal cross a nearby soybean field in daylight.

1996: Date unknown. In Chicken Hollow, about four miles southwest of Hillsboro, an Amish man saw a large black cat "bounding" from a nearby field into a wooded area, and his son saw a large tan cougar lying across a log in that same time frame.

1996: One summer morning, west of Hillsboro, Joe Laskowski and Kathy Laskowski looked around their farmyard to discover two large "lions," one tan and one black, distressing their small dog before it walked up a hill two hundred yards away. (See Laskowski also in 1993 entry.)

1998: Wonewoc Township on a back road near Elroy. Francis Stanek, Rich Stanek, and Ed Kolowrat were clearing brush when a black, cougar-like animal ran across a nearby field. They all agreed it was a cougar.

1998: Morning, Kouba Valley west of Hillsboro. An Amish farmer (neighbor of Amish farmer listed in 2001 entry) saw a tan mountain lion in his fields on separate occasions; one of them was also witnessed by his entire family. (See also 2009 entry.)

1999: In autumn, west of Hillsboro, Tom Wysocki was deer hunting in his woods when he saw a large, black cougar-like cat lying on a rock that overlooked a valley. He watched it for several minutes until it turned and saw him and then quickly slunk away.

2000: In autumn, Persuasion Woods west of Hillsboro, Ed Chalupecky was bow hunting when a large, tan, cougar-like animal walked in front of his truck, then walked away. (See additional Ed Chalupecky entries for 1991, 2011)

2000: In April, Karen Fernholz heard dogs barking from her house near Ironton and saw a black great cat about the size of a black lab.

2001: Date unknown. Kouba Valley west of Hillsboro, mid-morning. An Amish farmer saw a dark-furred cougar from inside his house, with both his naked eye and binoculars. It crouched as it watched the farm's cattle, which all ran to the other side of their pasture.

2001: Date unknown. Highway 82 east of Hillsboro. Wencil and Rita Mislivecek saw a tan cougar on the road. Wencil described it as twice the size of two other large cats with black fur he had observed on other dates. (See Wencil Mislivecek entries 2004 and 2014.)

2003: In early spring, in Burr Ridge near Valley, Arnie Lewis looked out his living room window and saw a large tan mountain lion moving up a hill six hundred yards away in daylight, also observed through binoculars.

2004: In early spring, at Weister Creek near Rockton, Angie Williams saw an "enormous" tan cat she estimated was as tall as the grill of her car cross her driveway as Williams was leaving her property in the late afternoon. It was only 50–60 feet away, she said, and she had no doubt as to what it was.

2004: In May, at the Chapparal Restaurant near Wonewoc, Wencil Mislivecek saw a black, cougar-like animal in a strawberry field. (See Wencil Mislivecek entries 2001 and 2014.)

2005: On a sunny November 24, Valley residents Jack and Carol Boaman saw a big tan cougar, weight estimated at 150 pounds, running east to west at the bottom of the slope his house sits on. The animal stopped near Boaman's barn, flattened itself to the ground, and then crept around the building before moving off into nearby brush.

2005: In September, three miles south of Hillsboro, Matthew Lambert came face-to-face with two cougars licking a salt block on his parent's property. He said one was tan, the other a very dark brown. One growled at him and then they ran off hissing when he fired a shot in the air.

2007: Date unknown. In Valley, Dan Obert and his father (Don Obert listed in the 1992–1993 entry), saw a "black cougar" chase a deer through a fence on their farm, explaining the deer was so frightened it beat its way through the fence rather than jumping. They later found tufts of black fur in the fence. The elder Obert added he had seen a black cougar behind the barn years earlier.

2009: Highway 80, southwest of Hillsboro. An Amish farmer (same man as in 1998 Kouba Valley entry above), was driving his buggy when he saw a large, black cougar-like animal cross the road ahead of him. He estimated its size as longer than a black lab, with a long tail that curled up.

2009: December, 4:30 p.m., Weister Creek, Rockton. David Waddell (son of Angie Williams, 2004 entry) was outdoors practicing coyote calls with a friend when they saw a large, tan cougar climb down from a tree—backward. The pair hurriedly left, and the animal, which Waddell described as 170 pounds with a body five feet long, disappeared. It was only one hundred to two hundred yards from the house.

2009–2010: Date uncertain. In August, north of Hillsboro, Kathi and Roger Sterba glimpsed a tan cougar from their kitchen window as it walked through a field to a woodline. Described as "bigger than any dog," this was their second sighting on their property. (See 1995 entry above.)

2010: One summer morning in Elroy, near the Baraboo River, Helen McDonald saw "an enormous black cat" drinking from a pond in her yard as she watched through a window.

2010: Summer, County Road FF near Hillsboro, at the intersection with Thew Road. Kathy Kolowrat saw a "dark tan" cougar emerge from the brush by an abandoned schoolhouse and walk onto the highway, where it stopped and looked at her in her car. It then leapt across a barbed wire fence and ran off.

2010: In mid-November, at Maple Ridge three miles east of La Farge, Steve Vesbach and several friends saw a large tan mountain lion sitting on a hay bale, illuminated by a large spotlight. It stood and jumped away, and Vesbach described it as being five feet long, three and half feet tall.

2011: Between Hillsboro and Tomah (State Highway 33), Ed Chalupecky saw a large, black unknown cat walking through a field as if looking for mice. (See also Ed Chalupecky entries 1991 and 2000.)

2011: In autumn at eight a.m. on Fox Ridge, three Amish sisters, Katie, Edith, and Arlene Yoder, were walking when they saw a large tan cougar run across the road one hundred yards in front of them and enter a pine grove.

2011: October, 6:30 a.m., White City, five miles southwest of Hillsboro. Francis Stanek saw a tan cougar larger than a German shepherd cross his driveway and enter a field that led to the woods. (See other Stanek entry 1998.)

2011: On October 16, just outside of Mauston, Clydesdale horse farmer Dennis Dodge caught a picture of a tan cougar on a trail-cam photo.

2011: On Dececember 5, between Mauston and Elroy, a woman saw a tan cougar chase three horses through her yard in daylight.

2011: In early winter, about one mile west of Union Center on State Highway 82, Janice Stowell was alerted to the sight of a large, tan cougar by the driver of another vehicle that had stopped to watch it running in the field below the road. The cat was four and half to five feet long, she estimated, and was headed for the Baraboo River.

2012: In summer, near Baraboo River in Elroy, Katherine Rick and a female relative watched a tan, cougar-like animal for about an hour from a distance of only a few feet as it took a cat nap in her yard. She estimated its size as the same size or a little bigger than a black Labrador retriever. She yelled at it and it left after about forty-five minutes, but it then lay down for another twenty minutes on an adjacent road.

2012: On November 22, near Valley, Ulla Olson and a guest saw two frenzied deer run across her yard, followed by a large tan cougar, limping. The cat turned onto Eastman Road and was soon out of sight.

2013: In winter, midday, at Hillsboro restaurant Beezer's Bar and Grill, Elroy dentist Chris Karas and Dan Winn saw a tan cougar "larger than most dogs" on an embankment viewed from restaurant window, as it climbed up into a nearby tree.

2014: One May afternoon, at a farm between Hillsboro and Elroy, Wencil Mislivecek was crossing a creek on a tractor and saw a large cougar-like animal two hundred yards away, about the size and color of a black Labrador retriever. It looked up and then walked toward him. The animal was "pure black," with a long tail the thickness of a broom handle, and remained in view for about ten minutes.

2014: In summer in Valley, Madeline Tengblad was out walking about one-quarter mile from her house when she saw a large tan cougar-like animal in a nearby hay field. She estimated it as about the size of a Labrador but longer.

2015: In June, rural Elroy woman (name withheld) saw a reddish brown, spotted, four-foot-long "huge cat" near her barn. It was chasing an Angus calf around a hay bale as if playing. Several larger cattle drove it away. She said the cat resembled a photo of a jaguar.

2015: In autumn, near County Highway O north of Hillsboro, a woman saw a "cougar" she described as a "really big animal with a long tail" that was a dark brown color, crossing a field as she drove by.

2016: In June, in Lime Ridge, Shannon Howell encountered a large, dark gray, cougar-like animal while walking her husky. She estimated its weight at 150 pounds and length at least five feet as it stood on logs on a neighbor's property, apparently watching something intently. Her dog pulled her back to the house. She said she had also recently seen a deer carcass jammed in a tree, indicative of a large cat's kill.

2016: On October 19, between Hillsboro and Kendall at State Highway 71 and County Highway FF, Anna Gilbertson saw a large "mountain lion" walking along the highway shoulder in the direction of Hillsboro. She slowed to look at the tan animal she described as roughly the size of a Great Dane only ten feet from her car, and reported her sighting to the sheriff's department.

2017: In May, near Wonewoc, Cody Revels and Katie Coleman experienced an extended encounter with a black panther near a fishing pond and captured it on cell phone video, which was later posted online for a limited time in *The Messenger of Juneau County*.

Sources for the above incidents include articles by Steven Stanek in various issues of the *Hillsboro Sentry-Enterprise*, and in *Fate Magazine*, December 2007, vol. 60, no. 12, issue 692.

Acknowledgments

I owe much gratitude to many people for the successful completion of this book. I thank fellow researchers, colleagues, and friends for everything from story and research contributions to creature-seeking and trail-hiking companions and much needed moral support: Steven Stanek, Terry Hooper, Barton Nunnelly, Lee Hampel, Sandra Schwab, Kim Poeppey, Sanjay Singhal, Jay Bachochin, Allison Jornlin, The Back Roads Lore crew, Corrine Mandera, the Unknown Creature Spot Facebook page gang, Pamela Roberts, Scott Corrales, Albert Rosario, Loren Coleman, Lon Strickler, Stan Gordon, William Kingsley, my wonderful husband Steven, and more people than I can name. I also, as always, express my extreme appreciation to all the encounter witnesses for sharing their experiences, and to my agent, Jim McCarthy, who gets me through it all. And finally, to the fine folks at Penguin Random House, who always work their magic to make my books the best they can be.

Endnotes

INTRODUCTION

1. Ivan Sanderson, *Abominable Snowmen: Legend Come to Life* (Kempton, Illinois: Adventures Unlimited Press), 2006, 382.
2. "Trail Spring (Nip'I Nagu)," *The Encyclopedia of Hoćak*, undated, https://hotcakencyclopedia.com/ho.TrailSpring.html, accessed November 10, 2017.
3. Carl Lindahl, John McNamara, John Lindow, *Medieval Folklore: A Guide to Myths, Legends, Tales, Beliefs, and Customs*, (New York: Oxford University Press, 2002), xviiii.

CHAPTER 1

1. Charles E. Brown, *Indian Folklore* (Madison: Wisconsin Historical Society Press, 1921), http://content.wisconsinhistory.org/cdm/ref/collection/tp/id/38839, accessed August 3, 2017.
2. Dorothy Moulding Brown, *Indian Legends of Historic and Scenic Wisconsin* (Madison: Wisconsin Historical Society, 1947).
3. "Several conspiracy-theory oriented Web sites are claiming a Biblical giant with flaming red hair was killed by U.S. soldiers in Afghanistan,"

Snopes, 2016, http://www.snopes.com/u-s-special-forces-killed-a-giant-in
-kandahar/, accessed September 12, 2017.

4. N. E. Genge, *Urban Legends: The Complete-As-One-Could-Be Guide to Modern Myths* (New York: Three Rivers Press, 2000).

5. Mack E. Barrick, *German-American Folklore: A Living Legacy in Proverbs, Riddles, Crafts and More* (Little Rock: August House, 1987), 169–172.

6. John Bierhorst, editor, *The Red Swan: Myths and Tales of the American Indians* (New York: Indian Head Books, 2002), 3.

7. "Introductory Note," *Völuspá.org*, undated, http://www.voluspa.org/voluspa intro.htm, accessed September 13, 2017.

8. H. R. Ellis Davidson, *Myths and Symbols in Pagan Europe, Early Scandinavian and Celtic Religions* (New York: Syracuse University Press, 1988), 190.

9. Nathan Klein, "Are You Ready for the Viking Apocalypse?" *Daily Mail*, November 19, 2014, http://www.dailymail.co.uk/news/article-2562584 /The-Viking-Apocalypse-Norse-myth-predicts-world-end-Saturday .html, accessed Octtober 11, 2017.

10. "A Rant About 'Ragnarok 2014,'" *A Clerk of Oxford*, http://aclerkofoxford .blogspot.com/2014/02/a-rant-about-ragnarok-2014.html, accessed October 11, 2017.

11. Bubba, "The Success of Fear, What the Slender Man Can Teach Us About Viral Marketing," *Branding Beat*, undated, https://www.qualitylogoprod ucts.com/blog/slender-man-viral-marketing/, accessed August 26, 2017.

12. Ron McGlone, "Strange Creature Reported in Carmel Area," *The Highland County Press*, http://highlandcountypress.com/Content/In-The-News /In-The-News/Article/Strange-creature-reported-in-Carmel-area/2/20 /25578, accessed August 26, 2017.

13. Ibid.

14. Kurt Broz, "Ohio 'alien' sighting may have logical explanation," *Doubtful News*, January 7, 2015, http://doubtfulnews.com/2015/01/ohio-alien -creature-sighting-may-have-logical-explanation/, accessed August 26, 2017.

15. Nick Sabo, "Alien Sighting North of Mount Vernon," *Mount Vernon News*, August 10, 2018, https://mountvernonnews.com/article/2018/08/10/alien -sighting-north-of-mount-vernon, accessed September 23, 2018.

16. Linda Rodriguez McRobbie, "The History and Psychology of Clowns Being Scary," *Smithsonian*, July 31, 2017, http://www.smithsonianmag.com /arts-culture/the-history-and-psychology-of-clowns-being-scary-2039 4516, accessed July 31, 2017.

17. "Quotes," *The Simpsons*, IMDb, 2011, http://www.imdb.com/title/tt206 3514/quotes/qt1588698, accessed July 31, 2017.
18. "Black-Eyed Children," *Wikipedia,* updated January 17, 2018, https://en.wikipedia.org/wiki/Black-eyed children, accessed January 22, 2018.
19. "Alfred Hitchcock Quotes," AZquotes, 2018, http://www.azquotes.com/author/6753-Alfred_Hitchcock, accessed January 24, 2018.

CHAPTER 2

1. Darrin Youker, "What's Legend Behind 'Meat Locker' near Wernersville?" *Reading Eagle*, November 11, 2011, http://www2.readingeagle.com/article.aspx?id=263279, accessed July 2, 2017.
2. Ibid.
3. "Is 'Wolf Woman' Sulking around the City? Various Area Persons Claim Seeing Creature," *Mobile Press Register*, April 8, 1971 (page unknown).
4. L. D. Bertillion, "The Lobo Girl of Devil's River," *A Treasury of American Folklore* (Guildford, CT: Globe Pequot, 2016), edited by B. A. Botkin, 758–763. Originally published in J. Frank Dobie and Mody C. Boatright, editors, *Straight Texas, Publications of the Texas Folklore Society*, Number XIII (Nacogdoches, TX: Texas Folk-Lore Society, 1937).
5. Ibid., 761.
6. Ibid., 763.
7. Robert Pyle, *Where Bigfoot Walks: Crossing the Dark Divide* (New York: Houghton Mifflin, 1995), 142–143.
8. James McCloy and *Ray Miller, Phantom of the Pines: More Tales of the Jersey Devil* (Wilmington, DE: Middle Atlantic Press, 1998), 93.
9. Charles J. Adams III, *Pennsylvania Dutch Country Ghosts, Legends and Lore* (Reading, PA: Exeter House Books, 1994), 147.

CHAPTER 3

1. Basil Johnston, *Ojibway Heritage* (Lincoln: University of Nebraska Press/Bison Books, 1990), 95.
2. James Gilland, "The Potential for Ambient Plasma Wave Propulsion," Ohio Aerospace Institute, October 11, 2011, https://www.nasa.gov/offices/oct/early_stage_innovation/niac/gilland_potential_ambient.html, accessed August 14, 2017.
3. Johnston, *Ojibway Heritage*, 101.

4. Jacques Vallee, *Passport to Magonia*, (Brisbane, Australia: Daily Grail Publishing, 2014), 162.
5. Ibid., 11.
6. Ibid., 11.

CHAPTER 4

1. David Kulzyck, "The Witchy Wolves of Omer Plains," *Strange Magazine* #15, Spring 1995, 25.
2. Lindsey Russell, "An Encounter with the Witchy Wolves?" Michigan's Otherside, undated, http://michigansotherside.com/the-witchy-wolves-of-omer-plains/, accessed July 27, 2017.
3. Tim Barnum, "Eerie Temperance Entertainment Calls Omer Plains Investigation a Great Success," *The Arenac County Independent*, March 23, 2009, http://www.arenacindependent.com/stories/Eerie-Temperance-Entertainment-calls-Omer-plains-investigation-a-great-success,79004, accessed September 28, 2014.
4. Ibid.
5. Ibid.
6. Brenda Peterson, *Wolf Nation: The Life, Death, and Return of Wild American Wolves* (Boston: Da Capo Press, 2017), 43.
7. Linda Godfrey, *The Michigan Dogman: Werewolves and Other Unknown Canines Across the U.S.A.* (Eau Claire, WI: Unexplained Research Publishing, 2010), 32–34.
8. Ibid., 34–35.

CHAPTER 5

1. Linda Godfrey, *Hunting the American Werewolf* (Madison, WI: Trails Books, 2006), 104–105.
2. Linda Godfrey, *Monsters Among Us* (New York: Tarcher/Perigee, 2016).
3. Lon Strickler, "The Morbach Werewolf: an Eyewitness Account," Profound History, January 5, 2018, https://www.phantomsandmonsters.com/2015/10/the-morbach-werewolf-eyewitness-account.html, accessed January 19, 2018.
4. Richard Hall, *From Airships to Arnold: Preliminary Catalogue of UFO Reports in the Early 20th Century (1900–1946)* (Fairfax, VA: UFO Research Coalition, 2000), 23, 32.
5. *Montague Area Centennial* (Michigan: White Lake Area Historical Soci-

ety, 1967), http://www.whitelakeareahistoricalsociety.com/wp-content
/uploads/2016/10/02.pdf, accessed November 30, 2017, chapter 2, 11.

6. Coral Williams, "Legends and Stories of White County, Tennessee" (un-published thesis), *The Heritage of Daniel Haston*, June 1930, http://www
.danielhaston.com/history/tn-history/white-county/legends-whiteco2
.htm, accessed January 22, 2018.

7. Scott Simon, "Cow Tipping, the Myth that Won't Stand Up," *Strange News*, NPR, September 7, 2013, https://www.npr.org/templates/story
/story.php?storyId=219963377, accessed January 22, 2018.

CHAPTER 6

1. Hannah Osborne, "Head Transplants," *Newsweek*, April 28, 2017, http:
//www.newsweek.com/head-transplant-sergio-canavero-valery
-spiridonov-china-2017-591772, accessed September 19, 2017.

2. Sarah Fecht, "Don't Lose Your Head," *Popular Science*, February 27, 2015,
http://www.popsci.com/no-human-head-transplants-will-not-be-possible
-2017, accessed September 19, 2017.

3. Montee Reel, "Famed Goatman Forever Held in Dusty Room," *The Wash-ington Post*, November 8, 2000, https://www.washingtonpost.com/archive
/local/2000/11/08/famed-goatman-forever-held-in-dusty-room/45fcae6c
-670e-41c5-b2fc-cdce14888a73/?utm_term=.a5de09394482, accessed Sep-tember 20, 2017.

4. Tyler, "Spooky Places in Roswell, NM," *The Pipeline*, March 30, 2014,
http://thepipeline.tumblr.com/post/81193761326/spooky-places-in
-roswell-nm, accessed September 19, 2017.

5. "Freaky Confrontations," *Phantoms and Monsters*, 2011, http://www.phan
tomsandmonsters.com/2015/09/freaky-confrontations.html, accessed Sep-tember 20, 2017.

6. Ibid.

7. "The Watts Valley Wolf Ape," *Weird Fresno*, September 15, 2008, http:
//www.weirdfresno.com/2008/09/watts-valley-wolf-ape.html, accessed No-vember 22, 2017.

CHAPTER 7

1. Linda Godfrey, *The Beast of Bray Road: Tailing Wisconsin's Werewolf* (Black Earth, Wisconsin: Trails Media, 2003), 58–65.

2. Linda Godfrey, *Strange Wisconsin: More Badger State Weirdness* (Madison: Trails Books, 2007), 110–111.

3. Ted Holiday and Colin Wilson, *The Goblin Universe* (Woodbury, MN: Llwellyn Publications, 1986), 112.

4. John Keel, *The Complete Guide to Mysterious Beings* (New York: Tor, 2002), 214.

5. Frederick Harris, "Exploring Native American Folklore: Little People and Giants" (graduate thesis, University of Montana, 2006).

6. "What's the Real Deal About the Atacama 'Alien'"? *IFL Science,* undated, http://www.iflscience.com/health-and-medicine/what's-real-deal-about -atacama-alien, accessed January 14, 2018.

7. David Bowles, "Mexican Gremlins?" Medium, December 29, 2016, https://medium.com/@davidbowles/mexican-gremlins-rq3-4add982d e8fd, accessed January 14, 2018.

8. "Legendary Native American Figures, Pukwudgie" Native Languages of the Americas, undated, http://www.native-languages.org/pukwudgie.htm, accessed January 31, 2018.

9. "Menehune, Mischievous Hawaiian Spirits," University of Southern California Digital Folklore Archives, May 12, 2016, http://folklore.usc.edu /?p=31075, accessed January 31, 2018.

10. Ivan Sanderson, *Abominable Snowmen: Legend Come to Life* (Kempton, IL: Adventures Unlimited Press, 2006), 1961, 121.

11. Ibid., 138.

12. Albert Rosales, *Humanoid Encounters 2000–2009: The Others Amongst Us* (Charleston, SC: Triangulum Publishing, 2015), 27.

13. Linda Godfrey, Richard Hendricks, *Weird Wisconsin: Your Travel Guide to Wisconsin's Local Legends and Best Kept Secrets,* Mark Moran and Mark Sceurman, editors (New York: Barnes & Noble Books, 2005), 56–59.

14. Mark Moran and Mark Sceurman, *Weird U.S.: Your Travel Guide to America's Local Legends and Best Kept Secrets* (New York: Barnes & Noble Books, 2004), 80–84.

15. Gerrit van den Bergh, Adam Brunn, "A 700,000-year-old Fossil Find Shows the Hobbits' Ancestors Were Even Smaller," *The Conversation,* June 8, 2016, http://theconversation.com/a-700-000-year-old-fossil-find -shows-the-hobbits-ancestors-were-even-smaller-60192, accessed January 16, 2018.

CHAPTER 8

1. "Guardian Gods," Internet Sacred Text Archive, undated, http://www
.sacred-texts.com/pac/hm/hm11.htm, accessed November 13, 2017, chapter 9, 122.
2. Patricia Dale-Green, *Lore of the Dog* (Boston: Houghton Mifflin, 1967),
184.
3. "The Foster Child of the Deer, a Zuni Legend," First People of America and
Canada—Turtle Island, undated, https://www.firstpeople.us/FP-Html
-Legends/TheFosterChildoftheDeer-Zuni.html, accessed September 3,
2018.
4. David Gordon White, *Myths of the Dog-Man* (Chicago: University of Chicago Press, 1991), 140–141.

CHAPTER 9

1. Ivan Sanderson, "The Dire Wolf," *Pursuit*, vol. 7, no. 4, October 1974 (privately published), 92.
2. Ibid., 94.

CHAPTER 10

1. Loren Coleman, *Mysterious America: The Ultimate Guide to the Nation's
Weirdest Wonders, Strangest Spots, and Creepiest Creatures* (New York: Paraview, 2007), 128–129.
2. Associated Press, "Strange Monster Reported Roaming in Arizona Hills,"
Journal-Times Sunday Bulletin, February 9, 1941, https://www.newspapers
.com/newspage/7991131/, accessed October 20, 2017.
3. Gerina Dunwich, *Phantom Felines and Other Ghostly Animals* (New York:
Citadel Press, 2006), 159.
4. Brad Steiger, *Shadow World: True Encounters with Beings from the Darkside*
(New York: Anomalist Books, 2000), 195.
5. Ernesto de Martino, *Primitive Magic: The Psychic Powers of Shamans and
Sorcerers* (Great Britain: Prism Press, 1988), 95.
6. "Legendary Native American Figures: The Water Panther (Mishipeshu),"
Native Languages of the Americas, undated, http://www.native-languages
.org/waterpanther.htm, accessed October 24, 2017.
7. Ibid.

8. Paul B. Jenkins, *History and Indian Remains in Lake Geneva and Lake Como, Walworth County, Wisconsin: Part One* (Lake Geneva, WI: Geneva Lake Historical Society, 1930).

9. Patty Loew, *Indian Nations of Wisconsin*, (Madison: Wisconsin Historical Society Press, 2001), 6–7.

10. Robert Birmingham and Leslie Eisenberg, *Indian Mounds of Wisconsin* (Madison, WI: University of Wisconsin Press, 2000), 120–121.

11. "Native American Lynx Mythology," Native Languages of the Americas, undated, http://native-languages.org/legends-lynx.htm, accessed October 24, 2017.

12. Associated Press, "Cougars on the Move in Midwest, Study Finds," *Milwaukee Journal Sentinel*, June 15, 2012, 3B.

13. Michelle A. LaRue, Clayton K. Nielsen, Mark Dowling, Ken Miller, Bob Wilson, Harley Shaw, and Charles R. Anderson Jr., "Cougars are Recolonizing the Midwest: Analysis of Cougar Confirmations during 1990–2008," *The Journal of Wildlife Management*, 76:1364–1369 (June 14, 2012), http://doi:10.1002/jwmg.396.

14. Linda Godfrey, *American Monsters: A History of Monster Lore, Legends, and Sightings in America* (New York: Penguin/Tarcher, 2014), 285–287.

15. Geoff Bartlett, "No Evidence of Panthers in Newfoundland Despite Reports, Say Wildlife Officials," *CBC News*, October 6, 2017, http://www.cbc.ca/news/canada/newfoundland-labrador/panther-newfoundland-sightings-wildlife-department-1.4343214, accessed October 24, 2017.

16. Ibid.

17. Mike Addison, "Black Cat Seen Near M6," *This Is the Lake District*, March 28, 2003, http://www.thisisthelakedistrict.co.uk/misc/print.html?nwid=712527, accessed March 29, 2003.

18. Ibid.

19. Ibid.

20. "Elusive Black Cat Shows Itself Again in Forest Lake," *Forest Lake Times*, March 5, 2003, http://www.forestlaketimes.com/2003/March/536crime.html, accessed March 13, 2003.

21. News Michigan Service, "Did They See Panther or a Big House Cat?" *Saginaw News*, October 4, 1990.

22. Steven Hepker, "The Celebrated Black Panther Surfaces Again," *Saginaw News*, February 17, 1990.

23. Frank Buckley and Gene Schabath, "Another Wild Cat On the Prowl," *Detroit News*, July 12, 1986, 1, 8A.

CHAPTER 11

1. "Flying 'Fence Posts' Seen Near Hillsboro," *Hillsboro Sentry-Enterprise*, February 26, 1948.
2. Ibid.
3. Ibid.
4. Ibid.
5. Steven Stanek, "A History of Air Disasters Over Hillsboro," *Hillsboro Sentry-Enterprise*, August 22, 1991, 5.
6. Ankan Sarkar, "Quartz Crystals at the Core of Earth are the Powerhouse of the Earth's Magnetic Field," *Science Times*, February 2, 2017, http://www.sciencetimes.com/articles/9341/20170223/quartz-crystals-at-the-core-of-earth-are-the-power-house-of-magnetic-field.htm, accessed November 15, 2017.
7. "Oh Deer: Mammals Use Magnetic Navigation, Too," *Evolution News and Science Today*, June 15, 2016, https://evolutionnews.org/2016/06/oh_deer_mammals/, accessed November 15, 2017; Petr Obleser, Vlastimil Hart, E. Pascal Malkemper, Sabine Begall, Michaela Holá, Michael S. Painter, Jaroslav Červený, Hynek Burda. "Compass-controlled Escape Behavior in Roe Deer," *Behavioral Ecology and Sociobiology* (August 2016), https://doi.org/10.1007/s00265-016-2142-y.
8. "Cougars in Wisconsin," Wisconsin Department of Natural Resources, October 25, 2017, http://dnr.wi.gov/topic/wildlifehabitat/cougar.html, accessed November 3, 2017.
9. Steven Stanek, "Mystery Cats of Wisconsin," *Fate Magazine*, December 2007, vol. 60, no. 12, issue 692, 59.
10. Ibid., 54.
11. Ibid.
12. Steven Stanek, "Video Captures Big Black Cat near Wonewoc," *Hillsboro Sentry-Enterprise*, May 18, 2017, 1.
13. Cody Revels, "Cody Grizzly Revels Submitted this Video of What He Believes To Be a Black Cougar," *The Messenger Of Juneau County*, May 8, 2017, https://www.facebook.com/messengerofjuneaucounty/videos/1508724772492319/, accessed November 3, 2017.
14. Steve Stanek, "Mystery Skull: Is It Proof of Lions in the Area?" *Hillsboro Sentry-Enterprise*, May 19, 2016, 1.
15. Olivia Munoz, "Scientist on Prowl for Proof of Cougars," *Saginaw News*, December 31, 2003, A1, A2.

16. Steven Stanek, "Mystery Critter Stirs Up Interest Across the State," *Hillsboro Sentry-Enterprise*, March 26, 1992, 1, 20.

17. Dianna Anderson, "Does Wisconsin Have Chupacabras?" *The Messenger of Juneau County*, July 21, 2011, 1.

18. Stan Gordon, "Unusual and Unexplained," *The Gate to Strange Phenomena*, April 2017, vol. 32, issue 4 (Richmond Heights, Ohio: privately published), 11–12.

19. Mike Burch, "Coyotes, Cougars, and Now. . . . Bigfoot!" *The Hillsboro Outlook*, September 12, 2012, 2.

20. Ibid.

21. Ibid.

22. Steve Stanek, "Cashton Bigfoot Recalled," *Hillsboro Sentry-Enterprise*, October 26, 1989, 1, 20.

CHAPTER 12

1. Edward Simon, "Why Bigfoot Sightings Are So Common Across Cultures," *The Atlantic*, October 25, 2016, https://www.theatlantic.com/science/archive/2016/10/sasquatch/505304/, accessed January 7, 2018.

2. "The Birth of Esau and Jacob," Bible Gateway, King James Version, Genesis 25:19–34, https://www.biblegateway.com/passage/?search=Genesis+25%3A19-34&version=ESV;KJV, accessed September 14, 2017.

3. Staff, "Werewolf Gene May Explain Excess Hair Disorder," Live Science, June 3, 2011, https://www.livescience.com/14430-werewolf-disorder-gene-discovered-excess-hair.html, accessed September 17, 2018.

4. Rob Riggs, *In the Big Thicket; On the Trail of the Wild Man* (New York: Paraview Press, 2001), 109.

5. Michael Heiser, *The Unseen Realm; Recovering the Supernatural Worldview of the Bible* (Bellingham, WA: Hexham Press, 2015), 92–96.

Index

About the Author

Linda S. Godfrey is one of America's top authorities on modern-day monsters and mystery creatures. A popular media consultant and personality, she has appeared on *MonsterQuest*, Fox News *Red Eye, Inside Edition, Monsters and Mysteries in America, The Jenny McCarthy Show*, NPR, *Coast to Coast AM*, and *Sean Hannity's America*. Her eighteen published books include *Monsters Among Us, American Monsters, Real Wolfmen, Weird Michigan, The Beast of Bray Road*, and many others.